The Royal Demesne in English Constitutional History

1066-1272

The Royal Demesne in English Constitutional History: 1066-1272

BY ROBERT S. HOYT

Associate Professor of History
The State University of Iowa

PUBLISHED FOR

The American Historical Association

CORNELL UNIVERSITY PRESS

ITHACA, NEW YORK, 1950

CORNELL UNIVERSITY PRESS
LONDON: GEOFFREY CUMBERLEGE
OXFORD UNIVERSITY PRESS

THIS VOLUME IS PUBLISHED FROM A FUND CONTRIBUTED TO THE AMERICAN HISTORICAL ASSOCIATION BY THE CARNEGIE CORPORATION OF NEW YORK.

PRINTED IN THE UNITED STATES OF AMERICA BY THE
VAIL-BALLOU PRESS, INC., BINGHAMTON, NEW YORK

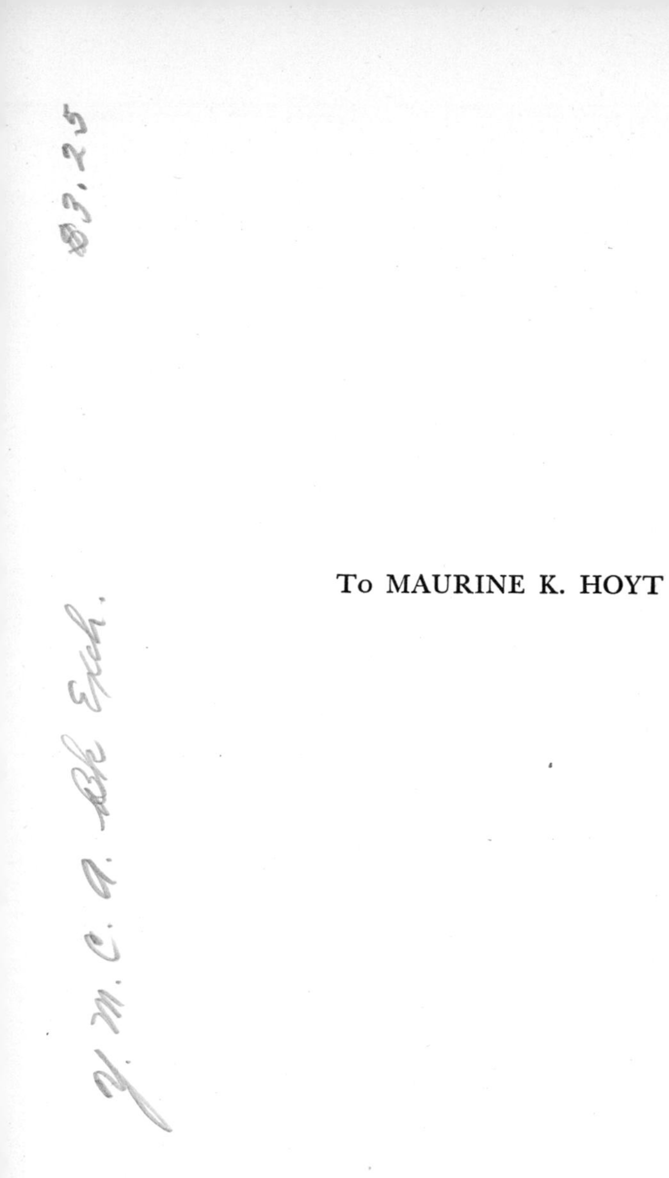

To MAURINE K. HOYT

Preface

My interest in the royal demesne in England grew out of a suggestion by Professor C. H. McIlwain that the legal peculiarities of the ancient demesne, and the relationship between the ancient demesne and the realm, needed a more thorough investigation than had yet been made. The literature on this subject hardly extends beyond the brief treatment by Vinogradoff, written in 1892, which in turn is derived from the works of Coke, Fitzherbert, and the legal writers of the sixteenth and seventeenth centuries. Maitland, who covered the same ground and accepted most of Vinogradoff's conclusions, noticed that "all this would make the ancient demesne of importance in the history of political arrangements," but his own interest was also restricted to the legal peculiarities of the ancient demesne. A review of this literature and investigation of the sources relating to the ancient demesne convinced me that it did not antedate the thirteenth century, and that the proper object of study was rather the royal demesne as a whole. As this work progressed, it became apparent that the larger importance of the royal demesne lay not in legal antiquities but rather in the new evidence it afforded for an understanding of the role and function of the English monarchy in medieval society. This has been my main interest. I have not attempted to write an exhaustive or definitive work on the royal demesne, and no one could be more acutely conscious than I of the number of special problems connected with the subject which invite further study from the legal, administrative, and economic points of view.

At every stage of the work which this volume represents, I have been deeply indebted for help, guidance, and encouragement, and it is a great pleasure to express, though it is difficult adequately to convey, the gratitude which I feel for the interest and support that I have received. To Professor McIlwain especially I am obligated for the inspiration which his teaching and direction of my early work, and his warm encouragement throughout, have given me. The manuscript of this work benefited from the incisive critique and suggestive ideas of Professor C. H. Taylor while it was being written. To Professor McIlwain, Professor J. R. Strayer, and Professor J. G. Edwards I am indebted for "aid and counsel" respecting my interpretation of particular documents as well as for specific criticism of Chapters II and III, V and VI, and VI, respectively. Above all, the extent to which I have been able to avoid errors of fact, reasoning, and interpretation is due to the kindness of Professor H. M. Cam, whose close reading of the whole manuscript has improved it in so many ways; I cannot adequately thank her for the interest she has taken in my work.

I am indebted to the Graduate College of The State University of Iowa for a grant in support of research, and to the efficient help of Mrs. Helen E. Shepherd, my assistant, during the academic year 1948–1949. That I could spend a year in England doing further research and completing the final revision of this work was made possible by a Fellowship of the John Simon Guggenheim Memorial Foundation and a grant from the Department of State, on the recommendation of the Conference Board of Associated Research Councils and the University of Manchester, under the terms of the Fulbright Act. To the staff of the Public Record Office I owe many thanks for their inexhaustible patience, courtesy, and assistance in making my work there as pleasant as it was profitable; I am particularly indebted to Mr. L. C. Hector and Mr. H. C. Johnson, Assistant Keepers of the Public Record Office, for assistance in transcribing the documents printed in Appendix E and for the many ways in which I profited from their knowledge and understanding of that field of scholarship which comprehends paleography, diplomatic, and history.

My thanks are due and gratefully extended to the Librarians and staffs of Widener Library, the library of The State University of Iowa, and the Library of the Institute of Historical Research for their courtesy and help. I also wish to thank Longmans, Green & Co., Ltd., for permission to reprint Chapter VI, which originally appeared in the *English Historical Review,* LXV, 145–174.

Finally, for whatever this work is worth, the credit in large measure is due to the encouragement and help of my greatest benefactor and sharpest critic, to whom this book is dedicated.

London, July, 1950 R. S. H.

Contents

The Royal Demesne in English Constitutional History

1066-1272

CHAPTER I

Introduction

IN THE political organization, as well as in the economic, social, and cultural life of western civilization, two great periods may be distinguished: the antique, dominated by the city-state; and the modern, dominated at least until the middle of the twentieth century by the national state. Between the collapse of a civilization based on the city-state and the origins of the modern national state in the later Middle Ages lies a period whose institutions were in large part determined by the relative influences exerted by the Church, the Empire, and the medieval monarchies. The Church and the Empire represented and expressed universal ideals which may be considered typically medieval. The medieval monarchies, lacking any such claims to universality, were equally typical—indeed, in no era has the principle of monarchy been so widely and so completely accepted.

The monarchies of western Europe played a central role in the transition from the antique to the medieval and from the medieval to the modern world. The "successor states," which inherited and built upon the debris of the Roman Empire in the west, afforded the Dark Ages their nearest approximation to political order. In contrast with the monarchies which built these half-Roman, half-Germanic kingdoms, the papacy was alternately struggling for survival or for freedom, while the Church was as much the tool as the counterpoise of royal power. In even greater contrast, the Empire was so moribund in the west that its mere survival was doubtful. In the more rapid transition at the end of the Middle Ages, the monarchies of western Europe again played a major role in building the modern national state. Where medieval monarchies were strong, strong national states emerged in modern times. The national state was a contradiction of the basic principles underlying the medieval Church and Empire.

The medieval monarchy, then, is for the historian a central fact in western civilization. The institutions and resources on which it was based, and the institutions which it built and used, all influenced the general course of European development. Everywhere, and in every period, the strength and influence of the medieval monarchy is related, more or less directly, to the extent of and its policy toward its landed endowment. In France and Germany, for example, the history of the crown lands is a well-known feature of the growth of the one and the weakness of the other nation. In England, the history of the royal demesne is just as closely related to the fortunes of the monarchy and the growth of the realm. This study is concerned with one period of that history, from the Norman Conquest to the accession of Edward I.

There are many developments—economic, political, legal, and administrative—which affected the royal demesne but must be excluded from our main interest. These developments lie beyond the scope of this study because they are features of the general history of the period rather than features peculiar to or especially characteristic of the royal demesne. We shall be concerned primarily with what is distinctive, or has been alleged to be distinctive, about the royal demesne. Upon the royal demesne, the monarchy was least restricted in its policy by ecclesiastical and baronial rights and interests, that is, by the relations between the secular and spiritual authority or by the contractual element in the feudal relation between lord and vassals. The purpose of the present work, therefore, is to appraise the nature and role of the monarchy from a new viewpoint. This is the main interest of the royal demesne in constitutional history.

In simplest terms, the royal demesne consisted of all the land in England which the king held *in dominio,* "in his own hand," land which is not held of the king by someone else. In this sense, the forests and the highways are part of the royal demesne. In Oxfordshire, for example, "the king's demesne forests have nine leagues in length and the same in breadth," according to Domesday Book.[1] And yet, although the royal forests and the highways are the king's, ordinary medieval usage does not include them among the *dominica regis.* There is a difference between the use of the word "demesne" as an adjective and as a noun. No king is said to hold Sherwood Forest or Watling Street in demesne, as he might be said to hold a manor in demesne. So also, a royal borough is the king's, or a king may be the paramount lord in a given borough; but boroughs, like highways and forests, are not so completely identified with the royal demesne in the narrower sense that a *tallagium dominicorum* is understood to include them as a matter of course. The king who orders a tallage to be collected will refer to the *civitates et burgi domini regis* in addition to the *dominica regis* upon which it will be levied.

The typical medieval Latin phrase which translates our "royal demesne" is *dominica regis,* and the plural usage, "demesnes," is a clue to the medieval concept of the royal demesne. The royal demesne was ordinarily conceived as a collection of manors; *dominica regis* were the *maneria regis.*[2] It was frequently the case that a royal manor coincided geographically with the vill or town, the agricultural or rural unit of population. Thus, the manor which is part of the *dominica regis* when considered singly might also be termed *villa regis* or, in an earlier period, *regia villa* or *cyninges tun.*

For the Middle Ages, the royal demesne was above all the sum total of these royal estates, the *villae* or *maneria regis,* the rural lands organized as manors. Other areas, both urban and rural, might fall under the demesne right of the king, or be spoken of as "demesne boroughs" or "demesne forests" in this adjectival sense; but they concern this study only in so far as they may throw light upon the royal demesne as the great bulk of the documents refer to it, the *Terra Regis* conceived as a group of royal manors.

Thus, the history of the royal demesne is primarily the history of

---

1 *Domesday Book: Seu Liber Censualis Willelmi Primi Regis Angliae* (Text, vols. I and II, ed. Abraham Farley, n.p., 1783; Indices and Introduction, vol. III, and *Additamenta,* vol. IV, ed. Sir Henry Ellis, Record Commission, n.p., 1816), I, fol. 154b.

2 The "narrow" or manorial sense of the word demesne will be discussed in the next chapter.

the monarchy in relation to its landed resources, and the words of Canon Foster apply equally well to our subject as to the English village of which he wrote: "It may be observed also that most of the documents on which English village history is based relate to the land, to its tenure, its assessments, its inheritance and descent, its manors. . . . Leave out the land, and but little remains. The history of an English village . . . is founded upon its soil." [3]

The history of the medieval English monarchy may have its most important ramifications in the history of governmental institutions or in political developments affecting the nation as a whole, but the monarchy also possessed its foundation in the soil, the royal demesne. The primary importance of the royal demesne for constitutional history does not lie in the agricultural or economic character of the crown lands, nor even in the extent or value of them. It is not what, or how large, was the royal demesne, but rather how the royal demesne was used and what happened upon it, that must engage our attention. Indeed, the size of the royal demesne at any given time in the Middle Ages is practically impossible to determine, with three partial exceptions. A mere list of royal manors —but no more than a list of their names—may be obtained from the early fourteenth century document, known as the *Nomina Villarum,*[4] relating to a parliamentary grant of foot soldiers to be provided for Edward II's Scottish war. A few more facts may be gleaned from the returns to the great inquests of the early years of the reign of Edward I which are preserved in the Hundred Rolls.[5] Both of these sources lie outside the chronological limits and the scope of the present work; and, furthermore, neither of them is so detailed or complete a record as that provided by Domesday Book. The record of the great survey undertaken in the last years of the reign of William the Conqueror includes the only systematic and approximately complete record of the medieval royal demesne. In every county, the description of the lands held begins with the *Terra Regis*. Under this rubric may be found the fullest description

[3] C. W. Foster, *A History . . . of Aisthorpe & Thorpe in the Fallows* (Lincoln, 1927), p. 1.

[4] *The Parliamentary Writs and Writs of Military Summons* (ed. Francis Palgrave, 2 vols. in 4 pts., Rec. Com.; n.p., 1827–1834), vol. II, pt. 3, Introduction.

[5] *Rotuli Hundredorum temp. Hen. III & Edw. I* (ed. W. Illingworth, 2 vols., Rec. Com.; n.p., 1812–1818).

of the manors of the royal demesne afforded by a medieval record.

Domesday Book is thus the point of departure for a study of the royal demesne. Beyond Domesday and into the "dark backward," the royal demesne as a whole recedes from view, although from that record and from scattered evidence relating to the royal vills of the Old English kings there may be drawn some useful information concerning the pre-Conquest crown lands. Both the Domesday evidence and that of the Anglo-Saxon charters suggest that the royal demesne in the later Old English period had been shrinking for a long time. In an earlier age the kings had possessed a landed endowment which rivaled the extent of William the Conqueror's *Terra Regis,* but it is unlikely that any of his Anglo-Saxon or Danish predecessors possessed so many or so widely distributed estates.

By the time of the Domesday survey, it is apparent that the royal demesne has been swollen in two ways. Political events and the introduction of feudalism both contributed to this process. The forfeitures (particularly those of the house of Godwin) and the escheats which attended the Norman Conquest and its aftermath added hundreds of manors, that is, separate estates, to the *Terra Regis*. Furthermore, the royal demesne was enlarged by the small holdings of many lesser persons among the dependent but free population. In the Norman mind these free men could have only the king as lord because they could be claimed by no other lord, in accordance with the feudal notions underlying the organization of Domesday Book. Their small holdings appear in Domesday Book as additions to royal manors—outlying members or the soke of royal manors—not as separate estates. Despite the judicial ties or the personal commendation which may have bound the holders of such lands to royal manors before the Conquest, we may well suspect that the lands of this population had not been conceived as forming part of the possessions of the Anglo-Saxon kings. The Anglo-Norman royal demesne was the beneficiary of the introduction of feudalism into England, by whose principles the ties of personal dependence and the tenure of land were joined. Whoever might hold his land from no other lord would thus appropriately be conceived as being a dependent tenant of the king's manor of which his land became a part.

In this connection, it should be observed that the very phrase "royal demesne" is intelligible only for the period following the Conquest. The phrase expresses a feudal concept. Lands, estates, or manors held in demesne are those which have not been subinfeudated. Where there has been no hereditable enfeoffment of land there can be no distinction between royal lands held in demesne and fiefs held by tenants-in-chief of the king. The Old English kings could only own the lands which they possessed—no proprietary rights could extend beyond the borders of their own lands. Here again, then, the royal demesne after the Conquest was the beneficiary of the introduction of feudal ideas. All land ultimately was held "of" the king, unless held "by" the king in demesne, and over all the soil of England the king was in one or the other sense the lord. As part of the rights and profits of feudal lordship (respecting the lord-vassal relationship), there was for the feudal monarch the additional possibility of the escheat of fiefs due to failure of heirs. Thus, leaving aside the abnormal but not infrequent possibility of forfeiture, the normal course of events might, and actually did, provide for a constant replenishing of the royal demesne after the introduction of feudalism which no Anglo-Saxon king could enjoy.

If there was not, strictly and feudally speaking, a royal demesne before the Conquest, we may on the basis of the Anglo-Saxon evidence legitimately speak of "crown lands"—lands which the king possessed in his official capacity only. They belonged not to him but to the crown, as distinct from the *propria haereditas* belonging to and disposable by the king as a person.[6] This distinction appears as early as the ninth century, but it "could not survive under a doctrine of feudal tenure, and lapsed with the Conquest," [7] for a time at least. How important this distinction was and how far the witan felt responsible for conserving the Old English crown lands, it would be difficult to conjecture. The great bulk of our information concerning the matter comes from surviving royal wills or references to royal bequests such as Asser gives in his Life of Alfred. Evidence of a different sort, such as that which reveals glimpses of

[6] J. E. A. Jolliffe, *The Constitutional History of Medieval England* (New York, 1937), p. 127, and references cited there.

[7] *Ibid.*, p. 128.

the role of the royal vill in the Anglo-Saxon administrative system, certainly contains no hint that there may be a distinction of this kind between the vills of which it speaks, or between them and other royal possessions. A king's town is simply a king's town, though some will have greater importance in the history of political arrangements than others.

A few more general characteristics of the Anglo-Saxon crown lands may be sketched here, as the background of the main period under consideration. Reference has already been made to the fact that up to 1066 the landed endowment of the English monarchy was steadily shrinking. The history of any great pre-Norman monastic foundation can illustrate the extensive alienation of the crown lands. The surviving charters, the histories and chronicles, and the lives of the Anglo-Saxon saints are full of evidence on this score. The identification and listing of all the recorded grants of royal lands to the Church would be, perhaps, the most impressive witness to the huge landed endowment of the early kings in England.

The original acquisition of these crown lands is obscured from view. From their vast extent one might surmise that, following the conquest of a given region by an Anglo-Saxon tribe, or the conquest of one kingdom by another, all the lands which by the terms of conquest or treaty were not left in the possession of previous owners became the property of the king. From these huge resources the king would immediately give tracts of land or estates (depending upon the condition of the conquered territory) to the chief men who helped him win the land or, after the introduction of Christianity, to the ecclesiastical foundations which might support his rule. The residue would thus become the original crown lands of the king. Provision would have to be made for members of the royal family, with the largest share of the royal estates descending to the succeeding king. Since many of these latter estates would be the seats of local government in accordance with the usage of the times, they would, after several generations, come to be considered as belonging to the crown rather than to the person of the king. They would stand in contrast with other estates which were not intimately associated with local government or which were acquired later by exchange or purchase or forfeiture. "However, it is much easier for us to dream dreams about such a transaction than to discover the truth." [8]

There is no doubt, however, that "far back in the Old English period the *cyninges tun* . . . had been a fundamental unit in the organization of justice and finance." [9] "The local administrative unit, therefore, was the royal vill with its adjoining and dependent territory, normally assessed as a hundred or some multiple of a hundred hides of land, and ruled for all purposes, whether fiscal, administrative or judicial, by a royal reeve." [10]

Whether the origins of the hundred are to be found in voluntary personal associations or in an earlier geographical district based on a royal vill whose court absorbed the functions of the voluntary associations,[11] there is no doubt of the close and enduring connection between many of the royal vills and the local government which finally took the form of the hundred. These vills are generally distinguished by their antiquity, their size (often including dependent hamlets or villages), and the occasional settlement of merchants who may have sought out the protection of the king's peace or merely been attracted by a concentration of wealth and population.

The crown lands of the Anglo-Saxon kings were intimately associated with the government. Royal vills were centers of local administration, and the private profits of all the king's land composed the great bulk of his government's revenues. Constant alienation, however, together with the rise of the great earldoms of the eleventh century, had reduced the advantage of the king over the greater men of the realm to a large extent. The Conquest redressed the balance and introduced a fundamentally different concept of the royal demesne, while at the same time it left unaltered the administrative role of the royal vill and the economic exploitation of royal manors as the basis of the monarchy.

---

[8] F. W. Maitland, *Domesday Book and Beyond* (Cambridge, 1897), p. 255.

[9] F. M. Stenton, *Anglo-Saxon England* (Oxford History of England, ed. G. N. Clark, vol. II, 2d ed.; Oxford, 1947), pp. 474f.

[10] G. O. Sayles, *The Medieval Foundations of England* (London, 1948), p. 183.

[11] Jolliffe, *Const. Hist.*, pp. 116–123, and Professor Cam's remarks on this theory in her review of Jolliffe's work in *English Historical Review*, LIV (1939), 483–489.

CHAPTER II

The Royal Demesne of the Norman Settlement, 1066-1087

THE extent and approximate value of the lands of William the Conqueror in 1086 may be determined easily, but beyond these two basic facts the nature of the Anglo-Norman royal demesne is obscure in the extreme. We may be sure that its administration and exploitation created less difficulty for the monarchy, and occasioned less resistance, than did the assertion of royal rights over the Church and the baronage. So also, the royal demesne of the Conqueror was the immediate basis of royal power, not only as the source of the bulk of his revenues, but also because it was closely associated with the whole administrative system. Its central importance for the reign has been widely recognized, even though the royal demesne itself is generally neglected in our accounts of the Norman settlement.[1] Perhaps this is because it was involved in no great political event or constitutional struggle. The chronicles of the period devote scarcely more than a passing observation to it. For our estimate of the nature and significance of the royal demesne, therefore, we must turn to Domesday Book and the other administrative records of the age.

To summarize the conclusions of this chapter, the available evi-

---

1 See, for example, the excellent account of the Norman settlement in Jolliffe, *Const. Hist.*, pp. 139–201. Although "the heart of the Norman monarchy is the royal treasure and the *terra regis*" (*ibid.*, p. 183), only two pages are devoted specifically to the royal demesne.

dence relating to the royal demesne of the Norman settlement emphasizes the fusion of private right and public authority which characterizes the feudal monarchy in all its activities. This evidence relates, on the one hand, to the administration, and on the other hand, to the taxation of the royal demesne. Neither with regard to administration nor taxation can the king as greatest landlord be distinguished from the king as suzerain ruler in his policy toward or treatment of the manors listed under the Domesday rubric, *Terra Regis*. Like any other feudal lord, he derived a direct income from the agricultural exploitation of the manors he held *in dominio*. Beyond that fact there was no fundamental distinction between the royal demesne and the rest of the realm. Nor was there any significant distinction between one or another part or kind of royal demesne. There was no "ancient demesne of the crown" or "land belonging to the nation," separate from the rest of the royal demesne, and of which the king was merely custodian during his tenure of the office of kingship. Such a distinction, had it existed, would have implied a distinction between private right and public authority, both of which in the Anglo-Norman period were actually fused in the person of the *dominus rex*.

DOMESDAY BOOK AND RELATED EVIDENCE

With these conclusions historians of Anglo-Norman institutions have by no means all agreed, either in general or in detail, as will appear below. The sources of the period offer difficult problems of interpretation and in some places may seem to indicate a wholly different character of the royal demesne. Indeed, there are occasional statements which on the surface would deny utterly the conclusions just stated. For example, there is the startling and unique heading of the *Terra Regis* section of the Exon Domesday survey of Devonshire: *Dominicatus Regis ad Regnum pertinens in Devenescira*. This would appear to be a plain statement that there were, in 1086, "estates . . . belonging, not to the King, but to the Kingdom." [2] Before examining the specific problem this statement involves, however, it will be advantageous to see what light can be

[2] Paul Vinogradoff, *English Society in the Eleventh Century* (Oxford, 1908), p. 326.

thrown on the nature of the royal demesne by a review of the evidence relating to its administration and exploitation.

The fusion which characterized the feudal monarchy is brought out most obviously in the farm of the king's manors. The sheriff was normally responsible for the royal revenues within his shire, including the farms of royal manors. But to this condition there were so many exceptions that it cannot be considered a hard and fast rule. The farms of particular manors may be found in the hands of sheriffs,[3] reeves or bailiffs,[4] private persons both important [5] and obscure,[6] and possibly the tenants of royal manors themselves.[7] This mixed system probably resulted merely from letting out royal estates to the highest bidder.[8] It was royal revenue, and not any distinction between persons or between official and unofficial capacity, which determined by whom the royal demesne was farmed.

The economic exploitation of some royal manors cannot be separated from their profits and revenues arising from jurisdiction or customary payments which were inherited from the Anglo-Saxon monarchy. This was true no matter who might be the farmer of such royal manors. "Public" officials farmed the "private" agricul-

3 For example, Roger Bigod, sheriff of Norfolk and Suffolk, and Ralf Taillebois, sheriff of Bedfordshire (*D.B.*, I, foll. 209, 218b; II, fol. 287). Farming activities are also suggested by two Berkshire *Terra Regis* entries: "Rex tenet in dominio Spersolt. Tres liberi homines tenuerunt T.R.E. pro III Maneria. Frogerus uicecomes post habuit & fecit unum manerium" (*D.B.*, I, fol. 57 [Sparsholt]); and ". . . dimidia hida fuit de firma regis, sed tempore Godrici uicecomitis fuit foris missa" (*D.B.*, I, fol. 57b [Shalbourn]). See also J. H. Round, "Introduction to the Domesday Survey," in *The Victoria History of the County of Buckingham* (ed. Wm. Page; London, 1905), I, 220f.

4 Domesday Book occasionally mentions reeves (*prefecti* or *prepositi*) in such a context that it is not clear whether a sheriff's official or an independent royal bailiff is meant (*D.B.*, I, fol. 30b [Ewell, Surrey]; II, fol. 287 [Bergholt, Suffolk]).

5 For example, Hugh de Port, the greatest lay tenant-in-chief in Hampshire (*D.B.*, I, foll. 38b, 39 [Eling and Holdenhurst, Hampshire], 219 [South Luffenham and Kelthorpe, Northamptonshire]).

6 For example, William, son of Stur (*D.B.*, I, fol. 52b [Bowcombe in Carisbrooke, Haldley, Lymerston in Brixton, and Shide, in the Isle of Wight]).

7 The practice certainly was rare and exceptional on royal manors, but can be found on several ecclesiastical or other private manors, some of which had been alienated recently. See Round, "Introduction to the Domesday Survey," in *A History of Hampshire and the Isle of Wight* (The Victoria History of the Counties of England; Westminster, 1900), I, 442.

8 *Ibid.*, I, 414.

tural profits of the king; so also, "private" persons farmed manorial profits which included "public" revenues. This fusion of administrative activities was neither a break from Anglo-Saxon practice nor was it unprecedented for the Norman kings. The ducal manors in Normandy were, before the Conquest, in the charge of *vicomtes* (*vicecomites*) of the administrative units into which the duchy was divided.[9] Nor was this system introduced into England by the Conqueror, as the antiquity of the hundred manor demonstrates. These hundred manors were the centers of hundred jurisdiction, to which were annexed the financial profits of both the hundred court and the ancient royal *feorm* or its commutation. When the hundred appears as the definitive unit of local government in England, in many instances the royal manor to which a hundred was thus annexed provided the name of the hundred.[10] Some royal hundred manors were centers of even larger areas, for the judicial revenues of several hundreds were annexed to them at the time of the Domesday survey.[11] The hundred manor, of course, was not peculiarly royal; where hundreds were in private hands, either singly or in groups, the normal center of administration was the most important manor of the lord of the franchise.

Royal hundred manors were sometimes used as more than centers of public local administration. They, as well as other important royal manors, could also constitute centers of groups of manors,

[9] W. J. Corbett, "The Development of the Duchy of Normandy and the Norman Conquest of England," in *The Cambridge Medieval History* (ed. J. R. Tanner, C. W. Previte-Orton, and Z. N. Brooke; Cambridge, 1926), V, 485.

[10] For a typical royal hundred manor of the old Wessex kingdom, see *D.B.*, IV, fol. 84b (Axminster, Devonshire, in the Exon Domesday). Various customary dues were paid there from private manors. See also, F. M. Stenton, "Introduction to the Domesday Survey," in *The Victoria History of the County of Huntingdon* (ed. Wm. Page, G. Proby, and H. E. Norris; London, 1926), I, 328; Wm. Farrer, "Introduction to the Domesday Survey," in *The Victoria History of the County of Lancaster* (ed. Wm. Farrer and J. Brownbill; London, 1906), I, 270f.; Stenton, "Introduction to the Domesday Survey," in *The Victoria History of the County of Oxford* (ed. L. F. Salzman; London, 1939), I, 374f.; and, for a review of the evidence as a whole, H. M. Cam, *"Manerium cum Hundredo:* the Hundred and the Hundredal Manor," in *Liberties & Communities in Medieval England* (Cambridge, 1944), pp. 64–90, reprinted from *English Historical Review,* XLVII (1932), 353–376.

[11] For example, *D.B.*, I, fol. 154b (Bensington, Oxfordshire). See also, Maitland, *D.B. and Bey.*, pp. 90ff., 288f.; Cam, *"Manerium cum Hundredo," passim;* and Cam, "Early Groups of Hundreds," in *Liberties & Communities,* pp. 91–106, reprinted from *Historical Essays in Honour of James Tait* (Manchester, 1933), pp. 13–26.

berwicks, or lands variously described ("sokeland," "appurtenances," etc.), associated together for purely economic exploitation.[12] The jurisdiction of such centers was manorial and economic and was confined to the appurtenant manors and lands, as in any private combination. There was no necessary connection with the hundred court, though the manorial court (if it existed at all in the eleventh century) probably coincided with the former.[13] This intimate association of some of the larger royal manors with the administration of one or more hundreds, this twofold function of the courts of the same manors—both hundredal and manorial—placed the royal demesne definitely within the normal county and hundred administration of the sheriffs and their bailiffs. Many of the latter thus acted as both "private" servants and "public" officials of the crown.

The surviving documents of the Conqueror's reign, which illustrate the administrative activities of the central government and its use of the normal administrative machinery of shire and hundred, make it clear that the royal demesne was not singled out for special treatment or excluded from the general administration of the realm as a special "immunity." [14] The *Inquisitio*

---

[12] Vinogradoff, *Eng. Soc.*, pp. 328–332.

[13] This cannot be demonstrated from the eleventh century evidence alone, but there are sufficient instances of a clear survival of this association of manorial and hundred court in the same royal hundred manor to justify the statement above. The most familiar case is that of Basingstoke, Hampshire, for which the pertinent references are: *D.B.*, I, fol. 39; *Rot. Hund.*, II, 220f.; F. J. Baigent and J. E. Millard, *A History of the Ancient Town and Manor of Basingstoke* (Basingstoke, 1889), pp. 68ff., 362 (extract from the Hampshire membrane, Pipe Roll, 13 John); Round, *V.C.H. Hants,* I, 401f.; and M. Curtis, "Basingstoke," *V.C.H. Hants* (ed. Wm. Page; London, 1911), IV, 127ff. For other instances of the mixed hundredal and manorial, economic and jurisdictional, rights annexed to eleventh century royal and private manors, see Maitland, *D.B. and Bey.*, p. 170; N. Nielson, "Introduction to the Domesday Survey," in *The Victoria History of the County of Kent* (ed. Wm. Page; London, 1932), III, 181; Stenton, *V.C.H. Oxford,* I, 374; and E. B. Demarest, "The Hundred Pennies," *E.H.R.*, XXXIII (1918), 62–72.

[14] Generalizing from the thirteenth century and later evidence, Vinogradoff declared, "the king's manor is treated as a franchise isolated from the surrounding hundred and shire," and that this (and other peculiarities of ancient demesne) was "a remnant of the condition of things before the Conquest" preserved on the royal demesne because "the king was decidedly considered as the one great safeguard of Saxon tradition" (*Villainage in England* [Oxford, 1892], pp. 92, 124f.). From the Domesday evidence he concluded that, of the three types of royal manors of the

Geldi[15] of the southwestern counties and the Northamptonshire Geld Roll,[16] both antedating the great survey, and the several "Domesday satellites" of the Conqueror's and later reigns, taken together create the impression that the monarchy was actively gathering—from its vassals, its tax collectors, and its subjects in the local courts—the information necessary to govern the newly conquered kingdom.[17] In each of these documents, the royal demesne is included if relevant to its purpose.[18] The *clamores* of the Domesday

---

eleventh century, one type consisted, in 1086, of "free tenements gradually passing under the manorial authority of the King and of his officers," and that "the freemen or socmen in question belong to the whole hundred" (*Eng. Soc.*, p. 330). These statements are difficult to reconcile, but the evidence he cited in support of the latter assertion is sufficient to establish that the royal demesne was not, T.R.W. at least, administratively separate from the hundred. In support of his theory of the "immunity" of the royal demesne, Vinogradoff appealed (*ibid.*, p. 326, n.3) to the following statement in Domesday Book: "Huius uillae uillani ab omni re uicecomitis sunt quieti" (*D.B.*, I, fol. 30b [Gomshall, Surrey]). Maitland, commenting on this passage eleven years before Vinogradoff wrote, observed that it was inserted in the record "as though it were no general truth that with a royal manor the sheriff had nothing to do" (*D.B. and Bey.*, p. 167). An exceptional or unique statement in Domesday ordinarily indicates an exception. Another Domesday reference which Vinogradoff quoted (in the same place) in support of his theory of "immunity" is not very useful because it, too, is unique, and because the only part of the manor exempt from geld or quit of service is the demesne of the manor (*D.B.*, I, fol. 163 [Tewkesbury, Gloucestershire]). That this was the normal and not a privileged condition, so far as geld is concerned, will appear below.

15 Not (as its name suggests) simply the returns to an inquest, but the record of a geld collection, hundred by hundred, which occasionally incorporates the testimony of "the English" and of local collectors on disputed or doubtful points. This testimony (and some of the other data) may have been taken by local inquest, either during the collection of the geld or afterward, but before the accounts as we now have them were being written; or it may have been supplied by the local tax collectors themselves, orally or in writing and without any inquest, when they paid in the sums collected and accounted for the rest. Between the actual collection and the date of the documents comprising the *Inquisitio*, some administrative activity had taken place, aimed at recovering sums not paid when due, and this activity may have involved an inquest.

16 A less detailed record of the collection of geld, also arranged by hundreds, c.1072.

17 V. H. Galbraith, "The Making of Domesday Book," *E.H.R.*, LVII (1942), 161–177; D. C. Douglas, ed., *Feudal Documents from the Abbey of Bury St. Edmunds* (The British Academy Records of the Social and Economic History of England and Wales, vol. VIII; London, 1932), pp. lxxi–lxxv; and Reginald Lennard, "A Neglected Domesday Satellite," *E.H.R.*, LVIII (1943), 32–41.

18 Thus, the *Inquisitio Comitatus Cantabrigiensis* (ed. N. E. S. A. Hamilton, Royal Society of Literature; London, 1876), probably a copy of the original Domesday returns, practically ignores the Cambridgeshire royal manors where William succeeded

survey prove conclusively that neither the commissioners nor the juries responsible for the information considered the *Terra Regis* outside the scope of their responsibility.[19]

We may now return to the problem of the *Dominicatus Regis ad Regnum pertinens in Devenescira* of the Exon Domesday.[20] The evidence so far reviewed has already made it apparent, in the words of Maitland, that "neither when it speaks of the time of William, nor when it speaks of the time of Edward, does our record draw any clear line between those manors which the king holds as king and those which he holds in his private capacity."[21] The Exon statement is there, nonetheless; and although it is unique as a heading, there are a few other manors or groups of manors which, in the second volume of Domesday Book, are said to be *de regno* or

---

Edward, and for this reason Salzman suggests that the document was "prepared for the use of the sheriff as the officer responsible for collecting gelds" (L. F. Salzman, "Introduction to the Domesday Survey," in *The Victoria County History of the County of Cambridgeshire and the Isle of Ely* [ed. L. F. Salzman; London, 1938], I, 337). By implication, royal manors did not pay geld and to that extent were not under the normal administration of the sheriff. But this interpretation seems to be neither necessary nor probable. (See Galbraith, "Making of Domesday Book," *E.H.R.*, LVII [1942], 170, 174f.) Further, it is difficult to imagine as exempt from geld the sokemen of Fordham and Isleham (*D.B.*, I, fol. 189b) who could "give and sell their lands to whom they would" and who "paid their amercements to the sheriff" (*forisfacturas suas uicecomiti emendabant*). And yet they are not mentioned in the *I.C.C.* Also, it is difficult to account, by Salzman's hypothesis, for the inclusion of the assessment (without further details) of the royal demesne in Soham and Kingston, and for the inclusion of the full Domesday return on the one and one-half hides of Chesterford (in Essex) that lie in Hinxton (in Cambridgeshire), which Salzman does not mention. The latter estate paid geld in Essex. See below, n.80, and Round, *Feudal England* (London, 1895), p. 116. Also, if the document was prepared for use in collecting gelds, as Salzman suggests, why did it alone, and no other geld record, omit the royal manors? Finally, if the demesne manors of the king were omitted because exempt from geld, why were the other exempt lands (Vinogradoff, *Eng. Soc.*, pp. 189f.) included? Until these questions can be answered, the exact purpose of the *I.C.C.* must remain obscure.

19 "In Bvruelle hundred clamant ministri regis super Hugonem comitem in Hecham et Welle terras iiorum fratrum Godric et Edric. et homines de Wapentac deratiocinauerunt eas ad opus regis" (*D.B.*, I, fol. 375 ["Clamores que sunt in Sudtreding Lincolie"]). "Duas carucatas terre quas habet Nigel in Sud dufelt. debent pertinere regis dominio in Poclinton" (*D.B.*, I, fol. 373 ["Clamores De Eurvic Scire"]). See also, *D.B.*, I, fol. 208 (Keyston, Gidding, etc., Huntingdonshire); II, foll. 276b (Bradenham, Norfolk, under "Invasiones in Nordfulc"), 447b ("Invasiones super Regem").

20 *D.B.*, IV, fol. 83.

21 Maitland, *D.B. and Bey.*, p. 167.

de regione or to "pertain" *ad regionem.*[22] What do these words, *regnum* and *regio,* mean? Are they synonyms or antonyms?

Only two alternatives have till now been suggested, one with some confidence and the other tentatively. Round treated *regio* as a mere scribal blunder for *regnum,* even though *regio* occurs three times and *regnum* but twice in Little Domesday; Maitland suggested that *regio* "may well stand for *kingship.*"[23] The difference between these two interpretations, in the present connection, is slight, for both would emphasize a distinction between royal demesne which belonged to the "kingdom" or "kingship" and royal demesne which did not. For both Round and Maitland, the words *fuit de* or *pertinuit,* when used with either *regnum* or *regio,* denote possession, and thus the manors so qualified belong to a special category of the royal demesne. The Domesday evidence would appear to be fragile support for even these cautious inferences, and, furthermore, the very infrequency of these references to *regnum* or *regio* would rule out any significance in the distinction which Round and Maitland thought they implied.[24]

There is a real distinction implied by *regnum* and *regio,* but it must be sought in a different quarter. A fresh approach, which no one seems yet to have explored, is provided by assuming that the Domesday scribes meant exactly what they wrote when they used the word *regio.* Instead of a blunder for "kingdom" or a crude expression of "kingship," it simply means region, i.e., *provincia, scira,* or *comitatus.* It is curious that (with one exception which does not concern the royal demesne) both *regnum* and *regio* occur only in what Professor Galbraith believes are "local Domesdays," preliminary digests put together locally from the "original returns" of a single Domesday circuit.[25] *Regio* has crept into the East Anglian

[22] "Terra Regis de Regione quam Rogerus Bigotus seruat," "Tornei manerium Regis de regione," and "Suafham pertinuit [*sic*] ad regionem" (*D.B.,* II, foll. 281b, 408b, 144); and "Terra Regis de Regno" and "Sparle tenuit R. E. et hoc manerium fuit de regno" (*D.B.,* II, foll. 289b, 119b). Where either phrase is used in conjunction with *Terra Regis,* it is part of a heading prefixed to a group of royal manors.

[23] Round, *Feud. Eng.,* p. 140; Maitland, *D.B. and Bey.,* p. 167.

[24] A *reductio ad absurdum* is reached when only two of the above passages are quoted "to warrant the suggestion that the demesne lands [of the king] were . . . the property of the nation" (Hubert Hall and S. R. Bird, "Notes on the History of the Crown Lands," *The Antiquary,* XIII [1886], 89).

[25] Galbraith, "Making of Domesday Book," *E.H.R.,* LVII (1942), 161–177. The

text (Little Domesday) to express the same distinction brought out more fully by the *mansiones de comitatu* which are found in the Exon Domesday but nowhere else.[26] In the East Anglian Domesday, *regnum* is opposed to *regio* just as in the southwestern Domesday *ad regnum* opposes *de comitatu*. This is a distinction between central and local administration, not a precocious political theory. *Mansiones de comitatu* and *maneria de regione* may have been meaningful phrases to the clerks of the Domesday circuits, but such manors are in fact *Terra Regis*, and the Domesday scribes at Winchester generally eliminated or ignored these local distinctions. Thus, in Great Domesday's *Terra Regis* sections there is no parallel to the clearly marked categories of royal demesne, arranged according to *antecessores* (as in the Exon Domesday) or according to farmers or *custodes* (as in Little Domesday). The central government will be no more interested in recording which manors have traditionally supported the local earl and which the king than it will be interested in categorizing royal manors in accordance with who held or who farms them. On the other hand, the clerks of Roger Bigod, sheriff of Norfolk and Suffolk, might well desire to stress the "comital" aspect of royal manors which have been assigned traditionally to the support of the local earl or sheriff.

For this explanation, as an alternative to the theories of Round and Maitland, no more than probability can be claimed. Leaving the realm of hypothesis, however, there is one final consideration which should dispel any real significance from whatever distinction may be read into the phrase *ad Regnum pertinens*. This is the fact that manors which *pertinuit* (i.e., T.R.E.) or were of the *regnum* or *regio* had been granted away by Edward. In fact, of the three manors in Norfolk and Suffolk which are individually mentioned as "pertaining" or "being" *ad regionem* or *de regno*, two were forfeited estates which Edward had alienated to Ralph

---

Exon Domesday is an original "local Domesday," and Little Domesday is a "fair copy" sent to Winchester but never edited, condensed, and incorporated into Great Domesday. The only other Domesday use of *regio* of which I am aware occurs in the customs of Yorkshire (*D.B.*, I, fol. 298b), where abjuring the realm seems to be contrasted with banishment from the *regio* by the earl or sheriff, again implying an equivalence between *regio* and shire.

[26] *D.B.*, IV, fol. 99.

the Earl. Therefore, both the paucity of evidence and the fact that two out of the three manors so denominated had been alienated vitiate any theory that "the germs of the later ancient demesne doctrine are clearly perceptible" in the Domesday references to *regnum* or *regio* or that "the main stock of Crown estates ought not to be alienated at all: they are described as belonging . . . to the Kingdom." [27]

The evidence which has so far been considered all relates to the administration of the royal demesne of the Conqueror. Both as a whole—in that the documents themselves and the administrative machinery which produced them dealt with the royal demesne as well as the rest of the realm—and with regard also to detailed problems, there appears to be in this body of evidence no fundamental distinction between the royal demesne and the rest of the realm, between one or another kind of royal demesne, or between the king's authority as "public" ruler and as the greatest "private" landlord.

It should be stressed, however, that the documents in which this evidence is preserved were concerned, perhaps primarily, with taxation. Whatever else Domesday Book was, it was also a "Geld-Book," at least in the sense that it served as "the 'book of hides' from which could be calculated the total number of hides for which each tenant-in-chief was liable." [28] Other, nearly contemporary documents record the assessment and collection of geld in particular years. To this side of the evidence we must now turn, for the evidence relating to taxation in these documents has been claimed to show a real and basic distinction between the royal demesne and other lands. The distinction is based upon the belief that the royal demesne, or at least the royal manors which had been held by Edward, were exempt from taxation.[29]

---

[27] Vinogradoff, *Eng. Soc.*, p. 326.

[28] Galbraith, *Studies in the Public Records* (London, 1948), p. 106. Professor Galbraith denies that the purpose of the inquest was a reassessment of the geld (*ibid.*, p. 105), and considers that Round's distinction between the inquest and Domesday Book is both "far-fetched" and "unreal" (*ibid.*, pp. 99, 101). Hence it is "a pointless exaggeration to call Domesday a geld book" (*ibid.*, p. 105). Compare D. C. Douglas, *The Domesday Monachorum of Christ Church, Canterbury* (London, 1944), pp. 25f.

[29] "Nor is there a lack of information to the effect that royal manors were in principle held to be exempted from the payment of geld because they were subjected

It is true that many manors listed under the rubric *Terra Regis* are specifically stated in Domesday Book not to be liable for geld. Of them it may be said that they are not and never were "distributed into hides," or the like.[30] They have never within memory been taxed to the geld or even assessed in hides. And it is true that the majority of these manors had been held by Edward and were ancient estates which from their first settlement had probably belonged to kings of the West Saxon monarchy. Does this evidence warrant the conclusion that the royal demesne as a whole, or that the "ancient demesne" of 1086, was exempt from geld as a principle underlying the Norman system of taxation?

Certainly it was not unusual that royal manors were exempt. Neither was it unusual, however, that royal manors, even those which Edward held, were subject to geld, and Domesday Book says so specifically, when speaking *de tempore Edwardi*.[31] If St. Edward taxed some of his ancient estates, is it reasonable that William the Conqueror would not? In some counties, Hampshire and Berkshire for instance, several royal manors are carefully distinguished in Domesday Book as exempt from geld; what are we to conclude with regard to the royal manors which are not so distinguished?[32] Finally, if royal manors were exempt from geld so were

---

to the king's farm" (Vinogradoff, *Eng. Soc.*, p. 182). So also, Round, writing of the manors held by Edward in Somerset, declared that they were "not liable to pay 'geld,' . . . a feature distinctive and peculiar to them" ("Introduction to the Domesday Survey," in *The Victoria History of the County of Somerset* [ed. Wm. Page; London, 1906], I, 394f.). Maitland was aware of the many exempt royal manors, but nowhere in his writings have I found that he enlarged this particular status of individual manors into a principle affecting the royal demesne as a whole. On the contrary, "the degree in which the various manors of the crown stood outside the national system of finance, justice and police we can not accurately ascertain. Some, but by no means all, pay no geld" (*D.B. and Bey.*, p. 167).

[30] For example, Axminster, Devonshire, "quam tenuit rex Edwardus ea die qua rex ipse fuit viva et mortua et nescitur quot hide ibi sunt quia nunquam reddidit gildum" (*D.B.*, IV, fol. 85); and Basingstoke, Hampshire, "Regale manerium fuit semper. Nunquam geldum dedit, nec hida ibi distributa fuit" (*D.B.*, I, fol. 39).

[31] For example, under "Dominicatus ad Regnum pertinens": Kerswell, Devonshire, ". . . quam tenuit Edwardus rex . . . reddidit gildum pro I hida et dimidia," and Teignton, Devonshire, ". . . quam tenuit Edwardus rex . . . reddidit pro I hida et I virga" (*D.B.*, IV, fol. 85 [Exon Domesday]).

[32] In Hampshire, of thirty-nine royal manors about which the evidence seems clear, twenty-eight were exempt or not hidated, while eleven were assessed in hides or said to pay geld. Of the twenty-eight exempt, thirteen were held by Edward and

manors in private hands, particularly those held by churches and monasteries.

But the problem of geld exemption has been oversimplified in the discussion so far. On almost every folio of the Domesday *Terra Regis,* as well as throughout the whole record generally, the evidence makes it clear that the problem of exemption cannot be stated in terms of the dilemma: "either fully assessed to the geld, or fully exempt." Actually, exemption was a relative matter. Full assessment or full exemption were only the two extremes of a condition which could be fixed at any point in between, and it is sufficient to call attention to the extensive "beneficial hidation" [33] found in Domesday Book in all parts of England, though particularly in the southern shires, to demonstrate that relief from taxation could be a matter of degree and was subject to the will of the king. Such relief may have been granted in accordance with some principle or plan, but from the evidence now available the salient feature of this reduction in assessment seems to have been royal grace.[34] It is, then, small wonder that royal manors, centers of administration and directly subject to exploitation by the servants

---

fifteen were not; of those not exempt, one was held by Edward and ten were not (*D.B.,* I, foll. 38–39b).

In Berkshire, out of forty-one manors, twenty were assessed in hides or said to pay geld; twenty-one were either not so assessed or said to be exempt. Of those assessed, eleven were held by Edward; of those exempt, only six were held by Edward. The entry concerning Cholsey is instructive: there were twenty-three hides, but it was assessed at twenty-two hides, and "out of the whole of this land the king has eleven hides which pay no geld." King Edward held it. In his introduction to the Berkshire Domesday, Round did not mention the Cholsey case, and I have not found that he noticed it elsewhere, but it is clear that he believed the manors held by Edward to be exempt from geld as a class (*D.B.,* I, foll. 56b–58; *The Victoria History of the County of Berkshire* [ed. P. H. Ditchfield and Wm. Page; London, 1906], I, 328; and Round, "Danegeld and the Finance of Domesday," in *Domesday Studies* [ed. P. E. Dove, 2 vols.; London, 1888], I, 102f.).

[33] Maitland, *D.B. and Bey.,* p. 264.

[34] Round cited the following cases of "special exemptions": "a geldo quietae concessu E. et W. regum," "rex concessit VI hidas quietas a geldo," "Wills. rex concessit III hidas ex his quietas a geldo," "quietae a geldo per W. regem" (*D.B.,* I, foll. 165, 169, 170 [ecclesiastical and lay manors in Gloucestershire]); "rex W. condonavit VI hidas quietas a geldo" (*D.B.,* I, fol. 186 [Herefordshire]); "fuit pro XV hidis, sed rex E. condonavit pro XI hidis ut dicunt" (*D.B.,* I, fol. 58b [Berkshire]); "T.R.E. se defendebant pro IIII hidis et una virgata, modo pro nichilo. Revocant regem pro geldo" (*D.B.,* I, fol. 43 [Hampshire]); (*Domesday Studies,* I, 98–101).

of the king, should benefit in greatest measure from this relief from public taxation. But this exemption of certain royal manors from the payment of geld was matched, or nearly matched, by exemption granted to manors held by private parties, either ecclesiastical or (more rarely) lay.[35] The distinguishing characteristic of the reduction of hidage on royal demesne is a distinction of degree, not of kind: exemption on many royal manors was often total, whereas exemption on private manors was usually partial.

It seems clear that there was no general distinction between royal lands and private lands, or between royal lands which Edward had held and royal lands which he had not held, with respect to Anglo-Norman taxation. The belief is widely held, however, that such a distinction can be shown for one type of royal manor, and, further, that administratively manors of this type enjoyed the status of an immunity, being extrahundredal and outside the sphere of shrieval authority. These are the royal estates which were subject to a special payment referred to in Domesday Book as the *firma unius noctis* or "farm of one day," or of fractions or multiples of one night's or one day's farm. The argument for immunity and geld exemption, for a special position of privilege and inalienability from the crown, for these manors is based upon the facts that in Domesday Book they give every appearance of being ancient settlements, that they render food rents and other primitive customary payments (although by 1086 these were generally commuted into cash), and that Domesday, while never saying that such manors pay geld, usually specifies that they either do not pay or that they are not assessed in hides.[36]

These facts must be granted; and it must also be granted that of all the *Terra Regis* these farm-of-one-night manors come nearest to justifying the theory that there was an "ancient demesne" in 1086. Indeed, historians who hold that belief have invariably based their generalizations respecting the "manors of St. Edward" upon the peculiarities of this particular group of estates. Of course, such a procedure is gratuitous because the two categories by no

---

[35] Maitland, *D.B. and Bey.*, pp. 448f.

[36] Vinogradoff, *Eng. Soc.*, pp. 182f., 384f.; Stenton, *Anglo-Saxon England,* p. 476; James Tait, *The Medieval English Borough* (Publications of the University of Manchester, No. CCXLV, Historical Series, No. LXX; Manchester, 1936), pp. 51f.

means coincide. It is for this reason that we have postponed any notice of this group of manors until having completed a preliminary survey of the evidence relating to administration and taxation of the rest of the royal demesne. The farm of one night presents a special problem, and must be treated as such, without generalizing from its peculiarities conclusions applying to the whole, or any other part, of the royal demesne.

In the first place, it may be noted that Domesday never draws a causal relationship between the night's farm and geld exemption, as have the proponents of the theory we are testing.[37] Second, the record never states that manors which pay the night's farm are extrahundredal or outside the normal administration of the shire.

Whatever was the nature of the Old English *feorm,* whether paid in kind or commuted into a money payment, the farm of one night found in Domesday Book [38] was so far from being extrahundredal that it is actually rendered by hundred manors, and it included the profits of local (i.e., hundredal) administration and justice.[39] The evidence is incontrovertible, for the post-Conquest period: the farm combined the private revenue of the king (from the agricultural exploitation of his manors) with the king's public revenue from his jurisdictional and administrative profits (customary payments and the *consuetudo placitorum* of the hundred court). This

[37] The theory rests upon such evidence as: "Rex Edwardus tenuit et nunquam geldauit, ideo nescitur quot hidae sint ibi. . . . Haec uilla reddit firmam unius noctis cum omnibus consuetudinibus" (*D.B.,* I, fol. 64b [Calne, Wiltshire]).

[38] That is, the *increased* render, T.R.W., still called the farm of one night, as in Hampshire. This may well indicate the addition of a new element in the farm, even perhaps the farmed profits of a hundred court.

[39] The connection between the post-Conquest (or at least post-1086) *firma unius noctis* and the local administration of the hundred is indicated in the references given above, footnote 12. Whether the *firma unius noctis* was a remnant of an ancient system of taxation (Demarest, "Hundred Pennies," *E.H.R.,* XXXIII [1918], 62–72), or whether the various customs recorded in Domesday Book were identical with, added to, or merely part of the farm, it is clear that "the old rent (*firma*) covered, not merely the income from the manor proper, but other revenue, which the king normally reserved for himself" (Carl Stephenson, "The *'Firma Unius Noctis'* and the Customs of the Hundred," *E.H.R.,* XXXIX [1924], 164, n.2). This other revenue could include the *consuetudo placitorum,* and the Domesday scribe adds, *ut dicunt prepositi et homines regis* and *calumpniantur hundremani et prepositus regis . . . ad opus firme Ermtone mansionis regis* (*D.B.,* I, fol. 105b, and IV, fol. 218). The reeve would hardly make this claim for Ermington had not this situation existed elsewhere.

is definitive evidence of the essential nature of the royal demesne under the Anglo-Norman monarchy: a fusion of private and public rights, of person and office, in the administration and exploitation of the royal demesne.

With regard to taxation, a good case may be made out for exemption of some particular manors because of the payment of the farm of one night, or the like. However, from the Domesday evidence it could be argued equally well that manors paid the farm because they were exempt from geld. In either case, the institution (as applied to royal manors) was practically restricted to the four adjacent counties of Dorset, Somerset, Wiltshire, and Hampshire. As such, it would then be a local custom of old Wessex and cannot support a generalization about the royal demesne as a whole or even the manors which Edward held.

One may doubt, however, that geld exemption was due to payment of the *firma unius noctis* alone, since practically none of these manors was hidated,[40] and many other manors, likewise neither hidated nor subject to geld, nevertheless did not pay the farm of one night. It may also be doubted whether the *firma unius noctis* as such entailed geld exemption or anything else. The phrase does not seem to have been a technical or precise term. The various payments in kind which in some counties are grouped together and called the farm of one night will in other counties appear separately or together, without any title, and the royal manors owing these payments are assessed to the geld.[41]

When all the relevant evidence is considered, it does not appear that Domesday Book justifies any basic distinction between royal manors which paid the farm of one night and those which did not, with regard to the administration or taxation of the royal demesne. The farm-of-one-night manors stand out, generally but not with-

40 There are a few examples of hidation applied to a manor owing the farm of one night; e.g., "Rex Edwardus tenuit. Ibi xlvi hidae fuerunt et sunt. . . . T.R.E. reddebat firmam unius noctis" (*D.B.*, I, fol. 20b [Eastbourne, Sussex]).

41 For royal manors assessed to the geld and also paying the corn, honey, and malt renders typical of the farm of one night, see *D.B.*, I, fol. 189 (Cambridgeshire *Terra Regis*). Oxfordshire and Northamptonshire paid a farm of three nights as counties (*D.B.*, I, foll. 154b, 219)—a fact which cuts across the neat formula that this farm, "in the domain of the sovereign, ministering to his private needs," entailed geld exemption (Vinogradoff, *Eng. Soc.*, pp. 182f.).

out exceptions, as large, old, and important manors, often the administrative centers of local government. Beyond this the evidence does not warrant any such concept as that of an "ancient demesne" of the Conqueror. These manors, like all the manors which Edward held, and like the other manors of the Domesday *Terra Regis,* when considered from the point of view of administration and taxation, suggest no significant distinction between the royal demesne and the rest of the realm, or between an "ancient demesne" and the rest of the royal demesne, or between a "private revenue" and a "public revenue" of the king. Both in administrative arrangements and in the liability for or exemption from taxation, the use and treatment of the royal demesne appear in Domesday Book to be subject only to the will of the monarch, unrestricted and uninfluenced by any of the distinctions or concepts which have been read into the evidence by Domesday scholars who were interested in broader subjects than that of the royal demesne. If one or another royal manor or type of royal manor enjoyed administrative immunity or geld exemption, such privilege rested not upon any custom derived from Anglo-Saxon times or any inherent principle of the Anglo-Saxon or Norman monarchy; rather, it sprang from the deliberate policy of the Conqueror and his government, whether that meant the acceptance or alteration of customary arrangements or the creation of a new arrangement.

Such are the conclusions to which a review of the Domesday and related evidence has led, but it must be admitted that some of the evidence is by no means categorical or unambiguous. Particularly may this be said of Domesday entries which give the hidage of a royal manor, but make no reference to geld at all. Royal manors which are not assessed in hides may safely be assumed to be exempt from taxation; the same may be said of manors which, although hidated, are specifically stated to be exempt. But private manors are also described in both ways. It is our contention, and will now be argued, that all other royal manors, like all other private manors, probably were subject to taxation.

The weight of the received doctrine of Domesday scholarship leans the other way, i.e., to the belief that the royal demesne (or at least what is called the "ancient demesne") was not, in principle and T.R.W. at least, subject to taxation. Fortunately, two documents survive from the reign of William the Conqueror which can provide a definitive solution of this problem, viz., whether the royal demesne or any part of it, T.R.W., was exempt from the geld on any principle different from that on which exemption was granted to various private manors. These documents are "the earliest English public records of which the text has survived." [42] They preserve an account of the collection of geld in several hundreds in five of the southwestern counties and in the county of Northamptonshire. These documents are the so-called *Inquisitio Geldi,* of 1084, and the Northamptonshire Geld Roll, of c.1072–1075.[43]

THE *INQUISITIO GELDI* AND TAXATION

The following typical entry is quoted from the account of the hundred of Lifton, in Devonshire, taken from the *Inquisitio Geldi:*

> There are twenty hides in Lifton hundred. From it the king has four pounds and fifteen shillings of his geld for sixteen hides less half a virgate. Of the four hides and half a virgate remaining (*remanentibus*), which have not rendered geld, the king has three hides *in dominio. . . .* Aluured Brito half a virgate *in dominio. . . .* For half a hide which Ralph holds of Baldwin the sheriff the king has not had his geld this year.[44]

[42] Stenton, *Anglo-Saxon England,* p. 636.

[43] *Inquisitio Geldi,* in *D.B.,* IV, 1–26, 59–75, 489f. (references, however, will be to folios of the *Inquisitio*); Northamptonshire Geld Roll, in A. J. Robertson, ed., *Anglo-Saxon Charters* (Cambridge Studies in English Legal History, ed. H. D. Hazeltine; Cambridge: Cambridge University Press, 1939), pp. 230–237. The question of the date of the *Inquisitio Geldi* has recently been reopened by Galbraith, who has rejected the generally accepted date of 1083–1084 and concluded that "the geld rolls 'in the form in which they have come down to us,' are not earlier than the Domesday survey" ("The Date of the Geld Rolls in Exon Domesday," *E.H.R.,* LXV [1950], 2). So late a date for the *Inquisitio,* and what Galbraith considers "the overwhelming probability that the geld rolls are dependent upon information contained in the raw material of the Domesday inquest" (*ibid.,* p. 12), would be even more plausible if the discrepancies both in hidation and in the tenants found in the two records could be explained away satisfactorily.

[44] "In hundreto listone sunt xx hide. Inde habet Rex iiii libras & xv sol. pro xvi hidis dimidia virga min' de Gildo suo. De iiii hidis et dimidia virga remanentibus, q' Gildum non reddiderunt, habet Rex iii hid' in dominio. . . . aluured' brito dim' virgam in dominio. . . . pro dim' hida quam tenet Radulfus de balduino uicecomite non habuit Rex hoc anno Gildum suum" (*D.B.,* IV, fol. 65).

The first fact stated by the entry is the number of hides in the hundred; then comes the amount of geld collected, together with the number of hides which have paid (from which data it may be determined that the rate was six shillings on the hide). The record then proceeds to account for the hides *remanentes,* the difference between the total and the number which have paid. In the Lifton case, some of the hides which *Gildum non reddiderunt* are said to be held *in dominio,* while from half a hide it is said that the king did not have his geld this year. Throughout the *Inquisitio,* the order of listing the items in the various entries may vary, and there may be given other or additional reasons to account for hides which have not paid geld. Almost invariably, however, there are a certain number of hides listed as not having paid and explained as being held *in dominio,* whether by the king or by others. In some entries all the hides of a hundred have paid except those held *in dominio.* Thus, for Uggscombe hundred, Dorsetshire, there are 104 hides; sixty-four have paid geld and forty are said to be held *in dominio.*[45] Now there can be no doubt (and no scholar has questioned) that the hides which the *Inquisitio* lists as held *in dominio* were exempt from geld, although we can search the document in vain for a specific statement to this effect. The hides *in dominio* are never qualified, never said not to have paid *hoc anno,* or the like, while all other hides *remanentes* are invariably qualified in some way which will tell why they have not paid—either they are specifically said to be exempt, and the reason is given, or they are said not to have paid *hoc anno* or otherwise specified as being "delinquent" in their geld.

The problem to be solved is the meaning of *dominium,* the nature of the hides which the *Inquisitio* notices as exempt because held *in dominio,* particularly the land so characterized and said to be held by the king. If the *Inquisitio* is referring to the same thing as Domesday Book, when the latter repeatedly states that the king holds one manor after another *in dominio,* then the *Inquisitio* is referring to what Domesday Book calls *Terra Regis,* and it might be argued that the royal demesne of the Conqueror was therefore exempt from geld.

The theory that the royal demesne was exempt from the Anglo-

[45] *D.B.,* IV, fol. 17b.

Norman geld seems attractive because it is not only simple and sweeping, but also logical, for why should the king subject his own property to a public tax as unpopular as the chroniclers indicate?[46] An immediate difficulty arises, however, when the consequences of such an interpretation are spelled out. It was not only the hides which the king held *in dominio* which were exempt, but also those which *habent barones regis in dominio*[47] or which *rex et barones sui habent in dominio.*[48] The *Inquisitio* draws no distinction between the exemption affecting the king and the king's barons, and the *barones* of the *Inquisitio* are all the king's tenants-in-chief, ecclesiastical and lay, no matter how humble.[49] Now tenants-in-chief certainly did pay geld for manors which they held "in demesne" directly from the king and did not subinfeudate. That the geld did not fall only upon the manors held by subtenants is clear from the most superficial analysis of Domesday Book. For example, in Devonshire, a county whose Domesday evidence can be checked against the data of the *Inquisitio,* Domesday specifically states that all but two of the manors held by tenants-in-chief paid geld.[50] There would seem to be a contradiction here: Domesday Book shows that manors held *in dominio* by a tenant-in-chief normally paid geld, whereas the *Inquisitio* records that a certain number of hides held *in dominio* by the same tenant-in-chief were exempt.

[46] "It was a principle of the Gheld-laws . . . the Ancient-Crown-Demesnes were to be absolutely ingeldable. . . . The Royal Demesnes of Dorset were non-hidated and ingeldable" (R. W. Eyton, *A Key to Domesday . . . Analysis and Digest of the Dorset Survey* [Dorchester, 1878]; p. 5, n.1, p. 80; Vinogradoff, *Eng. Soc.,* p. 326; Round, *Domesday Studies,* I, 102f.). See above, footnote 29.

[47] For example, *D.B.,* IV, fol. 19 (Godderthorne hundred, Dorsetshire).

[48] *D.B.,* IV, fol. 65 (Hartland hundred, Devonshire).

[49] Most of the *barones* of the *Inquisitio* can be identified among the Domesday tenants-in-chief. In the *Inquisitio,* tenure-in-chief seems to be the sole criterion of a baron: the priests of Taunton, Somersetshire (*D.B.,* IV, fol. 75), a widow, Ima or Emma (fol. 69), and Odo the Englishman, son of Edric (foll. 67b, 68b) are each barons. In Domesday Odo held four modest estates, one assessed to the geld at a hide and the other three at a virgate each (*D.B.,* IV, foll. 486b, 489). In the Exon Domesday he is classified as an English thane (fol. 481), and in the Exchequer Domesday as a king's thane (*D.B.,* I, fol. 87).

[50] The exceptions are the Abbot of Bucfast's manor of Bucfast (*D.B.,* IV, fol. 183) and Walter of Dowai's manor of Bampton (*D.B.,* IV, fol. 345b). The latter had been held by King Edward on the day on which he was alive and dead, and had been alienated by William.

The explanation of this seeming contradiction can only lie in the fact that the two documents were not referring to the same thing when they used the word *dominium*. Or, more accurately stated, the *Inquisitio* refers to only one kind of demesne, while Domesday Book uses the word in two senses. *Dominium* had two meanings when used to describe land, one that might be called feudal, and one that has a manorial reference. First, in the feudal sense, the term referred to a manor as a whole. A manor held *in dominio* was one which had not been subinfeudated to another person as lord of that manor.[51] Second, in the manorial sense, the term referred to only part of the manor. The part of the manor held *in dominio* was the land which was made productive by the labor of, but not occupied by, the peasantry of the manor. This distinction between feudal and manorial demesne provides the solution of the problem of exemption from geld. When the *Inquisitio* lists hides which are exempt because held *in dominio,* it refers not to *manors* held "in demesne," but rather to the *manorial demesne* of the manors held "in demesne" by the king and his tenants-in-chief.[52] The distinction made in the *Inquisitio* was not between geldable and ingeldable manors, but between exempt demesne and nonexempt *terra villanorum*.

---

[51] In order to keep the distinction clear in the following discussion, demesne in its feudal meaning will be referred to by the phrase "in demesne" in quotation marks. It should be added that in later usage, a free tenement within a manor could be said to be held "in demesne," but this distinction does not concern the present discussion.

[52] The distinction between baronial and other demesnes and the exemption from geld of baronial demesnes have both been denied. See Appendix A.

Maitland stressed the distinction between land *in dominio* and the *terra villanorum* within the Domesday manor. But he did not do justice to the Domesday distinction between a manor held *in dominium* and one held by a subtenant when he said: "There is already a slight ambiguity about the term *dominium.* We may say that a church has a manor *in dominio,* meaning thereby that the manor as a whole is held by the church itself and is not held of it by any tenant; and then we may go on to say that only one half of the land comprised in this manor is held by the church *in dominio*" (*D.B. and Bey.,* pp. 53f., 54, n.1). Repeatedly, Domesday Book uses the term without ambiguity but in the twofold sense in which *dominium* was understood, in connection with land. For example: "Comes de Ow tenet in dominio manerium quod uocatur Hou" (*D.B.,* I, fol. 18); "Ipse episcopus tenet Waltham in dominio" (fol. 40); "Ipsa abbatia tenet Bertune in dominio. . . . In dominio sunt iii carucae" (fol. 58b); "Osbernus episcopus tenet in dominio Bocheland. . . . Ibi nil in dominio" (fol. 58b); "Eiland . . . tenet Suenus in dominio. . . . ii carucae in dominio, et x carucae hominum" (*D.B.,* II, fol. 47).

The general rule suggested by a comparison of the evidence of the *Inquisitio* and Domesday, then, is that the hides which the former document lists as exempt because held *in dominio* do not refer to manors—the royal demesne as a whole, the *Terra Regis* of Domesday—but to the manorial demesne of royal manors. It may be added at once that there were also exempt manors in the southwestern counties, held by both the king and his barons, and that the *Inquisitio* duly records them as exempt, but not by listing all their hides as held *in dominio.* To this matter we shall return, but first, the implications of the general rule just stated should be noticed. If, in any hundred, the king is said to hold a number of exempt hides *in dominio,* the hides of those manors which are not part of the manorial demesne must be understood to pay geld, unless there is a special statement that they are exempt. Otherwise the hidage of the hundred cannot be accounted for, because the *Inquisitio* divides all the hides of a hundred into three categories: (1) the number which have paid, (2) the number *in dominio,* and (3) the number which have not paid, either because (a) stated to be delinquent and owing, or (b) specially exempt, in which case the reason is given. The sum of these three categories always (except for mere error) equals the total hidage stated at the beginning of the entry. Therefore, in every hundred in which the king is listed as having hides *in dominio,* he must have hides also in the first or the third category of the *Inquisitio.*[53]

Now there are many hundreds where the king holds hides *in dominio* and where the *Inquisitio* lists none for him in the third category (e.g., the hundred of Lifton, quoted above). We may therefore conclude that the royal demesne was subject to geld in the same way as all other lands. The distinction between the royal demesne and the rest of the realm, between the king and his vassals, was one of degree and not of kind. The *Terra Regis,* like the land of the barons and prelates and everyone else, was subject to geld with two qualifications. First, the manorial demesne of the manors held "in demesne" by the king and his tenants-in-chief was exempt

[53] I have found no royal manors in the five southwestern counties, covered by the *Inquisitio,* in which all the land was in the demesne of the manor, so this possibility need not be considered.

as a matter of course; and second, there were manors which were exempt as a whole, and of these it is not surprising that the king has more than anyone else.

Before taking up this second qualification, some additional light may be thrown upon the first by a comparison of Domesday Book and the *Inquisitio*. There are one or two Domesday statements that the manorial demesne of a manor held "in demesne" by a tenant-in-chief is exempt from geld. Such statements may be regarded as illustrating the general rule, but they cannot be taken to prove it. In fact, the rare or exceptional statement in Domesday usually implies an exceptional condition, and it so often implies the very opposite, as the general rule, that it must be explained away satisfactorily before the rule it seems to state may be accepted as having a general validity. In the Exon Domesday there occurs one almost perfect statement of what has been established independently (from the *Inquisitio*) as the general rule. It concerns the bishop of Exeter's great manor of Bishop's Tawton, in South Molton hundred, Devonshire: "In it are twelve hides, of which nine rendered geld in the time of King Edward, and the bishop had the other three remaining [hides] in demesne, and they never paid geld." [54] As an explicit statement regarding the payment of and exemption from geld within the manor, this entry is unique for the county and almost so for the whole Domesday.[55] It may therefore be granted that it implies an exceptional condition. The question is whether exemption of the manorial demesne or something else was the exceptional condition.

In the first place, it should be noted that the exceptional part of the Bishop's Tawton entry is not the distinction it draws between the hides in and outside the demesne of the manor. With respect to almost every manor assessed to the geld in Domesday,

[54] "In ea sunt xii hide de quibus ix reddiderunt Gildum tempore regis Edwardi, et alias iii remanentes habuit episcopus in dominio et nunquam Geldauerunt" (*D.B.*, IV, fol. 118).

[55] For other Domesday statements that the manorial demesne of a particular manor did not pay geld, see *D.B.*, I, foll. 163 (Tewkesbury, Gloucestershire), 167b (Guiting, Gloucestershire). The Tewkesbury case involved special arrangements, and Round was justified in criticizing Eyton for having relied upon it alone for his view concerning manorial demesne exemption. But explicit statements cannot be expected from Domesday Book on a matter which primarily affected collection rather than assessment of the geld. For a review of the evidence, see Appendix A.

the commissioners inquired into the extent of the demesne of the manor as well as whether the manor itself were held "in demesne" or by a subtenant. Therefore almost every entry in Domesday Book implies a distinction (1) between demesne and nondemesne within the manor, and (2) between a manor held "in demesne" and one held by a subtenant. For purposes of the geld, a distinction can only be made between liability and exemption. Why did the commissioners spell out this distinction in so many words in the Bishop's Tawton entry?

Turning to the *Inquisitio* entry for South Molton hundred, we find evidence which suggests an answer. The bishop is credited with three hides exempt because held *in dominio,* as we should expect; but the record further states that "for three hides which the men of the bishop of Exeter hold, the king did not receive geld." [56] Now Bishop's Tawton is the bishop's only manor in this hundred, and hence all these hides should lie there. If the bishop's men were delinquent in their taxes, is it not a surprising coincidence that they had failed to pay on exactly three, rather than some other number of hides? This coincidence, when read together with the almost unique Domesday statement concerning the exemption of manorial demesne, suggests that the men of Bishop's Tawton did not just happen to fail to pay on these three hides. Did they contest the liability of this land; that is, did they claim that the three hides which never paid geld were part of the *terra villanorum* rather than in the demesne of the manor? The advent of so many new and foreign lords and officials, following the Conquest, who were ignorant of local conditions, must have provided an opportunity for the English peasantry to try to escape from customary burdens or obligations of which their new masters were perforce ignorant. Domesday Book itself must be explained at least partly in terms of an effort to discover and enforce these rights and obligations, and the Domesday commissioners had judicial authority to settle disputes. The Bishop's Tawton entry in the Exon Domesday might very well incorporate the settlement of a dispute between the tax collectors and the bishop's men arising, perhaps, out of the geld levy recorded in the *Inquisitio*. The exceptional condition which the entry records, then, would be the settlement

[56] *D.B.,* IV, fol. 66.

of a dispute, and not the fact of exemption of the manorial demesne.[57]

Before leaving the subject of the exemption of manorial demesne, it should be noted that the general rule stated above cannot be demonstrated by a collation of the demesne figures given by the *Inquisitio* and those of Domesday Book because the coincidence of assessments recorded by the two documents is not significant. Indeed it is the discrepancy between the two records which strikes one immediately. For example, the *Inquisitio* states that in the hundred of Axmouth the king holds one hide in demesne.[58] Yet in Domesday Book, the king holds only one manor, the hundred manor of Axmouth, in this hundred, and the record states that "how many hides are there is not known because it never paid geld." [59] In the hundred of Exminster, the *Inquisitio* exempts the king from four and one-half hides held in demesne,[60] while Domesday Book lists within this hundred two manors under *Terra Regis,* Exminster, assessed at one hide (and possessing one virgate less a ferling in demesne), and Kenton, assessed at three hides and one ferling (and possessing a demesne of one hide).[61] The total Domesday assessment of the king's manors in Exminster hundred thus comes to four hides and one ferling assessed to the geld, of which one hide and three ferlings are held in demesne. The discrepancy here between the *Inquisitio* exemption and the total geld assessment is one virgate and three ferlings; the discrepancy when measured against the Domesday figures for the demesne of the manors is three hides, one virgate, and one ferling. Instances of these discrepancies could be multiplied,[62] and indeed they are the rule.

[57] This explanation would be strengthened if it could be shown that the bishop's men were farming the manor. Ecclesiastical manors farmed by the villeins were not unknown in 1086, but Domesday notices them only incidentally, and there must have been more of them than are actually recorded.

[58] *D.B.,* IV, fol. 68b.

[59] *D.B.,* IV, fol. 85.

[60] *D.B.,* IV, fol. 69.

[61] *D.B.,* IV, foll. 83, 94b.

[62] For example, in Lifton hundred the *Inquisitio* gives the king three hides in demesne; the Exon Domesday gives (for the manors of Lifton and Bradstone) one hide, one and one-half virgates assessed to the geld, of which one virgate is in demesne (*D.B.,* IV, foll. 65, 93). In Axminster hundred the figures are: *Inquisitio,*

Why this should be is an interesting subject for speculation. Certainly if two years separate the two documents many lands would have moved in and out of the king's and his barons' hands, and allowance must always be made for the number of errors contained in the record of the great survey as well as in such subordinate documents as the *Inquisitio.* There are, however, some intriguing hints which suggest that the two records may be speaking of two different assessments—the one based upon the other, of course, but different nonetheless.[63] Examples of the continuity of Domesday hidage are well known, in some cases reaching back to the eighth century and still recognizable at the end of the twelfth.[64] And yet, beneficial hidation and reductions in assessment are not uncommon in Domesday, and the possibility that at least some of these were accomplished during the Domesday survey itself cannot be ruled out. Pursuit of this line of inquiry, however, would lead too far from the present purpose and will be dealt with in another place. It is sufficient to notice here that the object of reassessment would not necessarily be simply the reduction (or even possibly an in-

---

twelve hides in demesne; Domesday (for Axminster, which is not hidated and does not pay geld, and Kilmington), two hides, of which one-half a hide is in demesne (*D.B.*, IV, foll. 68, 84b, 97). In Hartland hundred, the figures are: *Inquisitio,* ten hides in demesne; Domesday (for Hartland), nine hides, of which one is in demesne (*D.B.*, IV, foll. 65, 93b). These discrepancies can be illustrated by the figures concerning private lands. Odo the Englishman, referred to above, held manors in three different hundreds. The demesnes of two of his manors in one hundred were three virgates and three ferlings, respectively (*D.B.*, IV, fol. 486b), while the *Inquisitio* records an exemption of only three virgates and one ferling (*D.B.*, IV, fol. 67b).

63 Eyton's caution ("it is perhaps better to leave the apparent discrepancy between the Inquest and Domesday unexplored" [*Dorset Survey,* p. 133, n.6]) seems overly defeatist. It will be noticed that the Domesday figures for manorial demesne are lower than the exempt demesne of the *Inquisitio.* See the preceding footnote. Attention may be called to the interesting case of Walter of Dowai's hundred manor of Bampton (*D.B.*, IV, foll. 345b, 69). Instead of the almost invariable statement, in the past tense, of the geld paid T.R.E., the jury of the Domesday survey here stated, "how many hides lie in that land we know not, since it never paid geld," and yet it would seem that Bampton was then considered to be liable for geld, because the *Inquisitio* records Walter's exempt demesnes in Bampton hundred (two and one-half hides), although in Domesday he held no other manors in that hundred. Such a contradiction between the record of the Domesday survey and the record of the geld collection, when read together with the discrepancies noted above, would appear to be at least *prima facie* evidence that both liability and assessment were less rigid and unchanging than might be supposed.

64 Stenton, *Anglo-Saxon England,* p. 638.

crease) of the total assessment of the counties, hundreds, or vills but also the possibility of decreasing the hidage allotted to the exempt manorial demesne.[65]

It has been stated above that, although the hides listed as exempt because held *in dominio* refer only to manorial demesne, the *Inquisitio* does record the exemption of manors as a whole. It does this by listing the nondemesne hides of the exempt manor in what we have called the third category (above, p. 29), the category which neither has paid nor is *in dominio*, and by adding the statement that these exempt nondemesne hides *nunquam geldauerunt*, or the like. If, however, the hides which have not paid are *not* exempt, the *Inquisitio* invariably uses the phrase *non habuit rex gildum* or the like. The following entry illustrates the many instances where this usage distinguishes between exempt demesne, on the one hand, and nondemesne land which has not paid because exempt or because delinquent, on the other hand:

In hundreto Winnentone sunt xxx et vi hide et dimidia. Inde habet Rex de Gildo suo xxx et vi solidos pro vi hidis. Et Rex et barones eius habent in dominio xii hidas et dimidiam. De his habet Rex vii hidas in dominicatu, et sanctus achabran' i hidam, et sanctus Constantin' dimidiam hidam, et episcopus exoniensis iiii hidas. Excepto isto diminio habent homines comitis xv hidas quae nunquam reddiderunt Gildum testimonio anglorum. Et pro iii hidis de terra heraldi quas seruat B. uicecomes sub manu regis non habuit rex Gildum.[66]

It will be noticed that the hundred is assessed at thirty-six and one-half hides, of which six have paid, twelve and one-half are held

---

65 "The enlargement of the inland at the expense of the local peasant holdings meant, or at least threatened, the reduction of the area from which gelds could be taken, and the Domesday clerks, in noting cases where this enlargement had occurred, were recording manorial arrangements which directly affected the king's financial interests" (Stenton, *V.C.H. Oxford*, I, 394). Sir Frank Stenton cited the case of Fulk, the tenant of Roger d'Ivry at Brize Norton, Oxfordshire, who held in that manor five hides *in dominio, de terra villanorum* (*D.B.*, I, fol. 158b). "The point which the Domesday clerks wished to make was the possible reduction of the geldable area of a manor by the addition of peasant holdings to an exempt demesne" (*V.C.H. Oxford*, I, 394), that is, if and when the manor were held again in chief rather than from a mesne lord.

66 *D.B.*, IV, foll. 72f.

in demesne, and three hides of a royal manor in the custody of the sheriff have not yet paid as they should.[67] The remaining fifteen hides are specifically stated to be "in addition to that demesne" which has been listed in the preceding sentence, and they must therefore be nondemesne; but they cannot owe geld, for the invariable formula applying to land claimed by the *fegadri* (collectors) to owe but not yet to have paid is *non habuit rex gildum* throughout the *Inquisitio*. Therefore, since the sum of the royal and ecclesiastical demesnes equals the stated total (twelve and one-half hides), and the sum of the hides having paid, held in demesne, and still owing, are just fifteen short of the total assessment for the hundred, it follows that those fifteen hides are nondemesne lands which the English say have never paid geld and are returned in the *Inquisitio* as exempt.

Another exempt manor is indicated by the *Inquisitio* where it states that *Rotbertus de ob urgi villa* [sic] *habet iii uirgas quas tenet liberas de rege*.[68] The total assessment of this hundred is stated to be twenty-four and one-half hides, of which twenty-one hides and one virgate have paid, none are held in demesne by king or barons, and two hides and two virgates still owe. The total of these sums is just three virgates short of the total assessment; and thus Robert's three virgates can neither have paid geld, nor owe it, nor yet be the demesne of his manor. Thus, they must be exempt, held "freely of the king."

It would be unrewarding to attempt any test of Domesday manors stated to be exempt from geld, by collation with the *Inquisitio*. Too many Domesday entries merely state that such a manor did

[67] Other references to royal manors which were not exempt from geld may be seen in the following statements: "de v hidis de terra Haroldi quas tenent villani regis non habuit rex geldum" (*D.B.*, IV, fol. 13b); "de his denariis non fuerunt reddite iii libre et xiii solidi de cheneuuel regis" (fol. 1); "pro dimidia hide que iacet in uuincileia manerio regis non habuit Rex Gildum" (fol. 66b); and "pro i hida quam tenet Balduinus uicecomes de gildanti terra regis non habuit Rex Gildum" (fol. 72).

[68] *D.B.*, IV, fol. 75 (Milverton hundred, Somerset). No hides in this hundred are listed as held *in dominio* because no tenants-in-chief held any manors there "in demesne," and thus no manorial demesne was exempt. The king held Milverton "in demesne," but it was probably not hidated in 1084 (*D.B.*, IV, fol. 113). Eyton thought that Robert was a tenant-in-chief, but he probably held his exempt three virgates as a tenant of the count of Mortain, at *Welesforda*, where Bretel held the other

or did not pay geld, and there is reason to believe that this statement does not necessarily mean that the manor was geldable or exempt in 1086.[69] Furthermore, if an exempt manor were not hidated, no notice of it would have to be taken in the *Inquisitio,* which accounts only for the hidage of a given hundred.[70] Finally, there are the inevitable discrepancies between the two documents.

THE NORTHAMPTONSHIRE GELD ROLL

Thus far, the evidence considered has been wholly restricted to the southwestern counties mentioned in the *Inquisitio Geldi.* A review of the Northamptonshire Geld Roll, of a few years earlier, will confirm the conclusions based upon the *Inquisitio,* even though the data for Northamptonshire are neither so complete nor so detailed.

Perhaps it is this lack of detail which has led to the belief that the Geld Roll records, among other things, the exemption of *Terra Regis* as a whole from the geld.[71] The opening paragraph of the document lends credence to the theory that the royal manors were exempt: "To Sutton Hundred belong 100 hides . . . of these 21 hides and two-thirds of a hide have paid geld and 40 hides are inland and 10 hides are the king's own farm land (*kynges ahhen ferme land*) and 28 hides and one-third of a hide are waste." [72]

---

virgate of a hide which had been added to the count's estate at Ashbrittle (held of the count by Bretel) (*D.B.,* IV, foll. 92, 478b; see also, Eyton, *Domesday Studies: An Analysis and Digest of the Somerset Survey* [2 vols.; London, 1880], I, 170f.; II, 27f.).

[69] See above, footnote 63.

[70] This is proved by references to *carrucate nunquam geldantes* (e.g., *D.B.,* IV, fol. 14 [Melksham hundred, Wiltshire]), which are in addition to the sum of the hides listed, since this sum equals the total assessment given at the beginning of the entry. Thus the assessment in hides does not include nongelding ploughlands or nonhidated manors. Many (in some counties most) of the exempt royal manors were nonhidated, and thus would not have to be noticed at all by the *Inquisitio.*

[71] Round (*Feud. Eng.,* p. 152) implied as much by the form of the table in which he analyzed the Roll. See also his "Introduction to the Domesday Survey," in *The Victoria History of the County of Northampton* (ed. W. R. D. Adkins and R. M. Serjeantson; Westminster, 1902), I, 258f. Vinogradoff (*Eng. Soc.,* pp. 189ff.) stated, "the king's land does not pay. . . . The royal manors have also to be taken off, what remains as geldable" etc.; this is in connection with both the *Inquisitio* and the Geld Roll.

[72] Robertson, *Anglo-Saxon Charters,* pp. 230f.

The general similarity between the Geld Roll and the *Inquisitio* is obvious, but there are some crucial differences. The Geld Roll, like the *Inquisitio*, first gives the total hidage of the hundred, and then divides the hidage into three categories: (1) the number of hides which have paid, (2) the number which it terms *inland* (exempt manorial demesne), and (3) the number which have not paid. The sum of the three categories equals the sum given for the whole hundred (except for mere error). The Geld Roll, however, omits much information provided by the *Inquisitio*. Beside no mention of the rate, there is no breakdown of the hides of *inland* according to tenants-in-chief. Most important, the Geld Roll does not provide so complete a description of hides in the third category. The waste hides may safely be assumed to be exempt; also, the Geld Roll will often state that so many hides have not paid geld, or the like, which is reminiscent of the *Inquisitio*'s *non habuit rex gildum*. But what are we to think of the ten hides of the "king's own farm land"? First, was it in addition to whatever *inland* the king had in the hundred (i.e., was it *excepto isto dominio*, as the *Inquisitio* might say), or do the ten hides represent one or more whole manors, including both *inland* and what an English document might call *warland* (tenants' holdings, the *terra villanorum* of the *Inquisitio*)? Second, was it exempt from the geld, or was it delinquent and subject to geld?

The answers to both of these questions must be established before we can ascertain from this document whether or not the *Terra Regis* as a whole, the royal demesne, was exempt from geld in Northamptonshire. Addressing ourselves to the first question, then, it may be noted at once that nowhere in the Geld Roll itself is the question answered: the document assumes that the nature of the land listed under what we have called the third category is known. The answer, however, can be obtained by a collation of the Domesday *Terra Regis* and the lands which the Geld Roll ascribes to the king. The following table represents a preliminary collation, including all the hides mentioned in connection with the king in either document: [73]

[73] In the table, h. stands for hide; v., virgate; and b., bovate. The order of hundreds is that of the Geld Roll. See Appendix B.

HUNDRED	GELD ROLL	DOMESDAY
Sutton	10h.	3h.
Cleyley	nil	1h. 2v.
Gravesende	5h.	2h. 1v. 1b. and ⅕h.
Eadboldesstowe	5h.	2h.
Foxley	21h.	7h. 1v.
Towcester	20h.	7h. 2v.
Huxloe	nil	9h. 2v.
Willybrook	31h.	16h. 2v. 1b.
Navereslund	8h.	9h. 2v.
Nobottle-Grove	nil	2h. 2v.
Spelhoe	nil	7h. 1v. 1b.
Witchley	nil	35h. 2v. 1b.
Stotfald	nil	3h. 2v. 1b. and ⅓v.
Stoke	nil	2h. 3v.
Higham	nil	10h. 2v.
Mawsley	8h.	14h. 1v. 1b.
Corby	12h. 1v.	12h. 2v. 1b.
Rothwell	7h. 2v. plus	13h. 3v. and ⅓h.
Hamfordshoe	nil	2h. 2v. 1b.
Orlingbury	nil	6h.
Wymersley	nil	5h.
Geritone	(not mentioned)	1h.

The respective totals of the two columns of hidage are: Domesday Book, 177 hides and 37/60 hide; and the Geld Roll, 127 hides, three virgates, plus an unspecified amount in Rothwell (if the queen's land be included). These raw totals, however, need refinement. In addition to mere errors (for the Geld Roll, as well as Domesday, contains figures whose sum does not equal the alleged totals, as well as errors of omission and a vagueness which amounts to error when one attempts to put the record to use), there are two overriding considerations which rule out any correspondence between the hidage recorded in the two documents.

First, the general picture presented by a careful examination of the hidage which the Geld Roll calls *inland,* compared with the hide and ploughland figures of Domesday,[74] conveys the impression

[74] Especially such amounts of (assessed) land as one-fifth of a hide (Fawsley, *Gravesende* hundred), one-third of a virgate (Kelmarsh, *Stotfald* hundred), two-thirds of a hide (Rothwell and Orton, Rothwell hundred), and one-third of a hide (Loddington and Clendon, Rothwell hundred) (*D.B.*, I, foll. 219f.). These can be matched in other sections of the Northamptonshire Domesday (e.g., fol. 221, two-thirds of half a hide).

that there had been two reductions in the geld liability of the county.[75] One seems to have taken place prior to the date of the Geld Roll (by an arbitrary increase of the total *inland* allowed to various hundreds), and the second after the date of the Geld Roll but before Domesday (by an arbitrary series of reductions of the assessment of various hundreds, subpartitioned among the manors). Correspondence of assessment, even approximate, is therefore out of the question, particularly in view of certain difficulties of identification presented by the Northamptonshire Domesday.

The second factor which limits the value of a simple collation is the certainty that the Domesday *Terra Regis* includes more manors, in a greater number of hundreds, than the manors represented by the hidage ascribed to the king in the Geld Roll. Are we to assume that the Geld Roll specifically mentions all the royal demesne in Northamptonshire at the date of its compilation? Or should we assume that it does not necessarily allude to all, but only to that part of the royal demesne which it had reason to specify?

In order not to prejudice the validity of our final collation, regardless of the conclusion to which it leads, we must be sure that it is consistent with the former assumption, because both Round and Vinogradoff based their interpretation of the Geld Roll upon it. The date of the document, as Round implied, is crucial for the support of this first assumption. The latest *terminus ante quem* for which authority may be quoted is 1083, the year in which William's queen, Matilda, died.[76] One might be tempted to accept so late a date, since it would render almost impossible the theory that the Geld Roll records systematically all the *Terra Regis* in Northamptonshire as exempt from geld. If such a theory were to be maintained, then the even more difficult theory must be maintained, that in the brief and relatively peaceful period between 1083 and 1086 a veritable tenurial revolution took place in Northamptonshire. For the collation summarized above reveals that between the dates of the two documents the king would have acquired lands in eleven

[75] Round, *V.C.H. Northants,* I, 258–269, and, in greater detail, "The Hidation of Northamptonshire," *E.H.R.,* XV (1900), 78–86.

[76] Stenton, *Anglo-Saxon England,* p. 636, n.3; Robertson, *Anglo-Saxon Charters,* p. 481. Both base their acceptance of so late a date on the possibility that "the Lady, the King's wife" could be Matilda rather than Edith, Edward's widow, a view which Round did not share (*V.C.H. Northants,* I, 258).

different hundreds (one-half of the total hundreds in which he held lands in 1086). Inspection of the Domesday data further reveals that in these eleven hundreds there were thirteen separate estates, consisting of single manors or manors and their outliers.[77]

Actually, if we were to accept the assumption that the Geld Roll specifically mentions all the *Terra Regis* in the county, then we would have to accept 1072 as the most probable *terminus ante quem* for the document. In Domesday Book the king holds four large estates in Witchley hundred, and the Geld Roll mentions no royal demesne there. These estates are identified by Domesday as being formerly held by Edith, the Confessor's widow, and Earl Morcar. The Geld Roll would then be anterior to two important events, the death of Edith in 1075 (when her lands lapsed to the king) and the forfeiture of Earl Morcar's estates in 1071–1072.[78] It could then be argued more reasonably that lands mentioned in Domesday but not in the Geld Roll were all acquired after the date of the earl's rebellion—always assuming, that is, that the Geld Roll actually does mention all of the royal demesne.[79]

Alternatively, it may be assumed that the Geld Roll does not distinguish all the Northamptonshire *Terra Regis,* but only that part of it which was either exempt or delinquent. There are three reasons for preferring this second assumption: (1) All lands to which the Geld Roll ascribes ownership are in addition to the number of hides which it records as being *inland* or which it says have paid geld, i.e., they are in what we have called the third category, and if the *Inquisitio* and the Geld Roll are analogous administrative documents there is no foundation for believing that the royal demesne in

[77] Taking Tansor, Willybrook hundred, and Barnwell All Saints, Huxloe hundred, together because they "rendered" together, the other twelve are Passenham, Upton, Kingsthorpe, Ketton, Barrowden, South Luffenham, Casterton, Rothwell, Brixworth, Finedon, Hardingstone, and Brigstock, and their many "appendages."

[78] E. A. Freeman, *The History of the Norman Conquest of England* (2d ed.; Oxford, 1876), IV, 473ff. With Morcar's lands should be included those of his father Alfgar, since Domesday often lists lands under the name of the deceased instead of the heir and current lord. The fact that the King of Scots is mentioned as a landholder in the Roll also points to 1072, for in that year he may well have been granted lands in northern England by the settlement at Abernethy. See Stenton, *Anglo-Saxon England,* pp. 597f., 636, n.3.

[79] This assumption, of course, may be valid without the inference that the *Terra Regis* is all exempt.

the latter document is excluded from the first two categories. (2) Even between 1072 and 1086 it would be difficult to account for the apparently much more extensive royal demesne of Domesday Book. (3) References to the king's land in the Geld Roll involve only nine hundreds (compared with twenty-two hundreds in which Domesday records *Terra Regis*); in these nine hundreds it can be shown that only one estate is concerned in eight hundreds and two in the ninth hundred, thus implying that the Geld Roll references to the king's land actually concern particular estates rather than the whole of the royal demesne in each hundred (as a superficial reading of the document might suggest).

Whether we proceed upon one or the other assumption, in order to obtain a valid collation it is necessary to construct two lists of hidage which refer to the same royal estates. Wherever Domesday records *Terra Regis* and the Geld Roll does not, the hidage concerned must be deleted from the Domesday column of the table. This must be done hundred by hundred, with due attention to the manorial structure of the royal estates.[80] The following result is obtained:

---

80 The Domesday hidage has been reduced by the amount, in any of the hundreds listed, which belongs (1) to the *capita* of manorial groups possessing an outlier situated geographically in a hundred where the Geld Roll mentions no king's land, and (2) to the outliers of manorial groups whose *caput* is situated geographically in a hundred where the Geld Roll mentions no king's land. This must be done because assessment was territorial, while payment of geld was "seignorial" in that the *caput* of a scattered estate paid the geld assessed upon its members in several hundreds. The accuracy of this table—as of so many Domesday statistical problems—depends upon the application of this principle. The most familiar passage occurs in Cambridgeshire: "In Hinxton (Cambridgeshire) lies the *wara* of 1½h. of the manor of Chesterford (Essex) and it is valued in Essex" (*D.B.*, I. fol. 189b; *V.C.H. Cambridgeshire,* I, 361). The careful listing of the geographical location as well as the hidage of the members of such scattered manorial groups as Finedon is thus explained (*D.B.*, I, fol. 220). However, these cases, and the ones mentioned by Round ("Introduction to the Domesday Survey," in *The Victoria History of the County of Essex* [ed. Wm. Page; Westminster, 1903], I, 338), are dependent upon Domesday statements which might be open to a different interpretation.

It has not been pointed out hitherto that a mathematical demonstration of this principle is available in several passages of the *Inquisitio,* e.g., Whitestone hundred, Somerset (*D.B.*, IV, fol. 75): the total hidage is 115; fifty hides have paid, forty are in demesne, twelve have not yet paid, and thirteen *pay* in another hundred (although assessed in Whitestone hundred). The total of the itemized sums equals the total hidage of the hundred. Other examples: "Abbas abodesberie adquietavit in alio hundreto iii hidas terre et dimidiam quas ipse habet in hoc hundreto" (fol. 17b); "Con-

HUNDRED	GELD ROLL	DOMESDAY
Sutton	10h.	3h.
Gravesende	5h.	2h. 1v. 1b. and 1/5h.
Eadboldesstowe	5h.	2h.
Foxley	21h.	7h. 1v.
Towcester	20h.	7h. 2v.
Willybrook	31h.	9h.
Mawsley	8h.	4h. 3v. 1b.
Corby	12h. 1v.	3h. 3v.
Rothwell	7h. 2v.	1h. 1b.
Totals	119h. 3v.	40h. 3v. 1b. and 1/5h.

The totals of the two columns reveal an approximate ratio of three to one,[81] and this is brought out even more strongly by the fact that the king's land in *Eadboldesstowe* hundred pertained to his manor of King's Sutton, in Sutton hundred, and that together their hidage in the Geld Roll was fifteen hides, and in Domesday Book five hides. This three-to-one ratio might suggest that a general reduction of the hidage of royal manors had taken place between 1072 and 1086 in that proportion. But such an inference cannot be accepted until the nature of the Geld Roll hides is determined; and this three-to-one ratio provides the clue to their nature.

It will be noticed that there are some departures from the over-all three-to-one ratio which the table reveals as the general pattern. The adjoining hundreds of Mawsley and Rothwell show, respectively, the least and greatest reduction. Now the grouping of manors and holdings for both "public" and "private" liabilities is too familiar a feature of Domesday Book to insist upon. The details of these administrative groupings are now, in the great majority of cases, wholly lost. But if we suppose—hypothetically, and with no reason other than to test the evidence—that the royal demesne in

gregatores huius pecunie receperunt xii solidos pro terra alterius hundreti" (fol. 18). If assessment were not territorial and payment "seignorial," it would be impossible to determine the number of hides to delete from the Domesday data in order to establish the figures for the *Terra Regis* in Domesday which correspond to the royal demesne mentioned in the Geld Roll. Some of the hidage deleted in the Domesday column of the table, therefore, represents *capita* (or outliers) of manorial groups possessing outliers (or *capita*) situated in hundreds where the Geld Roll mentions no king's land.

[81] It would be unreasonable to demand more than a general pattern from Domesday and related statistics. Even the basic statistical fact of all Domesday, the five-hide unit, cannot without exception be applied to the hidated portion of Domesday.

the adjoining hundreds of Mawsley and Rothwell formed such a grouping, and then search Domesday Book for whatever light it might throw upon this hypothetical grouping, a striking fact emerges. The ploughlands which are outside the manorial demesne, recorded in Domesday Book, in the manors probably comprising the king's holdings in these two hundreds in 1072, are approximately three times as many as the Domesday hides assigned to the same manors. In Mawsley hundred (to which the Geld Roll attributes eight hides) there are sixteen Domesday nondemesne ploughlands,[82] and in Rothwell hundred (containing seven and one-half royal hides, according to the Geld Roll) there are two and one-quarter Domesday nondemesne ploughlands.[83] The combined totals conform much more nearly with the pattern suggested by the preceding table:

	DOMESDAY PLOUGHLANDS	DOMESDAY HIDES
Mawsley	16	4h. 3v. 1b.
Rothwell	2¼	1h. 1b.
Totals	18¼	6h.

The reappearance of this three-to-one ratio (established originally by comparing the total Geld Roll hides with the total Domesday hides), when comparing the Rothwell and Mawsley nondemesne ploughlands with the Domesday hides for those hundreds, suggests

[82] Faxton: "There is land for 12 ploughs. In demesne there are 3 ploughs." Wold and Walgrave: "There is land for 7 ploughs." The seven ploughlands at Wold and Walgrave, which belong to Faxton, include none in demesne. Thus, the sum of nine and seven is sixteen. Brixworth in Mawsley hundred must be excluded because its outlier in Hamfordshoe hundred is not alluded to in the Geld Roll. In Domesday, the two are given a common value T.R.E., and it must be supposed that they formed together one estate. Inclusion of Brixworth, then, would not conform with the principle on which the tables in the text are based (*D.B.*, I, fol. 219b; *V.C.H. Northants*, I, 306).

[83] Barford: "There is land for 2 ploughs." Rushton: "There is one sokeman having 2 oxen." Round interpreted the latter reference to mean a quarter of a plough team, implying a quarter of a ploughland. Since there is nothing in demesne here, the sum is two and one-quarter ploughlands. Rothwell and its many appendages are excluded because the Geld Roll does not mention king's land in *Stotfald* and Orlingbury hundreds, where it has outliers totaling nine hides, two virgates, one bovate, and one-third of a virgate. So also, three virgates in Rothwell hundred belonging to Edith's great manor of Finedon must be exluded (*D.B.*, I, foll. 219b, 220; *V.C.H. Northants*, I, 306ff.).

that there may be found here a means of identifying the Geld Roll hidage assigned to the royal demesne in that document. If both the Geld Roll hides and these ploughlands show the same ratio, perhaps they are equivalent. The following table, in fact, reveals the near identity between the Domesday nondemesne ploughlands, i.e., what the Geld Roll (if it had the occasion, since it is in the English language) might have called *warland,* and the Geld Roll hidage ascribed to the king. It is sufficient to notice that in four of the hundreds the two are identical, in a fifth case nearly so, and that the (now lost) administrative grouping of manors within and between hundreds may account for the seeming discrepancies, since the totals bear out the impression derived from the first four entries.[84]

HUNDRED	GELD ROLL HIDAGE	DOMESDAY WARLAND
Foxley	21h.	21
Towcester	20h.	20
Willybrook	31h.	31
Eadbaldesstowe	5h.	5
Corby	12h. 1v.	12
Mawsley	8h.	16
Rothwell	7h. 2v.	2¼
Gravesende	5h.	8
Sutton	10h.	4
Totals	119h. 3v.	119¼

[84] Working from a comparison of Domesday ploughlands and Domesday hides, Round evolved the theory "that the so-called ploughlands of the Northamptonshire Domesday are not ploughlands at all, but represent the old assessment" before the reduction implied by Domesday. To support his theory, however, he referred only to internal evidence in Domesday and to the fact that the total hidage of Domesday Northamptonshire was about half the total of the Geld Roll (Round, *V.C.H. Northants,* I, 264f.; see also Maitland, *D.B. and Bey.,* pp. 457f.). The table here presented confirms Round's theory (and identifies the "old assessment" from which the Domesday reduction was made) with external and independent evidence—but evidence that is fatal to the theory that *Terra Regis* was as such exempt, as will appear below.

Another result of the collation of the two documents is the revision it makes possible of Round's list of "the local manors of 'ancient demesne' (that is, those which had been held by the Crown before the Conquest)" (*V.C.H. Northants,* I, 273). Strangely enough, Green's Norton, the only manor which Domesday says King Edward held, is omitted from Round's list. If we accept his assumptions about the Geld Roll, manors which should be deleted are Hardingstone, Rothwell, Brixworth, Tansor, Brigstock, Kingsthorpe, Upton, and Barnwell. In addition to Green's Norton, King's Sutton and Towcester should be added as probably held by Edward (at least they were in the king's hands c.1072). See Appendix B.

Collation of the Domesday survey of Northamptonshire with the Geld Roll, then, leads to the conclusion that what the latter denominates as the king's land refers not at all to the total hidage of the king's manors in Northamptonshire, c.1072, but rather to that part only, of certain royal manors in nine hundreds, which was outside the manorial demesne, viz., the *warland* as distinct from the *inland* of those manors.

It must be emphasized that the conclusion reached so far by no means excludes the possibility that some, or perhaps all, of the king's manors in these nine hundreds were exempt as whole units from the geld collection recorded in the Geld Roll. To determine whether the Geld Roll supports the theory that the *Terra Regis* to which it refers was exempt from geld, we may turn to a review of the actual statements about the king's land which the Roll makes, now that the object of these statements is known to be not the total manorial holdings within a hundred, but only that part which was in addition to the manorial demesne.

The opening paragraph of the Geld Roll has been quoted already. Of the hundred hides in Sutton hundred, ten hides are said to be the *kynges ahhen ferme land.* This phrase is used again with reference to *Gravesende* hundred (now part of Fawsley hundred)—five hides are the *kynges agen ferme land.*[85] Domesday Book indicates that the king held land in these hundreds—presumably as well in 1072 as in 1086—only in the two manors of King's Sutton and Fawsley (and an outlier of Fawsley), manors which gave their names to the hundreds in which they lay, and which were possibly hundred manors.[86] It would be difficult to prove that they were not specially privileged and exempt *maneria regis.* And yet, were all manors which contained "the king's own farm land" exempt from geld? Before drawing this inference, and enlarging it into a general rule applying to all the *Terra Regis,* the one and only other reference to "the king's farm land" in the Geld Roll should be noticed, and a brief digression must be made in order to review any evidence in the *Inquisitio Geldi* or Domesday Book which can throw light on the problem.

First, under Corby hundred, the following significant statement is made in the Geld Roll: there are twelve hides and one yardland

[85] Robertson, *Anglo-Saxon Charters,* p. 230.
[86] See Appendix B.

of the *kynges fermeland weste & unwered,* which the editor of the document translates "which are waste and have not paid geld." [87] The implication seems plain enough: the twelve hides and a virgate (represented in Domesday by the manor of Gretton, of twelve non-demesne ploughlands) have not paid geld; and the reason is the usual one: they are waste.[88] If to be the king's farm land was sufficient to secure exemption, there would seem to be no reason for a geld record to notice whether the farm land were waste or not.

Second, the Old English word, *ferm* or *feorm,* rendered in Latin as *firma,*[89] does not in contemporary Latin documents seem to have referred, always and necessarily, to a privileged, exempt, or otherwise special kind of land. It is true that a few references in Domesday Book do seem to show a causal relationship between geld exemption and *firma regis* (e.g., *non geldum dabant quia de firma regis erant et ad opus regis calumnitatae sunt*).[90] Furthermore, this

87 Robertson, *Anglo-Saxon Charters,* pp. 236f.

88 The identification is supported by Domesday's statement that "very many things are wanting to this manor which in King Edward's time were appendant to it" (*V.C.H. Northants,* I, 305).

89 I have never seen an instance where *firma* was used as an adjective modifying *terra* (as in *fermeland*), but the equivalence of meaning is clear.

90 *D.B.,* I, fol. 60 (quoted by Vinogradoff, *Eng. Soc.,* p. 182, n.5). The entry is exceptional, if not unique, and should not be used to support a general rule. Against it there may be quoted many references to *firma regis* with no mention of geld, other than the usual statement of its assessment in hides and virgates. For example, in Haslingfield, Cambridgeshire, "the King holds 7h. and 1v. . . . This land was always of the King's farm" (*D.B.,* I, fol. 189b; *V.C.H. Cambridgeshire,* I, 361); the king holds Keyston, Huntingdonshire, and Edward held it, assessed at four hides to the geld with no hint of exemption (*D.B.,* I, fol. 203b), and we would never know it was and is part of the king's farm if that fact were not mentioned in passing as testimony of the shire under the *clamores* (fol. 208); so also, the king holds Shalbourn, Berkshire, which Edward held, and there is no mention of its not paying geld (though several other Berkshire estates are specifically said never to have paid), while its being in the *firma regis* comes out only incidentally in connection with a dispute (*D.B.,* I, fol. 57b).

Vinogradoff wrote that "royal manors were in principle held to be exempted from the payment of geld because they were subjected to the king's farm" (*Eng. Soc.,* p. 182). In addition to the passage quoted in the text, he referred to the following Herefordshire entry: "Lestret. Rex Edwardus tenuit. Ibi i hida cuius medietas erat in dominio regis et non geldat, alia medietas geldat. Hanc terram de firma regis dedit W. comes Ewen Britoni" (*D.B.,* I, fol. 184b). But this contradicts the theory in whose support it is quoted. Street was of the king's farm, and Earl William fitz Osbern gave it (*hanc terram*) to Ewan the Briton, but "now William holds it of Roger de Laci." See *The Victoria History of the County of Hereford* (ed. Wm. Page; London, 1908), I, 331.

meaning is clearly enunciated in one passage of the only other surviving geld record of this age, the *Inquisitio Geldi,* in which may be found the following statement: "In hundreto Witchirce sunt lxxx iiii hide & dimidia & i virgata preter firmam regis." [91] And the rest of the entry makes clear that the king's farm is not included in the eighty-four and one-half hides and one virgate of assessed land. Yet this entry is unique; its splendid isolation invites further inquiry. The fact that many manors in the king's farm were assessed in hides, even if others were not, need not be insisted upon for any student of Domesday Book. As a matter of fact, the king's farm is not even mentioned in the Northamptonshire Domesday—it is from the Geld Roll alone that one learns of the *firma regis* in this county.[92] This is a startling and inexplicable omission, if both the theory that the king's farm is exempt and also the theory that Domesday Book had a vital connection with geld assessment are maintained. The latter theory, of course, is easy to substantiate—but not in conjunction with the former, except by confusing specific and particular exemption with some general and overriding rule which cannot be supported by the Domesday evidence.

The remaining references in the Geld Roll to the royal demesne in Northamptonshire are even less congenial to a theory that the "ancient" demesne of 1072 or the manors belonging to the king's farm were exempt from geld because King Edward held them in demesne or in his farm. In all Northamptonshire, it is in Foxley

---

As usual, the half hide in demesne does not pay geld, while the other half does. Actually this is evidence that some manors of the king's farm paid geld in the normal way. Vinogradoff's interpretation assumes that *hanc terram* refers to *medietas . . . in dominio* rather than to the manor as a whole, but this is not in accordance with Domesday usage. Neither *medietas* is referred to by *hanc terram,* of course, but if a choice had to be made one would expect *hanc terram* to refer to the next preceding *medietas.* Vinogradoff's interpretation leaves the half hide which paid geld unaccounted for: if the geldable portion were not part of *hanc terram de firma regis,* who holds it T.R.W.?

[91] *D.B.,* IV, fol. 17.

[92] Domesday does record that Hugh de Port holds South Luffenham and Kelthorpe of the king at farm, and that Hugh fitz Baldric holds Casterton at farm (*D.B.,* I, foll. 219, 219b); but these manors were held, respectively, by Edith and Morcar, and thus have no relevance for the king's farm of the Geld Roll. Further, "holding at farm" and "belonging to the king's farm" are two different conditions: for the latter only has exemption been claimed. Green's Norton—held by Edward—is the real test case for Northamptonshire, and there is no mention there of the *firma regis.*

(now Green's Norton) hundred that the Geld Roll should be most likely to call attention to the king's farm, for Green's Norton in that hundred is the only manor listed under *Terra Regis* in Domesday which is said to have been held by Edward. Instead, however, the Geld Roll gives the number of hides in the *kynges ahhen land* in the very same words as it refers to the royal demesne in Towcester hundred, while in *Eadboldesstowe* hundred five hides are listed merely as "the king's." Finally, in the last three hundreds where the royal demesne is listed, Willybrook, Mawsley, and Rothwell, the plain implication of the Geld Roll is that the hides assessed to the king are geldable but have not paid as they ought, implying further that, if the king's land elsewhere has not paid, it is for a special reason and not by virtue of the king's ownership.

It has been seen already that in the *Inquisitio Geldi* land which is exempt is invariably listed as (manorial) demesne or stated "never to have gelded" or the like, while land which is subject to geld is invariably listed either as having paid or as a number of hides from which *non habuit rex gildum hoc anno,* or the like. So also in the Geld Roll, land which owes geld but has not paid is simply stated not to have paid (together with a notice of the owner), rather than being added to the *inland* or waste, thus:

To *Egelweardesle* hundred belong 100 hides . . . from 6½ hides at Norton not a penny has been received—Osmund, the king's writer, owns that estate. . . .

To Willybrook . . . the king owns the half hundred which has paid no geld.

To . . . Upton Green . . . 2½ hides have not paid geld, and that estate is owned by Richard Engayne.

To . . . *Navereslund* . . . 8 hides have not paid geld, and that estate is owned by the Lady. . . .

To Spelhoe . . . from 10 hides belonging to Abington—Richard's land—not a penny has been received, and from 6 hides belonging to Moulton—William's land—not a penny. . . .

To Mawsley . . . 8 hides which have not paid geld are owned by the king.

To Corby hundred . . . 5 hides have not paid geld—of these the Scottish king owns 3 hides and the Lady 1½ hides and Urs half a hide. . . .

To Rothwell . . . 15 hides have not paid geld—the king owns 7 hides and half a hide and the king's wife and Earl Robert's wife and William Engayne own 7 hides and half a hide.

To Orlingbury . . . 5 hides, owned by William Engayne and Witeget the priest, have not paid geld. . . .[93]

If these statements are compared without benefit of a previously formed conviction that the royal demesne was exempt from geld, it is difficult indeed to see any difference between the geld liability of the king and of Osmund, Richard Engayne, the Lady, Richard, William, the Scottish king, Urs, the king's wife, Earl Robert's wife, William Engayne, and Witeget the priest. The theory that they were all exempt from geld cannot be maintained, unless it be supposed that every hide in Northamptonshire which owed geld actually paid, for all the other hides are accounted for as *inland,* waste, or having paid. This is not only improbable in itself; it contradicts the evidence of the *Inquisitio Geldi,* which shows failure to pay in every county and in nearly every hundred it lists. Finally, the document plainly states that these hides "have not paid" or that from them "not a penny has been received"—not that they are exempt or do not owe—and it is gratuitous to read the idea of exemption into those statements.

Remembering that the hides to which the document refers (on the king's lands, at least) are hides of *warland,* then the conclusions to which the Geld Roll leads are the same as those indicated by the *Inquisitio.* The manorial demesne of the king's land is exempt; some of the king's manors are probably wholly exempt (though it is by no means certain that belonging to the *kynges ferme land* necessarily implies exemption); and the *warland* of other king's manors undoubtedly paid geld.[94]

[93] Robertson, *Anglo-Saxon Charters,* pp. 232–237; quoted by permission of the Cambridge University Press.

[94] A more general consideration may be noticed here, though there is no specific evidence to prove or disprove the point. Even admitting that hidation of royal manors is not inconsistent with exemption from geld, and even supposing (for argument's sake) that the demesne of the Geld Roll and the *Inquisitio* referred to manors and not to manorial demesne, it would be difficult to find a reason for the reduction of hidage of royal manors which may be found in several counties. If they did not pay, why change their assessments at all, unless to abolish them altogether?

The results of our investigation do not conform with some of the received doctrine of a previous generation of Domesday scholarship, and it has been necessary for this reason to examine the evidence in some detail. These conclusions not only throw new light upon the subject of taxation; they are essential for a proper interpretation of the constitutional significance of the royal demesne, and thus have important implications for the nature of the Anglo-Norman monarchy.

The royal demesne of the Conqueror, and his attitude or policy toward it—particularly its position in the administration of the realm and its liability to taxation—provide clear evidence, indeed evidence from which it may be demonstrated rather than merely inferred, that the Anglo-Norman monarchy recognized a distinction only of degree, not of kind, between its own landed endowment and the honors or fiefs of its tenants-in-chief or barons. Furthermore, this evidence reveals that fusion of "public" and "private" rights and interests which characterized the feudal monarchy in all its aspects. In this sense, the Anglo-Norman royal demesne was a feudal demesne, and the policy of the monarchy toward it was a feudal policy. It would be rash to exaggerate the differences between the crown lands of the late Old English kings and the royal demesne of the Anglo-Norman lord king—there was too much administrative continuity which bridged the Conquest. And yet the differences were real, and they were qualitative as well as quantitative. The Conqueror's demesne was not only larger and more valuable than the Confessor's landed wealth. We may search in vain, after 1066, for estates which belong to the "realm" or "kingship," crown lands which were distinguished from the *propria hereditas* of the king as a private person, and to this extent the advent of feudalism in England may well have diminished still further what little remained of the difference between office and personality in the Anglo-Saxon monarchy. So also, there was no "ancient demesne" in 1086, no royal estates which as a class enjoyed special immunity from the normal administration or exemption from taxation. If there had been, the privileges of ancient demesne tenure revealed by the evidence a century and a half later might indeed have been a survival of privileged conditions on the Anglo-Norman royal demesne. The irresistible inference of such an interpretation would be (and has been) [95] an appraisal of the feudal monarchy as essentially conservative, altruistically preserving upon its royal demesne the privileges it found there. Such an appraisal underestimates, as will appear, the initiative and resourcefulness of the medieval monarchy in exploiting and even going beyond the possibilities of its feudal rights and obligations.

No claim for novelty, of course, is advanced for the view that the Anglo-Norman monarchy was essentially feudal; yet it is new and unexpected (in view of the doctrine of Round and Vinogradoff) to find support for the feudal character of the monarchy in an analysis of the Domesday and related evidence concerning the administration and taxation of the royal demesne *tempore regis Willelmi*. Immunity, to a greater or lesser degree, is a normal condition of feudalism, and it is not surprising that some manors of the royal demesne occupy a privileged position; but so do many estates within ecclesiastical and lay honors. Such exemption from geld as may be found in Anglo-Norman England is no different in kind whether royal or baronial. Above all, the immunity found on royal manors does not spring from a clear distinction between the king in his public and in his private capacities. The institutions of the Anglo-Norman monarchy may reveal the king exercising higher power, enjoying rights of a transcendent kind—such as the right to levy, as well as to grant exemption from, geld—but the administration of the realm is based upon no distinction, and will nourish no distinction, between an "ancient demesne" of the crown and the private estates of the king.

[95] This is the position taken by Vinogradoff.

APPENDIX A

Were Manorial Demesnes Exempt from Geld?

IN one of the earliest articles he wrote on Domesday Book, J. H. Round committed himself to the view that "the whole scheme of the Danegeld contemplated the taxing of the hides in demesne just as much as the hides in villenage, as the normal condition of things." He dismissed the suggestion that "baronial demesnes" might have been exempt with the observation that "if this were the case, all calculations as to Danegeld would be most seriously affected." Then, without further allusion to the distinction between tenure-in-chief and subtenure, he passed in review the evidence which led him to conclude "that hides in demesne were not normally exempt" and could only be "made geld-free by a special act of the crown" (*Domesday Studies,* I, 92–98). Round's argument must be reviewed in detail, because it is crucial to the interpretation presented in the text, viz., that in the reign of William the Conqueror the manorial demesnes of manors held in demesne by tenants-in-chief were exempt from geld, and that no other land was exempt except by grant of the king.

First, it must be noticed that Round did not restrict himself to the period under consideration here. The greater, and more convincing, part of his argument rests upon twelfth century evidence, and it does not seem to have occurred to him that any changes in geld liability might have taken place. He quotes the coronation charter of Henry I, c.11: "Militibus qui per loricas terras usas deserviunt, terras dominicarum carucarum quietas ab omnibus geldis . . . concedo . . ." (Wm. Stubbs, ed., *Select Charters and Other Illustrations of English Constitutional History* [9th ed., rev., ed. H. W. C. Davies; Oxford, 1929], p. 119). For Round, this was simply a concession which was "subsequently cancelled by the crown." May it not rather have been a shrewd effort of the new king to gain support among subtenants by knight service by extending to them the demesne exemption already enjoyed by their lords —lords who would call upon their vassals for support against the king if they undertook a rebellion in favor of Robert of Normandy? When Duke Robert did invade England, in 1101, it was not the king's barons on whom Henry relied for support: "Of all their number the king could only trust a few personal friends" (H. W. C. Davies, *England under the Normans and Angevins* [13th ed., rev.; London, 1949], p. 123). As for the rest of the twelfth century evidence which Round produced, either it may be accepted without admitting its application to the period 1066–1086, or else it can be explained in terms of twelfth century economic developments whose origins are already to be seen in Domesday Book. Round did not consider the distinction between "assessed demesne" (*inland,* exempt demesne) and "agricultural demesne." As Sir Frank Stenton has pointed out, even in the Domesday survey the distinction was recognized between exempt demesne and land which a tenant held *in dominio, de terra villanorum,* that is, land formerly part of the holdings of the manorial peasantry and assessed to the geld as such, but later annexed or converted into demesne for agricultural or economic purposes. Round was not aware of how rapidly and extensively *terra villanorum* and waste land were being converted into demesne of the manor in the twelfth century, and before the evidence he cites can be accepted even for the twelfth century it would have to be demonstrated that it does not simply relate to such changes in the economic organization of the manor. (This is no criticism of Round, who was not an economic historian, since the significance of this development has been brought out by a later generation of scholarship [Stenton, *V.C.H. Oxford,* I, 393f.; M. Postan, "The Chronology of Labour Services," *Transactions of the Royal Historical Society,* 4th Series, XX (1937), 169–193].)

For the reign of William the Conqueror, it is the Domesday (and other contemporary) evidence on which Round's case must rest, and to this we must turn. Round appealed particularly to the Exon Domesday which "well illustrates what I have described as the bearing of the whole Survey. I select it because of its explicit phrase, 'reddidit gildum' " (*Domesday Studies,* I, 94). On manor after manor, it is necessary to add the demesne hidage to the villeins' hidage to obtain the total which *reddidit gildum T.R.E.,* and therefore, according to Round, all manorial demesnes paid geld T.R.W. and later. This is one of the rare instances when the great Domesday scholar fell into a trap of his own making, for if his interpretation of *reddidit gildum* here is correct, then he was wrong in thinking that the "ancient demesne" (manors held by both Edward and by William) was exempt from geld, for under the rubric *Terra Regis ad Regnum pertinens* each of the following manors was held by Edward and of each the Exon Domesday says that it *reddidit gildum* for so many hides: Tawton, Hemyock, Budleigh, Teignton, Kerswell, Colyton, Ermington, Awton, Diptford, Alvington, Plympton, Yealmpton, Walkhampton, Sutton, and Tamarton (*D.B.*, IV, foll. 83–87). It would seem safer, therefore, to accept *reddidit gildum* as a plain statement (in the past tense) of fact, i.e., the assessment T.R.E., without prejudice to the case in 1086, and turn to whatever other evidence is available.

Round cited the case of Count Eustace of Boulogne's manor of Loxton, Winterstoke hundred, Somerset, assessed at five hides, of which four were in demesne and one belonged to the villeins (*D.B.*, IV, fol. 282b). Now this is the only manor the count held in Winterstoke hundred, and he held the manor in demesne as a tenant-in-chief. The *Inquisitio Geldi* duly records the exempt demesne of Count Eustace, though the hidage shows a discrepancy (three hides and one ferling, fol. 77), which is not unusual; but in no other hundred of Somerset does the *Inquisitio* record the count as holding exempt demesne. On turning back to the Exon Domesday we find what the interpretation presented in the text should lead us to expect: all the other manors of Count Eustace were held of him by subtenants. (It may be remarked that Ida, Countess of Boulogne, held Kingweston, Bruton hundred, which *reddidit gildum pro v hidis . . . habet comitissa in dominio iii hidas i virgam minus* [*D.B.*, IV, fol. 283]. Turning to the *Inquisitio*, we find her credited with two hides and three virgates in demesne [*D.B.*, IV, fol. 82]. This was her only manor in Somerset, so there can be no doubt of the identification.)

The next case Round cited likewise conforms with the interpretation followed in the text. This was the manor of Hugh of Avranches, Earl of Chester, in Anstey, South Molton hundred, in Devonshire, which *reddidit gildum* for one-half hide, distributed between the demesne (one-half virgate) and the villeinage (one and one-half virgate). In this hundred Earl Hugh held one other manor, of the same name, but on it there was no demesne. Both manors he held as tenant-in-chief and in demesne (*D.B.*, IV, fol. 286). As expected, the *Inquisitio* credits Hugh with one-half virgate of exempt demesne in this hundred (fol. 66).

The next evidence cited by Round requires special examination, for the entry is quite exceptional in the whole of the Exon Domesday. This is the manor of Bratton, Lifton hundred, Devonshire, which Baldwin the sheriff held in demesne as a tenant-in-chief in 1086. Almost invariably the Exon Domesday records the geld assessment of manors in units of hides, virgates, and ferlings; yet of the one virgate to which Bratton was assessed, the record states that one-third of the virgate was in demesne and two-thirds of the virgate were the villeins' (*D.B.*, IV, fol. 288b). Round was especially sensitive to the unique or exceptional in Domesday language, but he does not seem to have been tempted to investigate this case. The assessment of Bratton can be understood only when compared with Baldwin's other holdings in Lifton hundred. When this is done, it becomes clear that Bratton does not support Round's interpretation.

BALDWIN'S MANORS IN LIFTON HUNDRED

Manor	*Assessment*	*Demesne*	*Ter.Vil.*	*Subtenant*
Okehampton	3v. 1f.	1v. 1f.	2v.	In demesne
Chidecot	½v.	(No hidage given)		Roger
Bowsleigh	1v.	1f.	1f.	Rolf
Dunterton	½h.	2f.	2f.	Ralf de Brueria
Bridestow	½h. ½f.	(No hidage given)		Ralf de Pomaria
land of 6 thanes	½h. 1½f.	(No hidage given)		six thanes
Week	½v.	(No hidage given)		Rainer
Lew	½h.	(No hidage given)		Roger de Molis
Wadlescot	1v.	(No hidage given)		Roger de Molis
Kelly	½h.	(No hidage given)		Motbert
Guscot	1v.	(No hidage given)		Colvin
Bratton	1v.	⅓v.	⅔v.	In demesne

The *Inquisitio* credits Baldwin with one and one-half virgates in demesne in Lifton hundred, which may be recognized easily as the one virgate and one ferling in the demesne of Okehampton (fol. 65). Leaving Bratton aside, no other demesne is exempt because all the other manors are held by subtenants: eight of them do not even have a demesne assessment. Now Bratton's demesne and *terra villanorum* assessments stand out in the above table in bold relief; the hidage is divided in a way which looks neither conventional nor traditional in Devonshire (there is another instance of tripartite division at Witheridge, Devonshire [*D.B.*, IV, fol. 96]). An explanation for this anomaly, however, is not hard to find: there are three ploughs on the demesne and six ploughs on the villeins' land of this manor. The fact that there is no trace of this odd assessment in the *Inquisitio* suggests that this manor was held by a subtenant in 1084, and that it (like the eight other manors) had no separate *inland* and *warland* assessments. Sometime after 1084 and before the Domesday survey the manor escheated and was retained in demesne by Baldwin, who naturally claimed exemption for his demesne ploughlands. Because they had never been assessed before, the new commissioners (possibly the Domesday commissioners themselves), unacquainted with or unimpressed by the virgate and ferling system traditional in these parts, split the manor in accordance with the ploughs in demesne and outside the demesne. All of this is, of course, hypothesis, but it accounts for the known facts, and it provides an explanation for the origin of the peculiar one-third virgate in the demesne of a Devonshire manor. Thus, the one-third virgate which Round called in witness of his theory, is best explained by contradicting it.

Possibly the strongest evidence Round cited was "the very remarkable entry at the end of the Survey of Huntingdon" (*Domesday Studies*, I, 96): "In Herstingest' Hundret sunt dominicae carucatae quietae de geldo regis. Villani et sochemanni geldant secundum hidas in brevi scriptas. Excepta Broctone ubi geldat abbas cum aliis pro una hida" (*D.B.*, I, fol. 203).

As Round pointed out, this is no general rule, but a "special arrangement, . . . essentially an exceptional state of things." For Round the special arrangement was the exemption of manorial demesnes which, according to him, were normally subject to geld. Is this necessarily so? As usual, Round ignored any distinction between the demesnes of tenants-in-chief and those of subtenants. A review of the manors which Domesday places within Hurstingstone hundred, Huntingdonshire, reveals that the tenants-in-chief there were the king, Countess Judith, the Abbot of Ely, and the Abbot of Ramsey. But only the Abbot of Ramsey had subtenants. Richard and Hugh, two knights of the Abbot, held three hides at Stukely, with three ploughs on the demesne (*D.B.*, I, fol. 204); Aluuold held one hide at Holywell; Eurard, Ingelran, and Pleines (who may be knights of the Abbot) held four hides at St. Ives. The special arrangement or exceptional state of things thus seems to have been that the Abbot of Ramsey, who possessed the bulk of the hundred in demesne but had enfeoffed several subtenants (possibly all by knight's service to acquit his service to the king), had secured a special exemption for the demesnes of the manors which he had subinfeudated. At the end of the county survey, Domesday supplies us with a commentary on the reference to Broughton in the passage quoted above, which may also indicate that the exemption of the demesnes in Hurstingstone hundred dates from before the Conquest (when the feudal rule concerning manorial demesnes of tenants-in-chief was not in effect). If this is so, Domesday is recording a pre-Conquest arrangement, a special case, and is thus preserving, in a sense, the "laws of St. Edward" where they do not conform exactly with new principles of geld liability.

Finally, Round admitted that "the levy-rolls of the Danegeld of 1084 distinctly show that, on that occasion, the hides 'in dominio' *were* exempted from the tax," but he explained this away as an exceptional "compromise—we might almost say a conspiracy" (*Domesday Studies,* I, 97) by which the barons agreed to the unprecedented rate of six shillings on the hide, in return for exemption of their demesne lands. Needless to say, this brilliant conjecture is not supported by any evidence, and Round submitted it only as a suggestion. Two considerations render it unlikely. First, we have already seen that the Northamptonshire Geld Roll is a strictly analogous document which—just like the *Inquisitio*—reveals the exemption of manorial demesnes of manors held in chief as the normal administrative practice. (It could be argued that if the documents were analogous, they might both record a special and exceptional exemption of manorial demesnes. But this interpretation would simply extend further an argument from silence.) Second, there is no evidence that this geld was collected elsewhere than in the five southwestern counties, where, except for Wiltshire, the assessment of land was generally very low and a higher rate might be expected. For lack of evidence to the contrary, then, the *Inquisitio* may be taken to record the normal conditions under which geld was levied, and under those normal conditions the demesnes of the manors which tenants-in-chief held in demesne were exempt.

The evidence of the earliest Pipe Rolls may be summarized briefly. In 1130, royal demesne (unspecified) or particular manors *in dominio Regis* were pardoned for part or all of their contribution to the Danegeld collected in the following counties: Oxfordshire, Wiltshire, Yorkshire, Cambridgeshire, Kent, Staffordshire, Gloucestershire, Northamptonshire, Norfolk, Suffolk, Buckinghamshire, Bedfordshire, Lincolnshire, Berkshire, and (possibly) Nottinghamshire (*Magnum Rotulum Scaccarii, vel Magnum Rotulum Pipae, de Anno Tricesimo-Primo Regni Henrici Primi* [ed. Joseph Hunter, Record Commission, 1833; *The Pipe Roll of 31 Henry I,* reproduced in facsimile from the edition of 1833; London, 1929], pp. 6, 23, 34, 46f., 66ff., 76, 79f., 86, 95, 99, 102, 104, 121, 126, 135). These pardons cannot be taken to mean that the royal demesne was exempt from geld in 1130, first, because no pardons were granted to the royal demesnes in about half the counties where geld was collected, and second, because the very fact of a pardon implies liability. It may be argued that these pardons apply only to escheats or vacancies temporarily in the king's hand, but that the rest of the royal demesne was all exempt. Such an impression is suggested by two Gloucestershire entries: "Et Idem Vicecomes reddit Compotum . . . de preterito danegeldum. . . . Et in Perdonis per breve Regis . . . In dominio Abbatiae de Cadomo dum fuit in manu Regis .xlij. s. . . . In dominio Regis de terra Rogeri de Berchelai .xxxvj. s. & iiij. d." (*P.R. 31 Hen. I,* pp. 79f.). But such an inference has not been demonstrated, and it leaves unexplained the absence of any pardons in half of the counties. Where the Pipe Roll mentions a manor by name, it might be established that it was or was not a recent escheat or vacancy; but in several instances, the entry reads merely *in dominio Regis* (e.g., *ibid.,* pp. 6, 95). All of these remarks may be illustrated as well by the first Pipe Roll surviving from the reign of Henry II (*The Great Rolls of the Pipe for the Second, Third, and Fourth Years of the Reign of King Henry the Second* [ed. Joseph Hunter, Record Commission, 1844; *The Pipe Rolls of 2–3–4 Henry II,* reproduced in facsimile from the edition of 1844; London, 1930], pp. 25, 27, 30, 37, 41, 47, 51, 55, 59, 62, 67).

According to Sir Frank Stenton, "the Pipe Rolls of the twelfth century prove that under Henry I and Henry II manorial demesnes were normally charged to the geld" (*V.C.H. Oxford,* I, 394, n.1.). Liability of manorial demesnes is clearly implied by pardons for so many shillings *in dominio terre* or *in dominicis Carrucatis* of the recipient of royal favor (*P.R. 31 Hen. I,* 23, 60, 66f., 74, 76, 79f., 95, 99, 102f.). The question is, however, whether these demesnes are in manors held in chief or from mesne lords (many tenants-in-chief, important men in the realm, held manors as subtenants also) and, also, whether these demesnes were annexed from the *terra villanorum* and thus, while in fact held *in dominio,* were not recognized as exempt in geld collection. Unfortunately, the brief notices in the Pipe Rolls are no help in establishing the nature of the manorial demesnes which are pardoned.

APPENDIX B

Terra Regis of the Northamptonshire Geld Roll and of Domesday Compared

THE following table presents a synopsis of the royal demesne hidage found in the two documents, together with the nondemesne ploughland figures given by Domesday in the hundreds where the king has land in the Geld Roll. The hundreds follow the order found in the Geld Roll.

	HIDAGE	PLOUGHLANDS	REMARKS
Sutton hundred			
Geld Roll: 10 hides are the king's own farm land			
Domesday:			
1. King's Sutton	3h.	4	
Cleyley hundred			
Geld Roll:	None		
Domesday:			
1. Passenham	1h.		
2. Pokesle	2v.		Belongs to Passenham
Total	1h. 2v.		
Gravesende hundred			
Geld Roll: 5 hides are the king's farm land			
Domesday:			
1. Fawsley	1h. 2v. plus 1/5 hide	8	
2. Sokeland	3v. 1b.		Soke of Fawsley
Total	2h. 1v. 1b. plus 1/5 hide	8	
Eadboldesstowe hundred			
Geld Roll: 5 hides are the king's			
Domesday:			
1. Whitfield	2h.	5	Belongs to King's Sutton

THE ROYAL DEMESNE

	HIDAGE	PLOUGHLANDS	REMARKS
Foxley hundred			
Geld Roll: 21 hides are the king's own land			
Domesday:			
1. Green's Norton, Blakesley, and Adstone	7h. 1v.	21	King Edward held
Towcester hundred			
Geld Roll: 20 hides are the king's own land			
Domesday:			
1. Towcester	7h. 2v.	20	
Huxloe hundred			
Geld Roll:	None		
Domesday:			
1. Islip	1h. 3v.		Belongs to Brigstock, in Corby hundred
2. Barnwell All Saints	6h. 1v.		Renders with Tansor, in Willybrook hundred
3. Outlier of Finedon	1h. 2v.		Belongs to Finedon, in *Navereslund* hundred, which Edith held
Total	9h. 2v.		
Willybrook hundred			
Geld Roll: The king owns the half-hundred which has paid no geld (this amounts to 31 hides)			
Domesday:			
1. Duddington	1h.	7	Belongs to Gretton, Corby hundred
2. King's Cliff	1h. 2v. 1b.		Earl Alfgar held
3. Nassington	6h.	14	
4. Apthorp	2h.	10	Belongs to Nassington
5. Tansor	6h.		Renders with Barnwell All Saints, Huxloe hundred
Total	16h. 2v. 1b.	31	(9h. omitting King's Cliff and Tansor)
Navereslund hundred			
Geld Roll: (The king's wife owns 8 hides)			
Domesday:			
1. Finedon	9h. 2v.		Has outliers in several hundreds; Edith held
Nobottle-Grove hundred			
Geld Roll:	None		
Domesday:			
1. Upton	2h.		
2. Harleston	2v.		Belongs to Upton
Total	2h. 2v.		

TERRA REGIS OF THE GELD ROLL AND DOMESDAY

	HIDAGE	PLOUGHLANDS	REMARKS
Spelho hundred			
Geld Roll:	None		
Domesday:			
1. Kingsthorpe	4h. 3v.		
2. Moulton	1h. 2v. 1b.		Belongs to Kingsthorpe
3. Weston	1h.		Belongs to Kingsthorpe
Total	7h. 1v. 1b.		
Witchley hundred			
Geld Roll:	None		
Domesday:			
1. Ketton	7h.		
2. Tixover	2h.		Belongs to Ketton
3. Barrowden	3h. 3v.		
4. Seaton	1h. 2v. 1b.		Belongs to Barrowden
5. Thorp	1h. 1v.		Belongs to Barrowden
6. Morcot	4h.		Belongs to Barrowden
7. Bisbrooke and Glaston	1h. 1v.		Belongs to Barrowden
8. North Luffenham	4h.		Belongs to Barrowden
9. South Luffenham and Kelthorpe	7h. 1v.		Edith held nos. 1–9
10. Casterton	3h. 2v.		Earl Morcar held
Total	35h. 2v. 1b.		
Stotfald hundred			
Geld Roll:	None		
Domesday:			
1. Kelmarsh	2h. and ⅓v.		Belongs to Rothwell
2. Oxendon	1h. 1v.		Belongs to Rothwell
3. Clipston	1v. 1b.		Belongs to Rothwell
Total	3h. 2v. 1b. and ⅓v.		
Stoke hundred			
Geld Roll:	None		
Domesday:			
1. Rockingham	1h.		Boui held
2. Stoke Albany	1h.		Soke of Corby, Corby hundred
3. Wilbarston	3v.		
Total	2h. 3v.		
Higham hundred			
Geld Roll:	None		
Domesday:			
1. Outlier of Finedon	10h. 2v.		Belongs to Finedon, in *Navereslund* hundred

	HIDAGE	PLOUGHLANDS	REMARKS
Mawsley hundred			
Geld Roll: 8 hides which have not paid are owned by the king			
Domesday:			
1. Brixworth	9h. 2v.		Has outlier in Hamfordshoe hundred
2. Faxton	2h.	9	
3. Wold and Walgrave	2h. 3v. 1b.	7	Belongs to Faxton
Total	14h. 1v. 1b.	16	(4h. 3v. 1b. omitting Brixworth)
Corby hundred			
Geld Roll: 12 hides and 1 virgate (yardland) of the king's farm land are waste and have not paid geld (and "the Lady" has 1½ hides which have not paid)			
Domesday:			
1. Gretton	3h. 3v.	12	Has outlier in Willybrook hundred
2. Corby	1h. 2v.		Has sokeland in Stoke hundred
3. Brigstock	3h. 2v.		Has outlier at Islip, in Huxloe hundred
4. Geddington	1h.		Belongs to Brigstock
5. Stanion	1v. 1b.		Belongs to Brigstock
6. Weekley	2h. 2v.		Earl Alfgar held
Total	12h. 2v. 1b.	12	(3h. 3v. omitting all but Gretton)
Rothwell hundred			
Geld Roll: Of 15 hides which have not paid geld, the king owns 7½ hides (and the king's wife owns an unstated part of the other 7½ hides)			
Domesday:			
1. Rothwell and Orton	8h. and ⅔h.		Has outliers in Stotfald and Orlingbury hundreds
2. Loddington	1h. and ⅓h.		Belongs to Rothwell
3. Clendon	½h. and ⅓h.		Belongs to Rothwell
4. Draughton	1h. 1b.		Belongs to Rothwell
5. Arthingworth	1b.		Belongs to Rothwell
6. Desborough	1b.		Belongs to Rothwell
7. Barford	1h.	2	Oslac White held
8. Rushton	1b.	¼	Soke of Barford
9. Outlier of Finedon	3v.		Belongs to Finedon, in *Navereslund* hundred
Total	13h. 3v. and ⅓ hide	2¼	(1h. and 1b. omitting all but Barford and Rushton)

TERRA REGIS OF THE GELD ROLL AND DOMESDAY

	HIDAGE	PLOUGHLANDS	REMARKS
Hamfordshoe hundred			
Geld Roll:	None		
Domesday:			
1. Holcot	2h. 2v. 1b.		Belongs to Brixworth, in Mawsley hundred
Orlingbury hundred			
Geld Roll:	None		
Domesday:			
1. Cransley	2h. 1v.		Belongs to Rothwell
2. Broughton	2v.		Belongs to Rothwell
3. Outlier of Finedon	3h. 1v.		Belongs to Finedon, in *Navereslund* hundred
Total	6h.		
Wymersley hundred			
Geld Roll:	None		
Domesday:			
1. Hardingstone	5h.		
Geritone hundred			
Geld Roll: (Geld Roll does not list *Geritone* hundred)			
Domesday:			
1. Outlier of Finedon	1h.		Belongs to Finedon, in *Navereslund* hundred

Note: Ploughlands have been omitted for those manors which belong to or have outliers in hundreds where there is no *Terra Regis* mentioned in the Geld Roll, as explained in the text, and for those manors which the king did not hold at the date of the Geld Roll.

CHAPTER III

Economic Exploitation of the Anglo-Norman Royal Demesne, 1066-1100

THE title, *dominus rex,* by which the kings of England were distinguished in the twelfth and succeeding centuries, has usually been noticed by historians who would emphasize those "private" rights of the king as landlord which cannot be dissociated from the king's "public" rights as ruler. The converse, of course, is equally true. The feudal king in his "private" capacity was not merely another, even if the greatest and wealthiest, landlord. The royal demesne, the immediate object of the seignorial exploitation of the Anglo-Norman monarchy, was, and was meant to be from the post-Conquest settlement on, the immediate and tangible basis of the feudal monarchy in England.

Yet of all the characteristics of the feudal monarchy, its "seignorial" policy is perhaps the most obscure. No important royal document—with the partial exception of Domesday Book—from the Conquest till well into the thirteenth century, has survived to reveal in any detail, as do the monastic cartularies and surveys, the relations between the king as landlord and his royal demesne. This chapter is concerned with reconstructing as much of that policy as may throw light upon the constitutional position of the Anglo-Norman monarchy and the social and legal conditions of the peasants dwelling within royal manors. This chapter, then, is a survey, and not the detailed investigation which would serve the purpose of administrative or economic history.

Nor is this chapter concerned—except occasionally and indirectly—with the relations between the king and that part of his demesne which was or was becoming urban. Generally, the relations between the king and the boroughs were complicated by two features which remove that subject from the scope of this survey. First, the king was usually the immediate landlord of only part of the boroughs of the royal demesne; second, the predominance of commercial life in the boroughs sets them apart from the rural demesne of the king. Not that a clear demarcation may be made between the rural and urban demesne: as will be noticed later, it is the very absence of any clear line separating them which provides valuable suggestions in interpreting the evolution of the rural demesne and of the royal demesne as a whole. But with the boroughs themselves this work is not directly concerned.

The annual and regular revenues derived from royal manors had two ultimate sources, in agricultural exploitation and in the profits of jurisdiction annexed to certain of the manors. These revenues could be, and sometimes were, paid directly into the Exchequer by royal officials (in the thirteenth century sometimes styled *custodes* or keepers) [1] whose job it was to collect and account for them. More usually, the manors and their profits were farmed, either grouped as a whole and incorporated within the farm of the county for which the sheriff was responsible, or let to farm, individually or in smaller groups, to individuals or to the tenants of the manors. In the latter case, the farm of specific manors was either in fee (i.e., perpetual to the farmer and his heirs) or for a limited term, either of years, or for life, or indefinitely at the will of the king.

This complicated and flexible lack of system is fully revealed in the Pipe Rolls, Close Rolls, and other records of the Exchequer and Chancery in the thirteenth century, and may be traced in the Pipe Rolls of the twelfth. Furthermore, with the single exception of an unequivocal case of a royal manor let to farm by the tenants, each of these methods of manorial exploitation is revealed in Domesday

[1] For example, Walter de Burgo, in *Close Rolls of the Reign of Henry III, 1237–1242* (Public Record Office; London, 1934), *passim; Rotulorum Originalium in Curia Scaccarii Abbreviatio* (Record Commission, 2 vols.; n.p., 1805–1810), I, 2; and *The Great Roll of the Pipe for the Twenty-Sixth Year of the Reign of King Henry the Third* (ed. H. L. Cannon, Yale Historical Publications, vol. V; New Haven, 1918), pp. 224, 255, 262f., 265, 267, 294.

Book in the eleventh century.[2] This should be emphasized because it illustrates the inadequacy of interpreting the development of the medieval monarchy in terms of an evolution from the simple and primitive to the complex and civilized.

Certain characteristics of the financial system found in Domesday suggest that it was in the administration of the royal demesne that several techniques and methods of later Exchequer practice were first developed. Round was of the opinion that the payment of money which was "weighed and assayed" or "blanch" was "peculiar to the king's demesne." [3] The change in payment from *ad numerum*

[2] The following examples may be cited from Domesday Book. (1) Manorial revenues accounted for directly by a "keeper": "Haec tria Maneria reddebant T.R.E. xxx lib. . . . Modo reddunt x lib. et vi solid. Willelmus peurel custodit" (*D.B.*, I, fol. 273a [Bakewell, Ashford, and Hope, Derbyshire]). (2) Manorial revenues included in the farm of the county: "Ipse comes Rogerius tenet de rege civitatem Sciropesberie et totum comitatum et totum dominium quod rex Edwardus ibi habebat cum xii M quos ipse rex tenebat cum lvii Bereuuichis ibi pertinentibus et alios xi M. . . . reddit ccc libras et cxv solidos de firma" (*D.B.*, I, fol. 254a [Shropshire farm]). See also Stenton, "Introduction to the Domesday Survey," in *The Victoria History of the County of Derby* (ed. Wm. Page; London, 1905), I, 300; and Round, *Feud. Eng.*, pp. 72f. (3) Particular manors farmed separately by individual farmers: "I Raginald have been paying yearly towards the king's farm 24 pounds for the estate of Ordulf" (*D.B.*, IV, fol. 97b, a difficult passage; this rendering follows the translation of O. J. Reichel, *The Victoria History of the County of Devon* [ed., Wm. Page; London, 1906], I, 412). (3a) The same, in fee farm: "Postea Willelmus camerarius tenuit de regina in feudo pro iii lib. per annum de firma et post mortem reginae eodem modo tenuit de rege" (*D.B.*, I, fol. 129b; for the interpretation of this passage, see Maitland, *D.B. and Bey.*, p. 152). (3b) The same, for a limited term: "Bercolt . . . quando Robertus Malet habuit reddebat totum simul . . . et tantumdem modo reddebat Rogero Bigoto. . . . Modo reddit ille Aluricus xl libras" (*D.B.*, II, fol. 287b [Bergholt, Suffolk]). The earliest instances of a royal manor farmed to the men of the manor which I have seen occur in the earliest surviving Pipe Roll: "[Homines R]egis de Tiwe reddunt Compotum de firma Manerii de Tiwe. In Thesauro xxxvj li. Et Quieti sunt" (*P.R. 31 Hen. I*, p. 6); "Homines de Cosseham . . . de firma ejusdem Manerii quod habent in custodia . . ." (*ibid.*, p. 23), and "Homines de Hareham . . . de firma ejusdem Manerii . . ." (*ibid.*, p. 24). The practice may go back to T.R.W., but if so it was rare.

[3] *V.C.H. Bucks*, I, 209. Round contended that payment in refined money was restricted to what he distinguished as the "ancient demesne" of King William, i.e., the manors where William succeeded Edward. This seems to be making too much of the point. It was not by the antiquity of the manor, nor was it by virtue of being held by Edward, that the method of payment was determined. For example, in Buckinghamshire, which Round took as illustrating his point, Aylesbury, held by Edward, renders fifty-six pounds weighed and assayed, T.R.W., and rendered twenty-five pounds *ad numerum*, T.R.E.; while Upton, where the same distinction in payment is employed, was held by Harold. Here as elsewhere the royal financial administra-

to *arsas et pensatas,* or the like, from T.R.E. to T.R.W., is typical of the royal estates in Buckinghamshire and Cambridgeshire, and it is an occasional feature of the *Terra Regis* sections of Surrey, Hampshire, Berkshire, Wiltshire, Somerset, Devonshire, Cornwall, Hertfordshire, Worcestershire, Bedfordshire, Lincolnshire, Essex, Norfolk, and Suffolk. It is found only rarely elsewhere in Domesday Book; but here, as in other respects, it is a mistake to assume that differences in Domesday phrasing or terminology necessarily coincide with differences in fact. The practice of requiring payment in refined money was probably much more common than Domesday reveals, particularly before the Conquest.[4] It would, therefore, be more accurate to say that the Conqueror's financial administration gave impetus to a tendency already appearing under his predecessor and that the requirement to render payment in money at full value was applied more uniformly on the royal demesne than elsewhere because it was subject to the full scope of the king's authority.

The salient feature of these payments in coin "weighed and assayed," etc., was that it was applied where the central government could anticipate the least opposition—such payment quite possibly being the condition of letting royal manors to farm. It is difficult to follow the argument that because the phenomenon is "so local and unsystematic . . . it is more likely to be the result of intelligent exploitation by the sheriffs" [5] than the result of royal policy. Eleventh century England is an unlikely place to look for "a common policy for the realm" and the monarchy would have been unique in western Europe had it had one. Except for Buckinghamshire and Cambridgeshire (in neither of which, however, is the rule without exception), the Domesday evidence as a whole suggests as "local and

---

tion fails to support the theory of an "ancient demesne" in 1086. The editors of the Dialogue of the Exchequer, while admitting a few exceptions, emphasize the *Terra Regis* as the object of monetary reforms in the early Exchequer, and conclude that payments blanch "were always confined to royal manors" (*De Necessariis Observantiis Scaccarii Dialogus* [ed. Arthur Hughes, C. G. Crump, and C. Johnson; Oxford, 1902], pp. 31–36).

[4] For example, "Sandford cum Wica. . . . T.R.E. xxv libre ad pensum et arsuram, quando rex recepit xx libre simili modo" (*D.B.,* I, fol. 39b); "Deneslai. . . . reddit per annum xiiii libras arsas et pensatas et v libras ad numerum. Similiter T.R.E." (fol. 132b); and "Mavrdine. . . . T.R.E. reddebat ix libras de candidis denariis" (fol. 179b).

[5] Jolliffe, *Const. Hist.,* pp. 183f.

unsystematic" an application of the principle on the county level as it does on the national. In other words, the sporadic occurrence of these payments argues as much against local initiative as against central. The strongest argument for "shrieval initiative" must be based on evidence like that provided by the Exon Domesday account of the *Terra Regis* of Devonshire. It seems fairly certain that the first nineteen manors listed were in the charge of Baldwin the Sheriff *ad firmam de rege*.[6] All but two of them are said to render money *ad pondus et arsuram*, or the like. In the next list of twenty-nine manors, Baldwin is identified as farming fourteen, all of which render refined money. Of the remaining fifteen manors, the payments of six are not qualified—we can only guess whether they paid *ad pensum* or *ad numerum;* and in five of these six, the farmer is not named—we can only guess whether any of them were Baldwin's. All in all, the sheriff would seem to be rather closely associated with payment in refined money in Devonshire. But we may be sure that if the sheriff in Devonshire was originally responsible for it, that sheriff was not Baldwin, for in at least three cases the manors already paid by weight when he received them. We may even doubt that Baldwin the Sheriff was a very strong supporter of the system, for in one of the four instances in which the farm had been increased during Baldwin's shrievalty, the Exon Domesday specifically says that it had been raised from ten pounds *ad pensum* to fourteen pounds *ad pensum* and ten shillings *numero*.[7] An argument in favor of local (as against central) initiative cannot go beyond inference, on the basis of this evidence, and there is no reason to believe that the sheriff was not simply carrying out the orders of the central government in every case of this kind recorded by Domesday Book. On Baldwin's own manors, which in Devonshire were more numerous than the king's, there is no trace of payment in refined money—though it must be conceded that Domesday would have less reason to notice the distinction on private estates than on the *Terra Regis*. However, in the case of Bampton, which Walter of Dowai had received in an exchange of manors with King William, Domesday does draw the distinction by stating that the manor "is worth eighteen pounds per annum, and when Walter received it, it was worth

[6] *D.B.*, IV, foll. 83–87, 93–97b.

[7] *D.B.*, IV, fol. 85.

twenty-one pounds *ad pondus.*" [8] Finally, it is relevant to notice that payment in weighed or blanched money may be found in Suffolk on royal estates which it would be difficult to prove had ever been in the charge of a sheriff. These are the forfeited lands of Earl Ralph which were in the custody of Godric the Dapifer.[9]

On the other hand, there is some Domesday evidence (as well as scattered evidence elsewhere) which points to the central government as the final authority in determining the question of the farm of a royal manor. Thus, the case of the Dartford dispute, which has been cited in support of shrieval as opposed to royal initiative, mentions the sheriff only casually, while the testimony of the French reeve and the English jurors as to the values they assign to the manor is duly recorded.[10] That a decision in the dispute is not recorded can only imply that the king or his officials, and not the sheriff, will determine the farm. The case may well illustrate "the chaos which existed in the fiscal scheme of a great royal manor," [11] although it is certainly not typical of the royal demesne as a whole in Domesday Book; but it even more clearly indicates the ultimate authority of

[8] *D.B.*, IV, fol. 345b.

[9] *D.B.*, II, 285bf.

[10] "Rex Willelmvs tenet Tarentefort. . . . T.R.E. valuit lx libre et tantundem quando Haimo uicecomes recepit. Modo appreciatur ab Anglis lx libre. Prepositus uero francigenus qui tenet ad firmam dicit quia ualet quater xx libre et x libre. Ipse tamen reddit de isto manerio lxx libras pensatas et cxi solidos de denariis xx in ora et vii libras et xxvi denarios ad numerum. Super haec reddit uicecomiti c solidos" (*D.B.*, I, fol. 2b). The sheriff takes his profit from the manor in the five pounds which the French reeve gives him, presumably, for the privilege of farming the manor. If the sheriff were responsible for requiring payment in "weighed" money, it is difficult to see why the five pounds are not also "weighed." It could be argued that Domesday would not record the character of the five pounds, since the payment is simply a matter between the sheriff and the reeve; but if that were so, why mention the five pounds at all? It is difficult to escape the impression that the reeve himself renders (*ipse reddit*) the sums mentioned directly to the central government, as was the case at Bergholt (noticed below) where "weighed" money is also required. If this is so, it is equally difficult to see what interest the sheriff had in whether the money were "weighed" or not—unless one would argue that the requirement goes back to a period antedating the arrangement recorded in Domesday and was originally the work of some unknown sheriff, but that is an argument from silence, to say the least. It is hazardous in the extreme to affirm that any particular arrangement or requirement does not occur in Domesday Book, but I have searched and have not found a single instance of a payment due to a sheriff in his shrieval capacity which is said to be made in refined money.

[11] Jolliffe, *Const. Hist.*, p. 184, n.3.

the king and his agents, thus supporting the implications of the testimony of the Anglo-Saxon Chronicle, that "the king farmed his land as dearly as he might . . . and cared nothing with what sin the reeves must exact it of poor men." [12] Altogether, it seems unlikely that the sheriff should have taught the royal treasury the value of requiring payments in blanched or weighed money. It is far more probable that sheriffs should have required such payments from individual manors which comprised their farm because they themselves were required to pay in coin of full value. In either case, the initiative is that of the royal government, payment in blanched coin is a development of the central government and not of the local government of the sheriff, and the scene of its earliest more than casual or exceptional application is the Domesday *Terra Regis*. The Pipe Rolls of the twelfth century reveal the Exchequer extending the requirement beyond the demesne, and thus applying to general administrative practice the experience gained where royal authority was least restricted, on the royal demesne.[13] Despite the difficulties of Domesday interpretation, it seems clear that such is the general conclusion to be derived from the evidence of the great survey.

Another administrative reform revealed by Domesday Book to be taking place, especially on the royal demesne, was the practice of commuting ancient customary payments in kind to payments in coin. This is connected with the growing insistence upon payment in money of full value,[14] and like the latter was based on precedent in the Confessor's reign. Commutation, indeed, as illustrated by Domesday seems to be generally at the end of a process reaching well back into Anglo-Saxon times; for only rarely does Domesday present a money tariff of specific items of a payment in kind, thus implying a recent commutation. Thus, the county of Oxford "renders a farm of three nights, that is, 150 pounds. . . . For weapons, 4 shillings; for the Queen's gift, 100 shillings by tale; for a hawk, 10 pounds; for a sumpter-horse, 20 shillings; for hounds, 23

[12] Anglo-Saxon Chronicle, 1086E, quoted by Jolliffe, *Const. Hist.*, p. 184, n.5.

[13] *Scac. Dial.*, pp. 36ff.

[14] For example, "Saham Manerium regis . . . reddit per annum xxv libras arsas et pensatas et xiii libras et viii solidos et iii denarios ad numerum de albis denariis pro frumento, brasio, melle et aliis minutis consuetudinibus. T.R.E. reddebat xxv libras ad numerum et iii dies firmam de frumento, melle et brasio et de omnibus aliis (consuetudinibus)" (*D.B.*, I, fol. 189 [Soham, Cambridgeshire]).

pounds in pennies of 20 to the ounce; and 6 sestiers of honey and 15 pence by way of custom." [15]

Commutation does not, however, seem to be connected with another Domesday feature of the financial exploitation of the royal demesne, viz., the even sums at which royal manors were so often farmed. These even sums were noticed by Round as "the most striking feature, perhaps, presented" by the royal manors of Domesday, and a feature which he believed "points to a primitive financial system." [16] Round's predilection to impute antiquity to anything characterized by an arbitrarily even scale [17] seems inadmissible in this instance. For if it be allowed that payment in kind is more archaic than payment in money, it will be found from a survey of the Domesday evidence relating to the commutation of the farm of one night and its variants that these archaic renders are almost invariably commuted for uneven figures probably representing the sums of a variety of small customs. This is illustrated above in the Oxfordshire schedule of commutation. Even sums, on the contrary, are rarely associated with the archaic farm of one night but almost always occur in connection with the ordinary farm of the manor.

It would, therefore, seem more historical and reasonable to suppose that the normal evolution of the rent from a royal manor was as follows: (1) a variety of renders in kind as the most primitive system; (2) a commutation of these renders in kind according to a tariff, which would produce an uneven sum as the money rent; and (3) the adjustment of this sum upward or downward in accordance with the economic condition of the estate and the method of administration (assuming that when a manor was under a bailiff who accounted for the itemized profits, the sum would tend to remain uneven; while if the manor were let to farm, in fee or for a term, an effort would be made to raise the rent to a larger even sum). Domesday implies that the third stage had been reached generally at the time of the survey, and the "roundness of the sums" [18] would point therefore to a recent development rather than a primitive financial

[15] *D.B.*, I, fol. 154b (following Stenton's translation in *V.C.H. Oxford*, I, 376, 401).

[16] *V.C.H. Northants*, I, 273.

[17] For example, "the five hide unit . . . was undoubtedly an old institution . . . the tendency in early days, no doubt, was to stereotype such figures, . . . the witness to a state of things prevailing in the distant past" (*Feud. Eng.*, pp. 92, 94).

[18] Round, *V.C.H. Northants*, I, 273.

system.[19] Again, the royal demesne is the scene of an administrative development which, while based on precedents of the Confessor's reign, is given impetus under the Conqueror.

The last feature of the "seignorial" administration of the royal demesne suggested by Domesday Book has already been alluded to in another connection.[20] This was the grouping together of several estates for purposes of exploitation. Working in the manner of Seebohm and Maitland, from the known to the unknown, it is possible to endow this widely noticed phenomenon with some significance which transcends the mere fact as revealed in the record of the great survey. It is a commonplace of the feudal period that escheated or forfeited honors were normally maintained in their integrity by the king, while in his hands. Although not without exception, this integrity of the feudal escheat is typical of the Anglo-Norman and Angevin monarchy, and its acceptance of this principle may well be considered as additional evidence of its feudal nature. It has not, however, been noticed that this principle, if not uniformly adopted by 1086, at least coincides with normal administrative practice of the Conqueror's reign as applied to the royal demesne. This was the administrative grouping of manors which may be found in all parts of England, and there is clear evidence that here again there were precedents going back beyond the Conquest, in some of the counties at least.

The researches of Eyton and Round have established that the

---

[19] It is gratuitous to add that I differ from J. H. Round on a Domesday problem only with hesitation and after a careful review of the evidence. The interpretation put forward here rests on a general survey of all the Domesday *Terra Regis,* of which the following entries may be taken as typical or pertinent: "Rex tenet Sumertone. Rex Edwardus tenuit. Nunquam geldauit. . . . Reddit per annum lxxix libras et x solidos et vii denarios" and "Rex tenet Cedre. . . . Reddit per annum xxi libras et ii denarios et obolum. . . . Sumertone et Cedre cum appendiciis reddebant firmam unius noctis T.R.E." (*D.B.,* I, fol. 86 [Somerton and Cheddar, Somerset]); "Cumbertone est dominica uilla regis. . . . Reddit c solidos ad numerum et tantundem reddebat T.R.E. Haec terra semper de firma regis" (*D.B.,* I, fol. 189b [Comberton, Cambridgeshire]); and "Rex tenet in dominio Stochae. De firma regis Edwardi fuit. . . . T.R.E. et post valuit xii librae. Modo xv librae. Tamen qui tenet reddit xv libras ad pensum" (*D.B.,* I, fol. 30 [Stoke, Surrey]). Similar references could be given at great length, but all to the same effect, that the commuted archaic farm is uneven, while the sum paid by *qui tenet de firma regis* is a round, even sum, and invariably in such cases the rent paid has lost all connection with the farm of one night.

[20] Above, pp. 12f., 17, 42f.

royal manors betraying the highest antiquity in the southwestern counties were normally grouped together for administrative purposes.[21] So also in the north, the royal manors of Derbyshire were farmed together in two large blocks, "for the sake of agricultural organization," both before and after the Conquest.[22] But the rest of Domesday Book need not be called to witness the general phenomenon. In this connection it should be noticed that the principle of "honorial integrity" generally controlled the assignment of honors and estates by the Conqueror to his tenants after 1066. It is true that the "average Norman baron had many English *antecessores,*" but, in reducing several thousand separate holdings "into less than two hundred major lordships," [23] the holdings of the Anglo-Saxon *antecessores* were generally granted by the Conqueror as a whole, though exceptions could be quoted at some length.[24] The converse of this general rule may be found in operation on the royal demesne in 1086, for escheated "honors" and lands were often treated administratively as separate entities. Except where all the royal manors of a whole shire were farmed together by the sheriff, escheats were not merged into the rest of the royal demesne, but were farmed as separate manorial groups kept distinct from manors

---

21 For example, Eyton, *Dorset Survey, passim;* and Round, *Feud. Eng.*, pp. 109–114. So far as I know, it has not hitherto been noticed that traces of a system of grouping may be detected in the nineteen royal manors listed under the rubric *Dominicatus Regis ad Regnum pertinens in Devenescira* in the Devonshire portion of the Exon Domesday. The sum of the payments of the first four manors make up an even farm of fifty pounds; the fifth and seventh manors combine to total fifty pounds, the eighth, ninth, and tenth likewise total fifty pounds; and the seventeenth and eighteenth manors on the list together total twenty-five pounds. This, however, leaves eight of the manors unaccounted for, and the geographical combinations of the manors hardly follow their grouping into fifty-pound farms. Another fifty-pound group could be made up from the boroughs of Lydford and Exeter together with Diptford and Bampton (which was not in the king's hands T.R.W.). All the remaining possessions would then total approximately forty-three pounds (*D.B.*, IV, foll. 83–88).

22 Stenton, *V.C.H. Derby,* I, 297, 311f.

23 Stenton, *Anglo-Saxon England,* p. 618.

24 Round accepted this principle, and depended upon it for many of his Domesday identifications of personal names. See, e.g., "Introduction to the Domesday Survey," in *The Victoria History of the County of Surrey* (ed. H. E. Malden; Westminster, 1902), I, 283f. Exceptions may be found especially among the estates of Harold, and the house of Godwin generally, where the confusion between private and "comital" possessions may well be the explanation. See Maitland, *D.B. and Bey.*, p. 168.

which already had been formed into administrative groups under particular farmers.[25]

The significance of this discussion now emerges in the light it throws upon what has been alleged to be a distinction between "ancient demesne" and the rest of the land in the king's hands in 1086, with its corollary that the political ideas of the Conqueror's generation included an understanding of the difference between "crown" and "king." The distinction between different groups of royal demesne manors certainly appears. But it arises from administrative convenience, and it conforms with the normal feudal practice of maintaining honorial integrity both in granting lands and in administering escheats. It is important to grasp the nature of this distinction, because it will have important implications in determining the validity of a theory of the privileges of ancient demesne which would find their origin in the Anglo-Saxon period and would trace them as a survival "from pre-Conquest conditions" found on "the manors of St. Edward." [26]

Whether there was, in 1086, any distinction other than a merely administrative one between one and another kind of royal demesne, the overriding consideration for the Norman monarchy must have been the total income to be derived from the whole demesne. In this regard, two separate problems must be dealt with: first, the at-

[25] Thus Queen Edith's lands in Witchley hundred, Rutland (but surveyed under Northamptonshire), consisting of eleven separate estates, were grouped around three centers at Ketton, Barrowden, and South Luffenham, which were farmed by Hugh de Port at ten, seven, and three pounds, respectively, totaling twenty pounds (*D.B.*, I, fol. 219). Baldwin, sheriff of Devonshire, farmed most of the manors formerly held by King Edward, but quite apart from them was his farm of the forfeited estates of the earls in that county for a flat 375 pounds, a fact which the Exon Domesday notes (*D.B.*, IV, fol. 97b). The estates of Matilda, the Conqueror's queen, were farmed as a block by Gotselin in the same county (*D.B.*, IV, foll. 108–110b). Geographical location certainly affected the composition of farm groups, but this factor can be used neither to affirm nor deny any special distinction between the groups. The Suffolk Domesday emphasizes the practice of group farming of escheated manors by arranging the *Terra Regis* estates in groups according to the "keeper" T.R.W. and the tenant T.R.E. Thus, "Terre Radulfi comitis quas godricus dapifer seruat In suthful In manu regis" (*D.B.*, II, fol. 284b); "Terra Matris Morchari comitis Quam Willelmus camerarius et Otho aurifex seruant In manu regis" (fol. 286b); and "Terre Stingandi quas Willelmus denoers seruat In manu RegiS" (fol. 288). Quite separate from these, at the head of the *Terra Regis* section, is a group of manors in which William succeeded Edward, the *Terra Regis de Regione quam Rogerus bigot seruat.*

[26] Vinogradoff, *Villainage*, p. 123.

titude of the monarchy toward exploitation of royal manors, that is, whether indeed "from the first days of the Conquest onwards, the king was the best of landlords"; [27] and second, what the actual and relative total revenues from the royal demesne amounted to, T.R.W.

The answer to the first question is important, for it too will have a direct bearing on the problem of ancient-demesne privileges. Did the Conqueror manifest a landlordly concern for the welfare of his demesne peasantry, so far as the exploitation of royal manors can show? Leaving aside "the tradition which ascribes to the Conqueror a law in favour of the tillers of the soil," [28] what does the administration of the royal demesne in 1086 indicate concerning the relationship between the king and the population of his demesne manors?

The only answer to be derived from the Domesday evidence is that the manorial population of the royal demesne was in the same position as the peasantry in general: the peasantry afforded a legitimate object of exploitation. In nearly every county there are signs of increased rents, of a widespread if not systematic effort to increase the revenues of the royal demesne. It is, of course, possible that the primary responsibility for such a situation rested with the sheriffs, bailiffs, and farmers, rather than with the king. But if so, it is clear either that these royal ministers were compelled to extract as much as they could because of the increased farms due to the monarchy, or else that the king was indifferent to, or unable to do much to soften, the effect which such exploitation inflicted upon the peasantry of his manors.

It is possible that the sharp rise in the total revenue from the royal demesne, in the period from 1066 to 1086, merely reflected an increase in agricultural values due to purely economic or general social and political causes, such as the re-establishment of peace and social stability or the growth of population and the rise of prices. But such an explanation does not accord with all the Domesday evidence, and it leaves out of account the clear indication of the dubious or worse activities of the king's ministers in charge of royal manors.

The interpretation here put forward seems to conform more

---

[27] Maitland, *D.B. and Bey.*, p. 65.

[28] *Ibid.*, p. 66. This "tradition" is embodied in the *Leis Willelme*, c. 29, and will be discussed below.

nearly with the Domesday evidence as a whole. However, it must be conceded that only a citation of all the values and renders and of all the activities of the king's ministers on the royal demesne of Domesday Book could demonstrate the point. It will, then, suffice for the present to illustrate this viewpoint by reference to typical or especially pertinent evidence.

The doings of Aluric the reeve (*prepositus*), as recorded by the survey of Suffolk, afford a view of the possibilities open to a minor royal official who was responsible to the sheriff, Roger Bigod. In the royal vill of Ringsfield, twelve free men who had rendered nothing T.R.E. were rendering fifteen pounds in 1086, "and this custom Aluric the reeve appointed for them in Roger Bigod's time." [29] In Barnby, eight free men who had rendered thirteen shillings and sixpence were paying an incredible thirty pounds, "and this custom Aluric imposed (*misit*) upon them in King William's time under Roger Bigod." [30] At Herringfleet, the farm of the manor had been twenty shillings "and afterwards in Roger Bigod's time Aluric the reeve increased (*crescebat*) [the sum] to one-hundred shillings." [31] It is tempting to speculate whether these exactions ever found their way into the king's own revenue. Lack of evidence rules out any dogmatic conclusion. Yet if the Aluric Wanz who in 1086 was the keeper of the king's manor of Bergholt is the same Aluric the reeve —and there is every reason to believe so, as will appear—the probability is that the exactions which fell ultimately upon the tenants of the royal manors resulted directly from increases in the farms due to the king. In the Bergholt entry a dispute is recorded, the details of which throw light on the question:

> When Robert Malet had it the whole together rendered 60 pounds by weight, and 8 pounds by tale . . . the same amount the manor rendered to Roger Bigod as the reeve himself says. But Roger says that it rendered 40 shillings more by tale and one mark of gold. But Aluric the reeve contradicts [him] and Roger is willing to prove [his saying]. . . . The said Aluric now renders 60 pounds by weight, and he so holds of the King by such agreement that he is bound to make the King

29 *The Victoria History of the County of Suffolk* (ed. Wm. Page; London, 1911), I, 420.

30 *Ibid.*, I, 421.

31 *Ibid.*, I, 423.

[payment of] 60 pounds out of the profit, and of this he vouches the King to warrant. So he says himself; and he says too that this does not hold good (*non remanet*) in that he does not make that profit.[32]

In the time of King Edward, the corresponding farm was thirty-three pounds, so that the three successive farmers T.R.W. were paying approximately double, with the "ultimate result . . . that the paying power of the population was overstrained, and the rents could not be gathered in." [33] The agreement with the king stipulated a payment so high that even the experienced Aluric could not extract it from the manor. The record of such a dispute in Domesday Book is rare, and it is not unreasonable to suppose that many an unrecorded case of local extortion resulted from the increases in the farms of many another manor of the Domesday *Terra Regis*.

Part of Aluric's difficulty may be indicated by the last few sentences of the Bergholt entry. The free men of the soke of Bergholt had paid to the reeve four pence each, T.R.E.; Roger Bigod's ministers had increased the payment to a lump sum of fifteen pounds. When he was succeeded by Robert Malet as sheriff the payment was further increased to twenty pounds. When Roger had the shrievalty a second time the payment continued at twenty, but "now Aluric Wanz holds them [the free men] by the like custom as T.R.E." [34] If the sokemen mentioned earlier in the Bergholt entry are identical with the free men of the soke of Bergholt dealt with here, their number had decreased from 210, T.R.E., to 119, T.R.W. Thus, Aluric would have suffered a loss of some eighteen pounds from this source of revenue. Roger claimed to have paid a total of ten pounds and a mark of gold more than Aluric had agreed to pay, and the difference may be represented by this restoration of the free men to "the customs of St. Edward."

This transaction, incidentally, cannot be accepted as evidence of a royal solicitude for the manorial population of the royal demesne, T.R.W., for the reason that the free men did not dwell upon the manor of Bergholt or its appurtenances, and (if they are identical

[32] *Ibid.*, I, 427. (The passage is reproduced by permission of the General Editor of the Victoria History of the Counties of England.) Notice the identification of Aluric the reeve with "the said Aluric [Wanz]" who is farming the manor in 1086.

[33] Vinogradoff, *Eng. Soc.*, p. 380.

[34] *V.C.H. Suffolk*, I, 427.

with the sokemen mentioned above) they are surveyed with their holdings quite separately from Bergholt and its appurtenances with the villeins, bordars, and serfs dwelling thereon. Furthermore, for an unstated reason—but one which may be implied by Aluric's and other reeves' behavior in these parts—of the 210 sokemen T.R.E., Domesday states "now there are only 119 . . . who have remained [attached] to this manor" (*qui huic manerio ramansi sunt*).[35] But where and why they left, and what happened to those who remained, is not recorded. Here it is enough to notice that despite their restoration to the customary free gift of King Edward's time, those who remained were still subject to the other phases of the rack-renting of a royal manor and its appurtenances which occasioned a quarrel between Aluric Wanz and Roger Bigod.[36]

Turning from East Anglia and its widely scattered free men to the more thoroughly manorialized county of Berkshire, Domesday Book presents less colorful but even more convincing evidence of exploitation. The royal demesne in this county was particularly extensive and valuable, being distributed among forty-three manors (besides the boroughs), whose total annual value exceeded 900 pounds, and whose average value was over twenty pounds.[37] One out of every four of these manors, according to the Domesday jurors, was paying to the king each year more than its annual value. The eleven manors in this category had an average annual value of twenty-seven pounds—some eight or nine pounds higher than the average annual value of the other thirty-two royal manors. But except for their generally greater value, there is nothing else peculiar to this group. They were large and small, and scattered geographically; they came to the Conqueror from diverse holders T.R.E. (King Edward held six of the eleven, while Harold, three free men, and Queen Edith held the others); and although nine of them are either said never to have paid geld or were not assessed in hides, two of them are not so distinguished and many of the other royal manors were equally exempt from taxation.

---

[35] *D.B.*, II, fol. 286.

[36] It is curious that Vinogradoff, who dealt with the dispute at some length (*Eng. Soc.*, pp. 379f.), does not seem to have noticed the significance of the Bergholt entry as a whole for his theory of ancient demesne privileges.

[37] For the data which follow, see *D.B.*, I, foll. 56b–58, or *V.C.H. Berks*, I, 327–335.

The following table provides an analysis of the eleven manors paying more than they were worth: [38]

Total value of the eleven manors	299 pounds
Total paid by the eleven manors	365 pounds
Average value	27 pounds
Average paid	33 pounds
Percent increase of payment over value	22%

Round's criticism of the work of Eyton has dispelled once and for all from Domesday scholarship the notion of symmetry, accuracy, or perfection in Domesday statistics. Still, the figures preserved by the record, when taken in the mass and not pressed beyond the limits of eleventh century administrative techniques, are not only valuable but incontrovertible for conclusions which are general rather than particular in nature. And the general picture presented by the Berkshire Domesday evidence clearly bears out what is suggested by the evidence from Suffolk: the royal demesne manors, with their peasants, were objects of exploitation and rack-renting.[39]

The same impression is derived from the survey of the neighboring county of Hampshire. In the words of Round,

> The raising of the rents exacted may, in some cases, have been justified, but that it was often grossly oppressive we know on the excellent authority of the Domesday commissioners themselves. Mapledurham (fo. 38) was over-rented by about 50%; Meon, worth 60 pounds, was paying 100 pounds and more, "sed non potest pati" (fo. 38); on manor after manor we find its estimated annual value contrasted with the sum, largely in excess, wrung from its tenants by the king's reeves. When we turn to the Isle of Wight (fo. 52), we find the first five of his manors valued as worth 50 pounds, yet paying 77 pounds. Keen and avaricious in money matters, the Normans loved the speculation of farming the king's manors; the baron, and even the prelate, took a hand in the game.[40]

[38] The figures are all approximate, to the nearest pound. The totals are not strictly accurate, because no correction has been attempted for the occasional notices of payments *ad pensum*.

[39] The only alternative is the supposition that the Domesday jurors were deliberately exaggerating wherever they believed their verdicts might obtain some relief. But this interpretation would only be a more elaborate statement of the position taken in the text, for it equally reveals the feeling that the king as landlord was more interested in profits than in being "the best of landlords."

[40] *V.C.H. Hants,* I, 414; passage reproduced by permission of the General Editor of the Victoria History of the Counties of England.

Left to the mercies of the avaricious baron and prelate, not to mention the routine exploitation of the royal reeve or bailiff, it is no wonder that the peasants of the royal demesne, like all peasants in England, might suffer "under the sway of foreigners, who may fairly be suspected of some harshness and greed." [41] No less remarkable is it that historians who would draw a distinction between conditions prevailing upon the royal demesne of the Conqueror and conditions prevailing elsewhere have done so, with Domesday Book before them, only by retreating from the evidence into the realm of theory.

A further statistical review of the Domesday evidence would only make more abundantly clear that the bulk of the evidence all points in one direction. The attitude of the monarchy toward exploitation of royal manors, as revealed by Domesday, hardly bears out Maitland's dictum that "the king was the best of landlords." Whether he left his manors to the mercies of a competitive farming system or operated them with royal bailiffs, the king was interested primarily in revenues, and only secondarily if at all in the welfare of his manorial demesne population.[42]

This is not to rule out any other than financial motives in the attitude of William the Conqueror toward his demesne manors. Political motives certainly played a part in his giving up most of the royal demesne in Sussex and in the three counties on the Welsh border which became "marcher fiefs of a special kind." [43] So also, William's retention in his own hands of extensive lands in Middlesex, Hertfordshire, Lincolnshire, Rutland, Cornwall, East Anglia, and Yorkshire, where King Edward had either few manors or none at all, was probably determined in part by an effort to extend the power of the king throughout the realm.

But the primary purpose of these additions to the royal demesne, which gave the Conqueror roughly "twice the amount of the Crown's revenue in King Edward's day as estimated by the Domes-

[41] Maitland, *DB. and Bey.*, p. 35.

[42] In his introductions to the Victoria County History Domesday sections, Round usually commented upon the evidences of manorial exploitation on the *Terra Regis*. See especially *V.C.H. Bucks,* I, 220f.; *V.C.H. Essex,* I, 357, 362f.; and "Introduction to the Domesday Survey," in *The Victoria History of the County of Bedford* (Westminster, 1904), I, 194f., 205f.

[43] Corbett, "Norman Conquest," *Camb. Med. Hist.,* V, 509.

day juries,"[44] was a greater endowment and income as the foundation of the Anglo-Norman monarchy. Furthermore, the king was not the greatest landlord by virtue of the increased number of his estates alone. As has been seen, the higher royal revenue was due as well to the increase in "the rents at which the manors were let to farm to the sheriffs and other reeves, who took charge of them as speculative ventures and recouped themselves in their turn by raising the dues and increasing the services exacted from the cultivating peasantry."[45]

The financial results of the greater extent and increased revenue of the royal demesne in 1086 may be shown in tabular form, based on the researches of W. J. Corbett (all values being approximate):[46]

Ecclesiastical property	19,200 pounds
English landholders	4,000 pounds
Baronies of Frenchmen	30,350 pounds
Odo of Bayeux and Robert of Mortain (king's half-brothers)	5,050 pounds
Royal officials and servants	1,800 pounds
Royal demesne	12,600 pounds
Total disposable revenue	73,000 pounds

The "crown and the royal house" and the royal ministers thus accounted for 19,450 pounds, more than all the ecclesiastical revenues and approximately 26½% of the total nonborough revenue of England. To include the boroughs would increase each category in the table, but the king would gain the most.

A much larger problem than concerns this chapter is implicit in these figures. Between a quarter and a third of the wealth of England was directly controlled by the king at the end of the Conqueror's reign. Why did the Anglo-Norman monarchy dissipate this huge wealth by alienation and turn with such vigor to the exploitation of its profits of justice and the incidents of feudal tenure (especially reliefs), in the period c.1087–1135? It is not enough to say that enforcement of judicial and feudal rights was necessary for political control of the kingdom—this is so obviously true that it answers the problem by avoiding it. The objects of

[44] *Ibid.*, V, 508.

[45] *Ibid.*, V, 509.

[46] *Ibid.*, V, 508. The figures represent annual values, omitting the boroughs.

such political control, or of what may be loosely termed the "centralization" of Henry I, were two in particular: first, an increase of royal revenue; and second, the enhancement of royal authority by bringing the king into a direct relationship (judicially especially, but also with respect to military obligations, etc.) with all free men.[47] Neither of these objects was nearer attainment by alienation of the royal demesne, and at first glance one would expect the monarchy to achieve the goal of greater revenue and political power by retaining and building up the royal demesne. But a solution of this problem lies primarily in a study of the relations between the king and the feudal baronage.

The contribution to be made from this survey of royal policy toward its demesne is suggested by the conclusions established thus far: the monarchy elaborated fiscal and administrative techniques —not innovations in themselves, but going beyond Anglo-Saxon precedent—on the royal demesne, which are later found in general use; the royal demesne of 1086 was not considered to contain a "public" element attached to the crown as distinct from the king, whose population enjoyed preferential treatment; the royal demesne was on the contrary exploited to the full for all it was worth and perhaps a little more; and the annual value of the royal demesne in 1086 made the king by far the wealthiest landlord in England. What must remain unknown, for lack of evidence, is the extent of the discrepancy between the total annual *value* of the demesne and the actual usable *income* derived from that source. In any case, demesne revenues had to be supplemented, as the records of the collection of geld under William demonstrate: the Conqueror's demesne did not free him from depending on other sources of revenue.

It may be suggested, then, that it was the inefficiency of royal administration that rendered the royal demesne of the Norman settlement constitutionally less significant than its great extent and value might imply. Certainly the whole Domesday survey reveals irregularity mixed with extortion on the *Terra Regis,* which, with the lack of system equally evident, together imply the need for administrative reform. Under Henry I—and certainly under the

[47] See Stenton, *The First Century of English Feudalism* (Oxford, 1932), pp. 216–222.

strong hand of Ranulf Flambard in the preceding reign—administrative reform is inseparable from financial profit. The author of the *Leges Henrici Primi* states as much in so many words, though he is concerned with the judicial aspect which became so prominent under Henry I. Administrative reform aimed at exploiting judicial and feudal rights gave the monarchy political power as well as financial profit; on the royal demesne there was still too great a danger that reform would profit the monarchy less than it would the semi-independent shrievalty which farmed the royal manors.

CHAPTER IV

The Royal Demesne of the Feudal Monarchy, 1100-1199

FOR the history of those medieval institutions which are fundamental in the growth of western civilization, the twelfth century is a period both crucial and tantalizing. It was a creative age, especially in England, where political and institutional growth was more precocious than anywhere else in Europe during the period, with the possible exception of southern Italy. Yet the historian who discerns clear indications of growth and development in the surviving evidence is confronted with often insoluble problems when he attempts to explain why, or even how, these changes took place. The chronicles and records of the twelfth century are sufficiently full to demonstrate the importance of the age, without being sufficiently clear and complete to reveal the full significance of those aspects which have a direct bearing on later developments.

These remarks apply particularly to the history of the royal demesne in the twelfth century, when the fuedal monarchy in England effected a basic and permanent change of policy toward its landed endowment. This change, in turn, had a basic and permanent effect upon the relations between the monarchy and the feudal society of which it formed the apex. Thus, the history of the royal demesne in this period is an important—though obscure—aspect of the general transformation of medieval England from an essentially feudal to an essentially national realm. The relationship of the royal demesne to this more general development may be seen best in an analysis of royal policy with respect to alienation of the royal demesne, centralization of administrative control of the demesne, and the development of a new kind of taxation on the demesne.

ALIENATION AND ITS CONSEQUENCES

Whatever were the possibilities of the extensive royal demesne of the Conqueror, as a foundation of the Anglo-Norman monarchy, it is clear that William Rufus, Henry I, and Stephen considered their demesne lands as a fund with which they could purchase even greater benefits, whether feudal or spiritual. Indications of extensive and deliberate alienation of the royal demesne are met on every hand in the period from 1087 to 1154.

There is, of course, no direct evidence that a policy of alienation was deliberately and consistently pursued. This is not an age of abundant administrative records or of competent theoretical treatises—witness the *Quadripartitus* in the realm of law.[1] The reconstruction of feudal policy, i.e., the governing ideas determining the action taken by the feudal monarchy and the feudal baronage, must be based on an evaluation of the fragmentary records of specific events and specific facts.[2] That the monarchy was quite aware of how alienation affected its resources cannot be doubted, in view of the *terre date* system, which is not only found in the earliest Pipe Roll [3] but is alluded to in Domesday Book itself.[4] Almost every alienation from the royal demesne involved an adjustment of the *firma comitatus* (or of the farmer or custodian whose debts appeared in the Pipe Roll), since a sum equivalent to the farm of the alienated manor had to be allowed to the sheriff (or eliminated from the special account of the farmer or custodian).[5]

1 "To have thought that a law-book ought to be written was no small exploit in the year 1118" (Sir Frederick Pollock and F. W. Maitland, *The History of English Law* [2d ed.; Cambridge, 1898], I, 101; also 97–104 *passim*).

2 This is well illustrated by Sir Frank Stenton's brilliant study, *The First Century of English Feudalism.*

3 *P.R. 31 Hen. I,* pp. 52 (Essex and Hertfordshire), 72 (Staffordshire), 90 (Norfolk and Suffolk), and *passim.*

4 "De hoc M tenet Giso episcopus unum membrum Wetmore quod ipse tenuit de rege E. Pro eo computat Willelmus uicecomes in firma regis xii lib. unoquoque anno" (*D.B.,* I, fol. 86 [Cheddar, Somerset]). See Round, *The Commune of London and Other Studies* (Westminster, 1899), pp. 73f.

5 "Warinus Vicecomes reddit Compotum de cc & xvj li. & xvij s. & iiij d. bl. de veteri firma. . . . Et In Manerio de Celeswrda quod Warnerius filius Ern' tenet ad firmam

The constitutional significance of this alienation of the royal demesne has not been adequately assessed. Alienation has usually been noticed primarily in connection with political issues, and in terms, which are anachronistic; or else it has been, for this period, passed over without serious consideration.[6] Thus Stubbs summed up the problem, looking back from the thirteenth to the early twelfth century and emphasizing Stephen's reign, in terms of political balance and struggle between the crown and the baronage.

> The most plausible means of making and keeping the king rich enough to pay his own way was doubtless to prevent him from alienating the property of the crown. . . . The outcry against foreign favourites, which had been raised at intervals ever since the Conquest, was the first expression of this feeling. The crown was very rich; so the nation was fully persuaded. The Conqueror had had an enormous income, William Rufus and Henry I had maintained and increased it. Stephen had begun the process of impoverishment, from which the crown had never recovered. . . . Royal demesne had been lavished on natives and aliens.[7]

If William Rufus and Henry I had increased the enormous income of the Conqueror, it was not by retaining or increasing the royal demesne, but the very reverse, that is, by exploiting the judicial and feudal possibilities of the monarchy and by letting more and more of the *Terra Regis* slip out of the king's hands. The fact of extensive alienation cannot be doubted. The process, indeed, had already begun under the Conqueror and was not without abun-

---

vij li. & xviij s. & iiij d. numero" (*P.R. 31 Hen. I,* pp. 12f.); "CHAERLEOLIUM. Hildretus reddit Compotum. . . . Et In Terris datis per breve Regis Ricardo militi xiij solidos & iiij d. terre" (*ibid.,* p. 140).

[6] For example, Jolliffe (*Const. Hist.,* pp. 199f.) sums up what he terms the "anti-feudal trend of royal policy" by stressing that "the demesne interest of the crown came progressively to the fore as its avowed preoccupation during three successive reigns," and refers to "the *terra regis* and the *jura regalia* as the most jealously cultivated *dominium*" under Henry I. The rest of the discussion of this period is devoted mainly to administrative developments relating to the *jura regalia* and hardly touches on the *terra regis.*

[7] Stubbs, *The Constitutional History of England* (3d ed.; Oxford, 1887), II, 584f. (Quotation used by permission of the Clarendon Press, Oxford.) In later editions, "natives and aliens" was changed to read "relatives and aliens," but this change does not affect the main point and is actually unwarranted if it is meant to exclude natives who were not relatives.

dant precedent in the preceding reign.[8] In alienation as in every other phase of the history of the royal demesne of the eleventh century, the Conquest provides no sharp break, no reversal of royal policy, to mark the Norman advent.

It is, then, incorrect to speak of "impoverishment" beginning under Stephen because of alienation of the royal demesne. Alienation did not begin under Stephen, and impoverishment in his reign was as much due to the breakdown of the whole royal administration and to the alienation of royal rights and revenues as it was due to any decrease in the extent of the royal demesne.[9] It should be added that no absolute distinction is intended between alienation of royal demesne as territory and alienation of royal rights and revenues. The territorialization of jurisdiction was the normal condition of feudal society: a grant of land normally, or at least very often, involved a grant of some jurisdictional rights and revenues. And yet there were degrees of jurisdiction. Furthermore, a distinction between land and jurisdiction, as well as a distinction between degrees of jurisdiction, was recognized and insisted upon in the reign of Henry I. The author of the *Leges Henrici* leaves no doubt that land and jurisdiction could be separated: the king has the soke of all lands he holds in demesne; he can give or retain the soke of manors granted out; and the soke, so far from "following" a granted manor automatically, is given or retained rather in accordance with the status of the grantee.[10] So also, "a great man may by purchase acquire soke . . . over lands that are not his own." [11]

Finally, it is unnecessary to insist, but it is well to notice, that setting the problem of alienation against a background made up of "the nation," "foreign favorites," "natives and aliens," and a "king

[8] Examples could be listed at great length from Domesday Book. More interesting is the fact that manors *ad regnum pertinentia* were alienated as well as those not so described. There was no inalienable "ancient demesne" in the eleventh century. See above, p. 17ff.

[9] For a careful and authoritative analysis of Stephen's relations with his barons, see Stenton, *First Century*, pp. 221–256.

[10] "Omnium terrarum, quas rex in dominio suo habet, socnam pariter habet . . . quarundam terrarum maneria dedit, sed socnam sibi retinuit. Nec sequitur socna regis data maneria, sed magis est ex personis" (*Leg. Hen.*, XIX, 2, in *Select Charters*, p. 125).

[11] Maitland, *D.B. and Bey.*, p. 82, referring to *Leg. Hen.*, XX, 2.

rich enough to pay his own way" and thus presumably "live of his own" (in the thirteenth century phrase) is out of chronological context with a period when a feudal lord—even the lord king—counted his vassals when he would weigh his strength. This was an age when the terms quoted were incomprehensible to the barons, either as valid issues of political controversy or even as words which carried significant meaning. Such is the whole tenor not only of the contemporary law books and charters but also of the best modern authority. It is beyond the scope of the present work to enlarge upon this general picture of the period. Here it need only be emphasized that alienation of the royal demesne in the late eleventh and early twelfth century was extensive and was characteristic of the contemporary feudal monarchy; it did not involve ideas or political issues to which the thirteenth century gave rise.[12]

The extent of alienation under William II, Henry I, and Stephen cannot be determined exactly, nor is any definite policy revealed, by the scattered evidence available. A threefold tendency might be suggested by some of the evidence but cannot be demonstrated. A review of the fate of the Domesday *Terra Regis* of Cambridgeshire,[13] for example, suggests, first, that certain large and valuable manors which embraced an entire village might, as one would expect, be retained in support of the monarchy, though any other distinguishing characteristics of such manors are elusive; second, that where a royal manor consisted of the greater part, but not all, of a village and its fields, there was greater likelihood of alienation; and, third, that scattered bits of *Terra Regis,* consisting of small fractions of villages, might often be retained by the king but put to the useful service of maintaining his ministers and clerks by being let to farm, much in the fashion of a petty serjeanty. But these tendencies fall far short of being a general rule or a royal policy. Rather, they reflect what must have been merely the day-by-day and common-sense use of a large fund of landed wealth which the monarchy might dispose of at will.

The three adjoining counties of Northamptonshire, Lincolnshire, and Leicestershire provide even better evidence of aliena-

---

[12] See Round, *Geoffrey de Mandeville* (London, 1892), pp. 99ff., 140–156; and Stenton, *First Century,* chs. V–VII.

[13] See Appendix C.

tion of the royal demesne in this obscure period, c.1087–1154. For each of the counties there is an early twelfth century survey which purports to give the hidage of the whole or part of the shire. They confirm the impression derived from the Cambridgeshire evidence.

Thus, the Northamptonshire Survey [14] shows that, by the date of its compilation sometime in the reign of Henry I, in half of the hundreds in which William the Conqueror held lands, all or more than half of the royal demesne had been alienated, while of the twenty-two tenurial or administrative units of the Domesday *Terra Regis,* only nine had been retained in the king's hands as held in 1086.[15] Among the more important alienations were the manors of Towcester, Brixworth, Faxton, Barnwell All Saints, Hardingstone, Tansor, Rothwell and Orton, and Weekley, which, together with lesser estates, represented approximately sixty-eight out of 141 Domesday hides or just under one-half of the royal demesne in 1086.[16]

The evidence of the Lindsey Survey, c.1115–1118, is even more startling, for not a single place held by the king in 1086 is included among the seven holdings comprising the royal demesne listed in that document.[17] It must be remembered that this survey is concerned with only part of Lincolnshire and cannot by itself support a general conclusion. Its evidence, however, is consistent with that of Northamptonshire, and it is borne out by the Leicestershire Survey of c.1124–1129.[18] The latter document also comprises but part of a county, viz., one whole wapentake and parts of two other wapentakes of Leicestershire. In the eight hundreds of the Survey which Round collated with Domesday Book,[19] the king held twenty-two separate manors or tenements in 1086, of which only ten remained in the royal demesne at the time of the Survey. In terms of Domesday carucates, this alienation represents

---

[14] *V.C.H. Northants,* I, 365–389 (translated, with an introduction and notes, by Round); see also Round, *Feud. Eng.,* pp. 215–224.

[15] See Appendix D.

[16] Subtracting the Witchley and *Geritone Terra Regis* from the Domesday total, since they are not included in the Northamptonshire Survey.

[17] *The Lincolnshire Domesday and the Lindsey Survey* (ed. C. W. Foster and T. Longley, The Lincoln Record Society, vol. XIX; Horncastle, 1924), pp. 237–260.

[18] Printed in Round, *Feud. Eng.,* pp. 197–203.

[19] *Ibid.,* pp. 205–209.

a reduction of the Domesday *Terra Regis* still in the king's hands at the end of the third decade of the twelfth century, from approximately ninety-nine carucates to approximately forty-five carucates, or an alienation of well over half of the Conqueror's royal demesne in less than two generations.

The charters of the Anglo-Norman period [20] and the Pipe Roll of 1130 reveal specific grants and refer to *terre date* which further illustrate the process of alienation. Examination of this evidence would only corroborate the general conclusions suggested by the early twelfth century surveys. That "the royal demesne had been granted away wholesale" [21] there can be no doubt. There was no distinction between "ancient" or "inalienable" royal demesne and any other lands held in demesne, so far as alienation was concerned. Finally, the revenue derived from the farm of the county was diminished substantially by alienation of royal demesne.[22]

Alienation of the royal demesne did not, however, mean a permanent loss of revenue corresponding to the value of the lands alienated. Alienation altered the position of the king from landlord to overlord: in place of the regular farmed revenues of his demesne manors, the king collected the occasional revenues due to any lord from his vassals, plus the taxes which fell upon the alienated lands held by knight's service. The constitutional significance of alienation of the royal demesne, then, lies in the further reason it provided for the development and exploitation of the feudal rights and profits of the monarchy. After 1154 the development of scutage into a normal feudal tax, the closer supervision of baronial administration and justice, and the extension of the royal administra-

[20] For grants from the royal demesne in the reigns of William I and William II, see H. W. C. Davis, ed., *Regesta Regum Anglo-Normannorum 1066–1154* (vol. I only; Oxford, 1913), nos. 86 (and App. XI), 87, 140, 163 (and App. XVII), 253, 257, 283, 301, 302, 340 (and App. LIII), 346 (and App. LVI), 378, 397, 400, 436, 438 (and App. LXXXIII). The following references may also be noted in connection with the alienation or the loss of royal demesne: Round, *V.C.H. Berks,* I, 293f., *V.C.H. Essex,* I, 337, *V.C.H. Bucks,* I, 209f., *V.C.H. Beds,* I, 195; Farrer, *V.C.H. Lancaster,* I, 280 and 291f.; Stenton, *V.C.H. Derby,* I, 298; H. P. R. Finberg, "The Early History of Werrington," *E.H.R.*, LIX (1944), 241; and M. M. Bigelow, *Placita Anglo-Normannica* (Boston, 1879), pp. 61, 69ff.

[21] Stenton, "Introduction to the Domesday Survey," in *The Victoria History of the County of Leicester* (ed. Wm. Page; London, 1907), I, 343.

[22] A statistical analysis of the reduction of the farm of the county, due to allowances for *terre date,* would not be very useful in establishing the extent of alienation, since the farm comprised more than the revenues of royal manors.

tion and justice into the machinery and (eventually) the substance of a common law, mark the growth of the Angevin monarchy. In each case, the depletion of the royal demesne helped provide an incentive for royal policy. This interpretation has not only the advantage of logic, but also the support of contemporary evidence.

> By the time of king Henry II, so much land had been granted to knights both by king Stephen and himself . . . that the returns of the Treasury were found hardly to amount to twelve thousand marks a year. One may therefore ask, or marvel in silence, how it was that king Henry II and his sons, in spite of their many wars, abounded so much in treasure. The reason is this, that as they had less in rents they took care to make up the total by occasional incomings and relied more on accessory than on the principal sources of revenues.[23]

Not only had the royal demesne shrunk and therefore diminished this source of revenue; the manors which the king retained were no longer producing the income they should have. The "state of confusion and disorganization" which characterized the Exchequer in the early years of Henry II's reign reflected the fact that "many years elapsed before the king succeeded in making his sheriffs render to him all that they ought to render." [24] The king's ministers spent much time and effort in re-establishing royal rights and revenues, and a considerable revenue was lost by allowance from the farms of the shires *in restauratione maneriorum comitatus* because of waste and destruction wrought during the preceding reign.[25]

This work of restoring the royal manors and of recovering royal rights and revenues was carried on by the same royal officials who were responsible for the growth of the Angevin judicial and ad-

---

[23] Giraldus Cambrensis, *De Principis Instructione,* III, 30, in *Opera* (ed. G. F. Warner, 8 vols., R.S.; London, 1861–1891), VIII, 316, as quoted and translated by R. L. Poole, *The Exchequer in the Twelfth Century* (Oxford, 1912), pp. 136f.; quotation used by permission of the Clarendon Press, Oxford. In a charter granted c.1186–1188, Henry II refers to the time of Stephen, when *multa dispersa fuerant et a dominiis alienata tum in feodis militum tum in Elemosinis Ecclesiarum* (*Ancient Charters Royal and Private Prior to 1200 A.D.* [Part I, ed. Round, Pipe Roll Society, vol. X; London, 1888], pp. 85f.).

[24] G. J. Turner, "The Sheriff's Farm," *T.R.H.S.*, NS, XII (1898), 128.

[25] For example, "Willelmus de Fraxineto reddit Compotum . . . de Noua Firma. In thesauro lx & xi li. . . . . Et In Restauramento Maneriorum lxxiiii li." (*P.R. 2–3–4 Hen. II,* p. 8); and "Et In Restauratione Maneriorum Regis totius Comitatus c & quater xx li. . . ." (*ibid.,* p. 38). See also, Turner, "Sheriff's Farm," p. 130.

ministrative system. From the barons in the Exchequer down to the hundred bailiffs, the king's ministers continued to represent him both as landlord of his demesne and as feudal king of the realm. The monarchy had not yet begun to make a significant distinction, in administration, between its demesne lands and the rest of the realm. Nevertheless, despite a considerable effort expended in restoring the royal demesne, the growth of royal power came to depend more than ever upon the exploitation of the feudal and royal rights which had no essential connection with the demesne, although in administrative practice there was no clear separation between exploitation of one and the other.[26]

Despite this, the royal demesne of the second half of the twelfth century has considerable importance in English constitutional development for two reasons, which must now be discussed. These are, first, the growth of central control and supervision of the administration of the royal demesne and, second, the development of a new kind of taxation which was restricted to royal boroughs[27] and the rural demesne.

CENTRALIZATION OF ADMINISTRATIVE CONTROL

The growth of control and supervision of the rural demesne of the king by his central government, in the reigns of Henry II and his sons, is a development roughly parallel with the growing direct contact between the central government and the chartered royal boroughs. In both cases, there was more development than innovation; likewise, in both developments the sheriffs and their shire and hundred officials were in varying degrees being replaced by commissioners sent out from the royal court, and by other persons (either local or specially appointed) in the financial relations between localities and the central Exchequer.

Central control of the royal demesne did not begin under Henry

---

[26] See below, pp. 94 *seqq.*

[27] As stated above, the present work does not concern itself, except indirectly, with the boroughs, which by the end of the twelfth century had become units in the feudal organization of English society, either as royal or seignorial demesne. An excellent summary may be found in Jolliffe, *Const. Hist.*, pp. 314–327, and Tait, *Med. Eng. Bor.*, pp. 342f. For the best general discussions, see Charles Gross, *The Gild Merchant* (2 vols.; Cambridge, 1890), Carl Stephenson, *Borough and Town* (Mediaeval Academy of America; Cambridge, 1933), and Tait, *Med. Eng. Bor.*

II; nor was its starting point the complete abondonment of royal manors to the sheriffs in return for a fixed farm. The Domesday commissioners compiled a rough equivalent of the later manorial extent of the lands of the king, as of others, and they exercised judicial power which is related to that of the later itinerant justices. The reign of William II presents no clear evidence of central intervention in the economic exploitation of the royal demesne, but this is not surprising. "The visitatorial system seems to have been established by the middle of Henry I's reign," [28] and in that period of undifferentiated governmental functions it would be difficult to suppose that the justices confined themselves to matters purely judicial.[29]

This is borne out by the surviving Pipe Roll of Henry I, which contains a notice of the work of two commissioners who were "apparently conducting an enquiry into the state of the king's lands, seeing to . . . the restocking of the king's manors, but also holding pleas." [30] This is the earliest direct evidence of the activity normally associated with the later itinerant justices who combined supervision of royal manors with the holding of pleas of the crown, in addition to other duties.

Another direct contact between the central Exchequer and the demesne manors did not wholly exclude the sheriff and his local administration. This was the payment of those profits of jurisdiction, of royal manors, which were not farmed by the sheriffs. Notices of these payments, for which the sheriffs were responsible, occur in the earliest Pipe Roll.[31] What later came to be known as purprestures,[32] perhaps the most important class of these profits

---

[28] N. D. Hurnard, "The Anglo-Norman Franchises," *E.H.R.*, LXIV (1949), 440, n.3.

[29] The Pipe Roll of 31 Henry I indicates that the same men who held pleas attended to other business of the king *(ad Necessaria Regis facienda)* (*P.R. 31 Hen. I*, pp. 131, 33).

[30] Jolliffe, *Const. Hist.*, p. 195. "Et In Restauratione Maneriorum Regis per W. Espec' & Eustacius filius Johannis xxiij li. & xvij s. numero" (*P.R. 31 Hen. I*, p. 24).

[31] "Et Idem Vicecomes reddit Compotum de xx m. arg. pro j murdrum in hundredo de Caudona. . . . Et In perdonis per breve Regis. In dominio Regis de Humintona & de Hareham xlv s. & viij d." (*P.R. 31 Hen. I*, p. 20); "Pro j murdrum in hundredo de Cudeluestan. . . . Et In Perdones per breve Regis . . . In dominio Regis xxxj s. & vj d." (*ibid.*, p. 74).

[32] Fines paid for encroachments on the royal demesne, i.e., occupation without warrant.

of jurisdiction from the royal demesne, probably began to be levied in the reign of Henry I, though not under that name. This was certainly one of the purposes of the survey of Winchester made by five commissioners of Henry I early in the twelfth century.[33]

Before the reign of Henry II, however, and certainly during Stephen's reign, it is fair to say that except for occasional intervention by special commissioners the sheriffs as farmers or custodians stood between the central government and the bulk of the royal demesne manors. The significant developments were rather by way of controlling the sheriffs (particularly under Henry I) than by establishing direct exploitation of the royal demesne. Typical of this stage of royal policy was an Exchequer tradition the details of which may well be doubted, but which illustrates well the considerable reforms known to have occurred at the beginning of the twelfth century. According to this tradition, the revenues from royal manors were paid only in kind until the reign of Henry I. Victuals were brought at stated times directly to the royal court for its daily use. Henry, plagued by the *multitudo colonorum de fundis regiis* who came to his court or met him when traveling and complained of their difficulties in rendering the payments in kind, sent prudent and discreet men throughout the realm who, having viewed each manor, converted the payments in kind to money values for which henceforth the sheriffs were to be responsible at the Exchequer in their farms of the shires.[34] This tradition may well have preserved and confused some memory of a survey undertaken to convert the last payments in kind (noticed occasionally in Domesday Book) into money renders. The kernel of historicity in the tale is its emphasis upon the separation of the royal court from the direct exploitation of the royal demesne and upon the supervision exercised by special commissioners over the work of the sheriffs.

After the accession of Henry II, the Exchequer intervened much more effectively in the exploitation of the royal demesne in two ways. First, it established direct relations with the bailiffs and other subordinate officials immediately responsible to the sheriffs; and, second, it withdrew altogether the farm or custody of certain royal

[33] "The Winchester Survey," ed. Round, *V.C.H. Hants,* I, 527–537.

[34] *Scac. Dial.,* pp. 89f.

manors from the control of the sheriffs and their subordinates, placing them in the charge of persons who accounted for their issues directly to the Exchequer. And this was not all. The "first sign of differentiation" in the Pipe Rolls, beginning in 1165, reflected the inauguration of inquiries into purprestures on the royal demesne which "became a regular duty of itinerant justices" from that time on.[35] Henceforth the Pipe Rolls contained special sections headed *"de purpresturis,"* or the like, kept separate from the rest of the county accounts because not forming part of the county farm. The justices who inquired into purprestures brought the central government into immediate contact with the royal demesne, and the Dialogue of the Exchequer (written only a dozen years after the first Pipe Roll entry) expressly attributes this direct intervention by the central government to the "negligence of the sheriff or of his ministers." [36]

What Stubbs took to be a general resumption of crown lands in 1154–1155 should rather be interpreted as a precedent for the regular inquiry into purprestures whose financial results the Pipe Rolls begin to record ten years later. William of Newburgh explicitly states that Henry "ordered that all royal demesnes, with full integrity, be resigned by any trespassers whatever (*quibuscunque detentoribus*), and be restored to their former right and status"; and then he goes on to refer to barons who claimed to hold demesne lands by "charters which they had obtained from King Stephen by force or bargaining"—that is, had extorted from or wheedled out of him as the price of their support.[37] Henry II's justice may have been summary and comprehensive, but William of Newburgh hardly justifies Stubbs's statement that "royal estates, by whatever charters of the late king they were conferred, must be restored." [38]

---

[35] H. G. Richardson, Introduction to *The Memoranda Roll for the Michaelmas Term of the First Year of the Reign of King John (1199–1200)* (P.R.S., NS, vol. XXI; London, 1943), pp. xxiif.

[36] "Per negligentiam vicecomitis vel eius ministrorum" (*Scac. Dial.*, p. 132). According to Glanvill (IX, 11), purprestures were determined by sworn inquest (*De Legibus et Consuetudinibus Regni Angliae* [ed. G. E. Woodbine, Yale Historical Publications, Manuscripts and Edited Texts, vol. XIII; New Haven, 1932], p. 132).

[37] "Praecepit ea [regia dominica] cum omni integritate a quibuscunque detentoribus resignari, et in jus statumque pristinum revocari. . . . Chartas, quas a rege Stephano vel extorserant vel obsequiis emerant" (Will. Newb., II, 2 in *Select Charters*, pp. 151f.).

[38] *Const. Hist.* (5th ed.; Oxford, 1891), I, 489. To cite one example, William of Ypres,

This was not so much a resumption of royal demesne as it was a revocation of bad charters and the confirmation of such arrangements as were acceptable as legally valid. It was the illegality, not the mere fact, of alienation that Henry moved swiftly to correct. Until this was accomplished the Exchequer could not account properly for the county farms and *terre date;* in this sense, the whole transaction was a "restoration" as much of the Pipe Rolls as of royal estates.

In 1176, by the Assize of Northampton, royal bailiffs were directed to answer directly to the Exchequer for all revenues, both rents and "perquisites," in their bailiwicks, "except those which pertain *ad vicecomitatum.*" [39] The effect of this provision was to exclude the sheriff from receiving demesne revenues unless they comprised part of the farm of the county or were payable to him in his official capacity (i.e., the occasional revenues to which the demesnes might contribute along with hundred or shire and for which the sheriff had to account at the Exchequer, plus perquisites of the shrievalty which did not reach the Exchequer). This seems to represent an increasing control of the local administration over that indicated by the great general inquest touching administrative grievances in 1170, usually referred to as the Inquest of Sheriffs. By one of the articles of that inquiry, the barons conducting it were required to obtain evidence from sworn juries as to the condition of buildings and the stocking of royal demesne manors.[40] In 1170 and 1176, precedents were thus set for the later routine supervision of the royal demesne by the itinerant justices of the general eyre. From the reign of Henry II on, the itinerant justices went behind the sheriff to investigate the conduct of bailiffs and also to inquire into the condition of royal manors. They had authority and were under orders to determine not only what grievances

---

a notorious adherent of Stephen, retained his lands in Kent. See *The Red Book of the Exchequer* (ed. Hubert Hall, 3 vols., Rolls Series; London, 1896), II, 648ff.; and *P.R. 2–3–4 Hen. II,* pp. 65f., 101f.

[39] "Item baillivi domini regis respondeant ad scaccarium, tam de assiso redditu, quam de omnibus perquisitionibus suis, quas faciunt in bailliis suis; exceptis illis quae pertinent ad vicecomitatum" (Ass. North., c.10, in *Select Charters,* p. 181).

[40] "De dominiis domini regis inquiratur si curiae sint clausae de fossatis et hais, et si sint ibi grangiae et bovariae et bercheriae, et aliae domus et instauramenta sicut dominus rex praecepit antequam transfretaret" (Inq. of Sher., c.14, in *ibid.,* p. 177).

should be redressed but also—and it was here especially that the sheriffs' power was curtailed—to determine how much should be allowed from the farm of the county in restocking royal manors. The whole of this program of central control was made possible by the use of the procedure by sworn inquest.

The earliest surviving articles of a general eyre, those of 1194, illustrate the system in full operation. The itinerant justices were directed to inquire *diligentissime* into the amount of the fixed rents (money payments from manorial tenants) of each single manor held in demesne; the value of all other things (mills, markets, fishponds, etc.) which might produce income in the aforesaid manors; the number and value of the ploughs, not merely valued at the standard rate of twenty shillings, but in relation to their productivity when used on the actual land, good and bad, of the manor; and, finally, they were directed to inquire into the stock on each manor and the amount and value of stock which each manor could maintain. A written report of all these amounts and values was to be sent in to the Exchequer.[41] With these data at its command, the Exchequer could, of course, increase the revenue of the royal demesne in several ways. Fraud could be detected more easily.[42] Allowances from the farm of the county for restocking could be held down to the actual needs of the royal manors. Allowances for *terre date* could be determined more accurately. No less important, the various miscellaneous manorial profits could be more fully exploited.

The increased revenue and more efficient exploitation of the royal demesne, which this centralization of control made possible, were not, however, its most important constitutional results. The same administrative techniques which, applied to royal justice, ulti-

[41] "Inquiretur etiam diligentissime quantus sit assisus redditus per singula maneria in demenio, et quantum valeant omnia alia in praedictis maneriis assisa, et quot sunt carucae, et quantum singulae valeant, non aestimantes eas ad pretium xx. solidorum tantum, sed secundum quod terra fuerit vel bona vel mala, crescat vel decrescat pretium. Illi vero qui firmas suscipient, firmas suas instaurabunt. . . . Inquiratur etiam de quot bobus et averis singulae carucae valeant instaurari, et quot et quantum instauramentum singula maneria possint sustinere. . . . Et cum omnia praedicta instaurata fuerint et appretiata, omnia inbrevientur aperte et distincte et deferantur ad scaccarium" (Articles of 1194, c.23, in *Select Charters,* p. 255).

[42] For a case of fraud, detected in 1173–1174, and copied by Swereford into the Red Book of the Exchequer, see *Red Book Exch.,* II, ccxiv.

mately developed in England a common law, created even more rapidly and strikingly a "common royal demesne." Centralization transformed the demesne from a congeries of more than two dozen parts (represented by the individual sheriffs with whom almost alone, for all practical purposes, the Exchequer had dealt) into a single whole whose several parts were under the common administrative control of the Exchequer. The sheriffs became only one group out of three main groups of officials subordinate to the central government in the administration of the royal demesne. The second group was that of the bailiffs of royal estates over whom the Exchequer gained direct control through the procedure by inquest and the new officials, the itinerant justices. The third group, gaining in prominence from the middle years of Henry II's reign on, consisted of individuals who acted as farmers or custodians of particular royal manors which had been removed from the farm of the county. They, of course, accounted directly to the Exchequer.

It would be an oversimplification to say that an independent system of manorial administration, co-ordinate with that of the sheriffs, was established by the growing practice of letting out royal manors to individual farmers or placing them under special custodians. The sheriff was by no means wholly excluded from control of manors which had been removed from the farm of the county. Indeed, sheriffs sometimes acted as farmers or custodians of such manors, though not in a shrieval capacity.[43] And in matters not directly concerned with the farm, the sheriff continued to exercise all of his authority. If a farmer or keeper failed to pay, it was the sheriff's duty to distrain for the payment,[44] as for any other debt. He was responsible for payments of purprestures, tallage, *superassisa,* and amercements from manors excluded from his farm.[45] He could be directed to hold local sworn inquests into the value of lands which had been, or were about to be, granted at farm to others.[46] The sheriff also could be called upon to hold inquests

---

[43] Any Pipe Roll of the reign will provide numerous examples, e.g., *P.R. 2–3–4 Hen. II,* p. 79 (Boseham, Sussex), and extract from P.R. 8 Hen. II, in *Select Charters,* p. 159 (Norton, Oxfordshire).

[44] "Preceptum est eidem Vic. quod distringat tenentem quicunque sit pro predicta firma" (*Mem. Roll 1 John,* p. 78). There had been a dispute as to who owed the farm for the preceding year, the new farmer having refused to pay.

[45] *Ibid.,* pp. 7, 46 (for good examples), and *passim.*

[46] *Ibid.,* p. 44.

either into the general conditions of royal manors (like the inquiries conducted by the itinerant justices) or for judicial purposes under orders from the central courts.[47]

Evidences of these latter activities reveal the interesting fact that for judicial purposes some royal demesne manors were grouped together to form a single unit, just as others were for economic exploitation. The "four hallmotes of Havering, Writtle, Newport, and Hatfield Regis" sent four men to Westminster in the Hilary term, 1199, each man representing one of the royal manors, and each having taken part in the inquest held by the sheriff at a joint meeting of the four hallmotes.[48] Behind the brief record of this judicial event—an interesting incident but unimportant in itself—may be detected the beginning of a development whose constitutional significance still lay in the future. Legally, or for judicial administration, the royal demesne was beginning to be treated as an entity, as a common denominator whose numerators were particular royal manors. This case concerned a tenement in Havering, and judgement depended on the verdict of the neighborhood. The "neighborhood" of Havering was not the three geographically adjoining vills, for Havering was a royal manor. Its judicial neighborhood consisted of the three other royal manors which were occasionally combined with it for judicial purposes. This is in contrast with the diversity of means adopted by the Exchequer in the purely economic exploitation of the king's landed resources. In 1199, Writtle was farmed by Thomas de Neville,[49] apart from the county farm; Hatfield was about to be granted at farm to the prior of Hatfield; [50] Havering was farmed at will by the canons of St.

---

47 P.R.O., Rentals and Surveys, Roll 74, referred to and quoted from by G. H. Fowler, "Luton Names in the XIIth Century," in *The Publications of the Bedfordshire Historical Record Society,* II (1914), 267ff.; and *Placitorum in domo capitulari Westmonasteriensi asservatorum Abbreviatio* (abstracted *t. Eliz.* by Arthur Agarde, Rec. Com.; n.p., 1811), p. 61.

48 *Curia Regis Rolls of the Reigns of Richard I and John* (ed. C. T. Flower, 8 vols., P.R.O.; London, 1922–1938), I, 77. The defendants in another action before the justices at Westminster, a few years later, *ponunt se super juratam iii villarum Litton & Hocton & Lecton* (*Plac. Abbrev.*, p. 95). The first reference in the preceding footnote also probably refers to a joint session of the hallmotes of Luton, Houghton Regis, and Leighton Buzzard, in Bedfordshire.

49 *The Great Roll of the Pipe for the First Year of the Reign of John* (ed. D. M. Stenton, P.R.S., NS, vol. X; London, 1933), p. 102.

50 See below, footnote 53.

Bernard, while Newport was still under the sheriff and within the farm of the county.[51]

The primary (though not the only) reason for the withdrawal of certain manors from the farm of the county and their assignment to particular farmers or keepers was to increase the revenue from the royal demesne. This would be a logical consequence of centralization of control under the Exchequer. In addition to the routine inquiry into royal revenues by the itinerant justices, the Exchequer itself sent out officials [52] to investigate the possibilities of increasing manorial profits. Likewise, special inquests were held locally to determine the amount particular manors had been contributing to the farm of the county, preliminary to their being removed from the *corpus comitatus* and granted at farm at a higher rate to a private party. In this kind of a transaction, the Exchequer dealt directly with the locality involved, sometimes calling up representatives of a sworn jury of knights to deliver their verdict at the Exchequer itself.[53]

That such methods were profitable may be illustrated by the manor of Calstone, in Wiltshire, which had been contributing six pounds and ten shillings to the farm of the county. It was transferred to a private farmer whose revenues were found upon inquiry to have amounted to ten pounds, six shillings, and eight pence. Still later, a third farmer was extracting more than forty-seven pounds (in the reign of Richard I). This increase in revenue was due in part, however, to considerable restocking of the manor previously accomplished by the sheriff.[54] On the basis of this information, by 1199 the Exchequer had transferred Calstone to a fifth farmer who

[51] *P.R. 1 John,* p. 103.

[52] Normally this was the responsibility of the sheriff; but see *Cl.R. 1237–1242,* p. 221, and *Introduction to the Study of the Pipe Rolls* (P.R.S., vol. III; London, 1884), p. 89.

[53] "Ricardus de Essartis et Ricardus de Calne uenerunt super scaccarium . . . et dixerunt ex parte militum de uisneto de Hadfelde quibus preceptum fuit ut ueredictum suum mandarent quantum manerium de Hadfeld portat in corpore comitatus quod manerium illud portat quater xx li. et x li. per annum" (*Mem. Roll 1 John,* p. 84). Hatfield Regis was granted to the Prior of Hatfield, to hold at farm for one-hundred pounds (an increase of ten pounds), *ad voluntatem regis* (*Liber Feodorum: The Book of Fees Commonly Called Testa de Nevill* [3 vols., P.R.O.; London, 1920–1931], II, 1347).

[54] *Three Rolls of the King's Court in the Reign of King Richard the First: A.D. 1194–1195* (ed. Maitland, P.R.S., vol. XIV; London, 1891), p. 79.

was paying in more than twenty-one pounds.[55] Thus the royal revenue from this manor tripled, and this increase was presumably based upon the returns of an inquest delivered to the Exchequer by itinerant justices.

Political or personal considerations might, of course, interfere with the purely financial motive which guided the Exchequer. Manors were granted in fee, or in alms, to defeat or modify what appears to have been the consistent Exchequer policy. Thus, the royal manors of Diptford and King's Kerswell, in Devonshire, had been granted in fee by Henry II to his uncle, the Earl of Cornwall, and the sheriff allowed for these *terre date* from his farm of the county. When the Earl died, the manors escheated and were granted at farm to William fitz Stephen, who accounted for them at the Exchequer separately from the farm of the county for three years. Then for sixteen years they were placed back in the farm of the county, until in 1194 Richard I granted them to Henry Fitz-Count, and once more the sheriff was allowed for *terre date*.[56] Such instances of royal manors being granted out, escheating to the crown, farmed at will, placed back in the *corpus comitatus,* or placed under a special custodian could be multiplied at great length from the Pipe Rolls.

It would be unrealistic, then, to discuss the royal demesne manors simply as objects of exploitation by the Exchequer, and the history of that exploitation as a series of reforms or experiments which made for greater and greater efficiency. Just as the Exchequer was dependent upon the general administrative and judicial reforms —particularly the sworn inquest and the growth of an itinerant judiciary—so also its actions were at all times limited by royal will and its administrative control of the demesne subject to higher decisions. At any time, "in obedience to a royal writ," payments of the farms of particular manors could be made in the king's chamber (which was still itinerant with the court) without even having gone through the Exchequer accounting system or having been entered on the Pipe Roll.[57]

---

55 *Mem. Roll 1 John,* p. 63.

56 Turner, "Sheriff's Farm," pp. 136f.

57 T. F. Tout, *Chapters in the Administrative History of Mediaeval England* (6 vols.; Manchester, 1920–1933), I, 103ff. This is one reason why it would be futile to attempt any calculation of the revenues from royal demesne manors.

So far, the administration of the royal demesne has been discussed without reference to one element which must now be considered in order to account completely for the growth of the system of farming to particular individuals outside the farm of the county. The royal demesne was not static; not only did alienation take place constantly, but the reverse process was no less constant. Manors were being added to the demesne by escheat, forfeiture, and wardship. In all three cases, and especially in the last, these manors were usually only temporarily included in the royal demesne. Eventually, a separate system was worked out, under special officials (the escheators), for the administration of this "temporary" royal demesne—a development, incidentally, which aided no little in the growth of the idea of the unity and permanence of a crown endowment distinct from the casual lands held by the king as feudal lord and which thus made possible the later concept of an "ancient demesne of the crown."

At about the same time and with the same administrative technique (sworn inquest before itinerant justices) that the central government was using to strengthen its grip upon local administration and to bring the Exchequer into direct contact with subordinate officials of the royal demesne, the central government was tightening its control of escheats and wardships.[58] Strictly, these royal rights over minor heirs and widows were purely feudal rights; further, the lands of wards were not legally royal demesne at all, though escheats might so be considered. But in a time of undifferentiated government, it would be anachronistic to draw a sharp distinction between the king's feudal and his domainial or seignorial rights, and particularly so with regard to the administrative practice of the government. Thus, the stricter enforcement of the feudal rights of the monarchy had important consequences for the exploitation of the royal demesne.

The earliest detailed record of governmental concern for royal escheats and wardships is the so-called "Ladies' Roll" of 1185. It consists of an enrolment of the returns to an article of the general eyre of that year, and the roll provides ample evidence that lands temporarily in the king's hands due to escheat or wardship were often, even regularly, placed under farmers or custodians

[58] For example, Ass. North., c.9, in *Select Charters,* p. 180.

who accounted for the farm or the issues of their manors directly to the Exchequer.[59] It would be impossible and unimportant, in view of the scanty evidence surviving, to attempt to establish relative priority in the use (or even widespread use) of this administrative system for the royal escheats and wardships as against the ordinary royal demesne. The practice is found both on ancient royal manors and on escheats in the evidence going back to Domesday Book and beyond.[60] But lands which were only temporarily in the king's hands especially lent themselves to being kept by particular persons, separately from the farms of the counties. The annual roll, the great roll, of the Exchequer was complicated enough without the endless modifications which would have been entailed in each sheriff's account were escheats placed in the farm of the county. As special accounts they could be handled more easily. This is not to say, however, that administrative convenience determined royal policy. On the contrary, it would appear that escheats and wardships were utilized by Henry II and succeeding kings primarily as a means by which to reward court favorites or to provide support for royal officials of the central government.[61] In any case, the general impression to be derived from the evidence is that the elaboration of royal control of escheats and wardships led to a general practice of letting them to individual farmers or putting them under special custodians and that this practice came to be applied more frequently to manors which had long been in the royal demesne and incorporated in the farm of the county. In an age of rising prices, this was more profitable, since either the farms could be increased without reference to the established sher-

---

59 *Rotuli de Dominabus et Pueris et Puellis de XII Comitatibus* (ed. Round, P.R.S., vol. XXXV; London, 1913), *passim*, and especially (for examples of lands or manors alienated by the king since 1087) pp. 27f., 32, 87. Failure to mention a farmer or custodian in the roll does not mean the land was in the *corpus comitatus:* many entries are too brief, and many lands have fallen to the crown too recently to have been assigned custodians or farmers. See also *Red Book Exch.*, I, 650, 661. Although the earliest surviving record of its kind, the "Ladies' Roll" marks no innovation; compare Ass. North., c.9, and see Cam, *Studies in the Hundred Rolls* (Oxford Studies in Social and Legal History, ed. Vinogradoff, vol. VI; Oxford, 1921), 11f., 17.

60 See above, pp. 11, 72ff.

61 For typical examples, see *Rot. de Dom.*, p. 32; *Mem. Roll 1 John*, p. 26; and *Rotuli Litterarum Clausarum* (ed. T. D. Hardy, 2 vols., Rec. Com.; n.p., 1833–1844), I, 3, 4, and *passim.*

iffs' farms or the whole of the issue could be taken in from a custodian. Further, as noticed already, such a practice guaranteed direct Exchequer control.

As the Pipe Rolls become more detailed, toward the end of the twelfth century, there are more frequent notices of payments made by particular persons for particular manors, though a Pipe Roll entry will rarely tell the status of the manor, i.e., whether in the king's hands by escheat, wardship, or as an ordinary part of the royal demesne.[62] The earliest surviving Memoranda Roll, dating from the last year of the century, leaves no doubt that the system of direct farming and custody under the Exchequer was not only widespread, but that it had been in operation on the royal demesne long enough to have created many a complicated account of which written memory was carefully preserved for the use of Exchequer officials.[63]

Two features of this development afford particular interest for the constitutional history of the period. The first is the practice of farming royal manors to the tenants themselves. Precedent for this can be found not only in the *firma burgi* which the majority of the larger royal boroughs enjoyed by 1200, but also upon the rural royal demesne, at least as early as the last years of the reign of Henry I.[64] It must be admitted at once, however, that there is no evidence that Henry II's government encouraged the system or even took the initiative in adopting it in particular cases. Most of the evidence relating to the farm of royal manors by their tenants before 1189 concerns either those which have been called "*quasi*-boroughs" [65] (possessing burghal or urban features) or those which were subfarmed to the tenants by farmers who were directly responsible to the Exchequer.[66] Farming to the tenants of a manor was no new thing in the reign of Henry II; on ecclesiastical estates

62 Except for accounts relating to important escheats, which were placed upon a separate *rotulus* at the beginning of the Pipe Roll (the *Rotulus Honorum*), thus removing them altogether from the regular accounts arranged geographically by county.

63 *Mem. Roll 1 John,* pp. 7 (Brill), 23 (Milton and Weston), 24 (Aylesham), 46 (Higham Ferrers, Houghton, and Paulerspury), 63 (Stokes, Allington, Lydiard, Seend, Devizes, Combe, and Marlborough), 64 (Brill).

64 *P.R. 31 Hen. I,* pp. 6, 23f.

65 Tait, *Med. Eng. Bor.,* p. 210. See also below, Appendix E, no. 8.

66 *Rot. de Dom.,* p. 32.

it went back at least to 1086.[67] It may well have been the successful experience of the farmers who subfarmed to the tenants (many of the former were themselves royal officials) which led the government to adopt the practice by the end of the century. Chronologically, this development parallels the sudden increase in grants to royal towns of the *firma burgi* and other privileges under Richard I. It is not difficult to detect the same motive behind Richard's grants to his urban and rural demesne: increased revenues. Already by 1199 there are signs that the tenants of royal manors who had secured their own farm were having difficulty in meeting the sums due, either for the fine exacted for the grant or for the annual payment of the farm.[68]

The second feature of the development of direct farming and custody of royal manors before 1200 which possesses a constitutional interest was the effect it had upon the development of the Exchequer as a law court, not that the Exchequer was becoming, at so early a date, a separate court: rather, the king's justices were sitting in the king's court, often under the presidency of the justiciar, which was held in the Exchequer at Westminster. Their business might be to hear litigation, or it might be purely administrative. They might hear the petition of the men of a royal vill to have their own farm,[69] or, later, the returns of an inquest on the basis of which they would establish the rate of the farm.[70] Records of such business might be kept on the plea rolls or upon the Memoranda Roll

[67] *D.B.*, I, foll. 41b, 127b; Round, *V.C.H. Hants,* I, 442; L. F. Salzman, "Introduction to the Domesday Survey," in *The Victoria History of the County of Sussex* (ed. Wm. Page; London, 1905), I, 367f.; and Vinogradoff, *Villainage,* p. 182.

[68] *Mem. Roll 1 John,* pp. 37, 77. The sheriff of Norfolk and Suffolk (quite possibly not a disinterested party in this transaction) tells the Exchequer officials that the men of Orford cannot pay their fine for forty marks *pro habenda uilla sua in manu sua.* In Huntingdonshire, the men of Alconbury *nihil reddiderunt de fine suo de xl m. pro habenda uilla sua ad firmam.*

[69] The men of Kingston-on-Thames, in 1194, offered thirty marks to have their farm again as they had it under Henry II (*Rotuli Curiae Regis* [ed. Sir Francis Palgrave, 2 vols., Rec. Com.; n.p., 1835], I, 15).

[70] See the returns of an inquest concerning what the king has in demesne, and what had been alienated, at Kingston-on-Thames, 1200, in *C.R.R.,* I, 252. The jurors state that the hundred always has belonged and should belong to the royal demesne of Kingston. John later granted the men their farm for a fine of sixty marks (double what they had offered in 1194). The farm was also increased. See Richardson, Introduction to *Mem. Roll 1 John,* p. xv.

of the Exchequer,[71] or both. Furthermore, in a dispute over rents or services between the tenants and the farmer of a royal demesne manor, the justices sitting in the Exchequer could provide a speedy and authoritative settlement which would not endanger the king's revenues.[72]

The growth of central control and supervision of the administration of the royal demesne, under Henry II and the absentee King Richard I, went hand in hand with and depended upon the same new methods and royal officials as the better known growth of royal justice and general administration which built the common law and increased the power of the Angevin monarchy. In the latter more general development, the monarchy had before it two particular goals, the increase of royal revenue and the development of direct relations between the king and all free men, whosesoever vassals they might be—a relationship symbolized by the oath of liege homage [73] and made real by the new protection for free men provided in the king's courts. Centralization and direct control of the royal demesne, by achieving the same two goals with regard to the king's own manors, thus contributed to the rise of the Angevin monarchy. But the royal demesne played an even more significant role. Upon the demesne the monarchy had a relatively free hand in working out its administrative reforms; from the demesne it was relatively unhampered in building up its revenues. It would be impossible to demonstrate any priority for the royal demesne in the development and application of Henry II's reforms, and it would merely misconstrue their nature to claim that they were applied first on the demesne and then extended to the rest of the realm. And yet the earliest of that judicial activity for which the reign became so important concerned the restoration of the royal estates, and the earliest elaboration of the Pipe Rolls—the basic

---

71 *Mem. Roll 1 John,* p. 23.

72 For example, *ibid.,* pp. 78f.

73 "Item Justitiae capiant domini regis fidelitates . . . ab omnibus, scilicet comitibus, baronibus, militibus et libere tenentibus, et etiam rusticis. . . . Habent etiam Justitiae praecipere, quod omnes illi qui nondum fecerunt homagium et ligantiam domino regi, quod ad terminum quem eis nominabunt veniant et faciant regi homagium et ligantiam sicut ligio domino" (Ass. North., c.6, in *Select Charters,* p. 180). The reference to "rustics" (i.e., villeins) probably betrays more the spirit and the hope than the accomplishment of the royal government; if anywhere at all, it was probably on the royal demesne that such was taken from manorial peasantry.

records of the Exchequer—came in response to the use of judicial inquests into encroachments upon the royal demesne. It is not too much to say, then, that the royal demesne in the second half of the twelfth century provided not only revenue with which to support, but also an extensive area in which to experiment with, the rapidly growing administrative system which became the strongest element of the Angevin monarchy.

Sir Maurice Powicke called attention to an essential difference between administration in England and that of continental rulers, when he wrote that

> in England the unit was the shire, throughout the continental domains it was the city, castle or royal vill. . . . In England the sheriff was responsible for the royal dues and for the administration of royal justice within the borders of his shire. . . . For all continental lands . . . the geographical divisions were secondary and subject to change . . . the power of the overlord had grown through the development of the demesne, combined with the activities of a central civil service.[74]

In the light of the foregoing discussion, the nature of this contrast may, perhaps, be more sharply defined. The growth of the English king's power involved a limitation of the sheriff's responsibility for revenues from the royal demesne, as well as for the administration of justice.[75] But although the power of the king did grow "through the development of the demesne, combined with the activities of a central civil service," in England the development of the demesne was "intensive" rather than "extensive": it involved the increase of revenue through more efficient exploitation rather than an increase in geographical extent.

THE DEVELOPMENT OF ROYAL TALLAGE

Professor Powicke's distinction is a useful one when attention is shifted from the administration and economic exploitation of the royal demesne to the next subject which must be discussed.

[74] F. M. Powicke, *The Loss of Normandy (1189–1204)* (Publications of the University of Manchester, Historical Series, No. XVI; Manchester, 1913), pp. 34f.

[75] "Et nullus vicecomes sit justitiarius in vicecomitatu suo, nec in comitatu quem tenuerit post primam coronationem domini regis" (Art. of 1194, c.21, in *Select Charters,* p. 254). The whole system of an itinerant judiciary would tend to limit the sheriffs' importance in the administration of justice.

This is the development of a new kind of taxation which was collected from royal boroughs and the rural royal demesne. For taxation, the administrative unit was geographical, the shire; and the sheriff's responsibility (at least after assessment had been completed) was primary. This was true whether the tax was "national" (based on all land, like the geld, or Danegeld), "feudal" (based on the knight's fee, like scutage or the extraordinary feudal aid), or the tax which in the thirteenth and later centuries was called tallage and was levied upon the royal demesne. Royal tallage, the *tallagium dominicorum nostrorum* [76] of the Close Rolls of Henry III, must be considered a tax and must be clearly distinguished from the seignorial tallage which all feudal lords could take at will from the peasants of their demesne manors. Only as thus distinguished do the real constitutional implications of tallage emerge, and only thus does the role of the royal demesne in constitutional history become clear.

There are several reasons why royal tallage must be considered to have been a tax, though it may be admitted that it shared with ordinary "manorial" tallage certain features which in some measure help to set apart royal tallage from other taxes of the Middle Ages. Most important of these features was the arbitrary element in tallage which was not present in the extraordinary feudal aid. The king by his mere will could order a tallage of his demesnes to be assessed and levied; [77] he resisted successfully any effort on the part of his barons to impose consent as a condition.[78] This was the characteristic of royal tallage which has led historians to identify it, or nearly so, with the right of the lord of a manor to "tallage his villeins high and low." [79] Such an impression might, indeed, be derived from some of the thirteenth century evidence, but before reading this interpretation back into the twelfth century it is well

---

[76] *Cl.R. 1227–1231* (P.R.O.; London, 1902), p. 309.

[77] "Praeterea tailleantur omnes civitates, et burgi et dominica domini regis" (Art. of 1194, c.22, in *Select Charters,* p. 254). "De tallagio ultimo assiso per preceptum nostrum . . ." (*Cl.R. 1227–1231,* p. 153).

[78] Compare c.32 of the Articles of the Barons with c.12 of Magna Carta (*Select Charters,* pp. 288, 294).

[79] Thus Stubbs referred to tallage as "levied by the feudal right of the king as lord" (*Const. Hist.,* I, 671), by which he could have meant only the king's rights as manorial lord of his peasants, not as feudal lord of his vassals.

to review briefly the evidence from Domesday Book to the end of Richard's reign.

With one or two rare exceptions, the word tallage, as *tailla*, occurs in Domesday Book only in the survey of Lincolnshire, and even there it throws little light on the present problem since it is not mentioned on the *Terra Regis*. This *tailla* bears a clear resemblance to the later manorial tallage of unfree peasants.[80] The fact that it occurs in the manorial descriptions as of 1086, but not T.R.E., suggests that the word, if not the payment, was "a Norman importation." [81]

After Domesday Book there are some few references to tallage before the reign of Henry II, but they also seem to refer to private and manorial tallage of villeins and have no special connection with the king.[82] The origins of royal tallage can in no way be traced through the evidence back to any of the early twelfth century references where the word itself actually appears.

In the second half of the century, the word begins to appear more frequently, in both official and private sources, until by the time of Richard I it is a common term. And yet even in this period royal tallage is by no means an easy thing to identify and define. For example, the Templars and Hospitallers possessed the privilege of having one man free from tallage in every royal borough.[83] Under Richard I, and possibly earlier, they protected themselves by ob-

---

[80] According to Sir Frank Stenton, "this 'tailla' should not be identified with that taillage of later medieval custom—the sum exacted by a lord from his unfree tenants. . . . The 'tailla' should rather be regarded as a sum of money paid directly to the lord, by both free and unfree tenants" (Introd., *Lincolnshire Domesday,* p. xxiii). According to Professor Stephenson, it was an imposition collected from all peasants on a manor, later becoming fixed for free tenants and, as a mark of servile status, an unrestricted exaction from the unfree ("Taxation and Representation in the Middle Ages," in *Anniversary Essays in Mediaeval History by Students of Charles Homer Haskins* [ed. C. H. Taylor; Boston, 1929], p. 305).

[81] Stephenson, "Taxation and Representation," p. 305.

[82] The reference to tallage of free men in a collection of laws ascribed to William the Conqueror cannot be used as evidence for the period before 1154. "Uolumus etiam firmiter precipimus et concedimus, ut omnes liberi homines tocius monarchie regni nostri habeant et teneant terras suas . . . libere ab omni exactione iniuste et ab omni tallagio" (*Willelmi Articuli Londoniis Retracti,* c.5, in F. Liebermann, ed., *Die Gesetze der Angelsachsen* [Halle, 1903], I, 490). This chapter certainly belies the ascription of these articles to the Conqueror, and Liebermann assigned them to c.1210.

[83] Richardson, Introd., *Mem. Roll 1 John,* p. xcvj. Cf. *ibid.,* pp. 11f.

taining a special writ from the justiciar addressed to the sheriff and, in so many words, directing the exemption from tallage to be observed.[84] And yet this precision belies the terms of the original grant of privileges to the two orders as they are enumerated in their charters. For example, the Templars' earliest charter, granted by Stephen in 1154 and confirmed in the same year by Henry II, freed them "from all other exactions," while Henry II's later charter (confirmed in 1189 by Richard) granted exemption "from all secular service and exaction and servile work and from all other occasions and secular customs." [85] The Dialogue of the Exchequer, touching on these privileges, refers to them in general and vague terms, though it does explain why exemptions granted by charter were secured in specific cases rather by writ than by the production of the charter.[86] Tallage, according to this evidence, was a species of the genus "secular exaction" or the like. But it is unprofitable to pursue further this line of inquiry, for these and similar records all assume that the meaning of *tallagium* is well known and they provide no hint of its exact nature.

The clue to the meaning of "tallage" is the chroniclers' use of the term. Throughout the twelfth century, and even as late as 1297, they still spoke of tallage in a vague and general sense, corresponding with taxation or levy of any kind.[87] In contrast, official records of 1297 refer to tallage as one particular and specific kind of tax. The chroniclers were preserving the original loose and nontechnical meaning of the term, which can be found not only in the chron-

[84] "Vic. . . . ostendit breue Justic' per quod precipiatur ut faciat eis habere in singulis burgis unum hominem qui debet esse quietus de huiusmodi taillagiis et exacionibus" (*ibid.*, p. 22). "Wulfwardus Fullo reddit compotum de iiii m. de dono. In perdona Militibus de Templo iiii m. per libertatem quam habent habendi i hominem quietum de tallagio in quolibet burgo regis" (*The Great Roll of the Pipe for the Twentieth Year of the Reign of King Henry the Second* [P.R.S., vol. XXI; London, 1896], p. 23). This is the earliest occurrence of *tallagium* which I have found in the Pipe Rolls.

[85] These charters are printed from a fifteenth-century register in B. A. Lees, ed., *Records of the Templars in England in the Twelfth Century: The Inquest of 1185* (The British Academy Records of the Social and Economic History of England and Wales, vol. IX; London, 1935). The passages quoted are: "omnibus aliis exaccionibus" (p. 137), and "omni seculari seruicio et exacione et opere servili, et de omnibus aliis occasionibus et consuetudinibus secularibus" (p. 139).

[86] *Scac. Dial.*, p. 98.

[87] J. G. Edwards, "*Confirmatio Cartarum* and the Baronial Grievances in 1297," *E.H.R.*, LVIII (1943), 154ff.

icles but also in the official records of the twelfth century. In other words, the precise and restricted meaning of "tallage" does not appear, even in official documents, until many years after royal tallage had begun to be levied. In the Close Rolls of the middle of Henry III's reign, *tallagium* and *auxilium* could still be used interchangeably.[88] In 1198, a tax of five shillings was collected "from every carucate or hide of land in all of England." Roger of Howden refers to this levy in one place as an "aid" and a few sentences later calls it a "tallage." [89] These two terms, technically and in accordance with later official usage, should stand in direct contrast with each other. And yet the Exchequer documents concerned with this tax use the word "tallage" in the same vague and general sense. The commissioners responsible for the collection are "assigned for making a tallage of the carucates" or "to place tallages upon the tillage of the ploughs." [90]

This vague and nontechnical twelfth century usage suggests that the origin of royal tallage may be found, earlier in the century, in a tax which did not bear that name. The Pipe Rolls bear out this impression by their use of *tallagium* as the equivalent of both *auxilium* and *donum*. The Articles of 1194 directed the collection of a "tallage"; the Pipe Roll of 1195 records the sums paid in by way of *donum*.[91] The Pipe Roll of 1188 contains headings, *De tallagio dominiorum Regis,* under which are listed the amounts owed by the men of various royal vills *de dono*.[92] The equivalence of "tal-

---

[88] R. S. Hoyt, "Royal Taxation and the Growth of the Realm in Mediaeval England," *Speculum,* XXV (1950), 47, n.23.

[89] "De unaquaque carucata terrae sive hyda totius Angliae quinque solidos de auxilio. . . . et libera feoda ecclesiarum parochialium de hoc tallagio excipiebantur" (Rog. Hov., IV, 46, in *Select Charters,* pp. 249f.).

[90] "Assignati ad taillagium faciendum de carucatis . . ." and " . . . ad ponenda tallagia super wainagia carucarum . . ." (*Book of Fees,* I, 4ff.).

[91] *Select Charters,* p. 254; *The Great Roll of the Pipe for the Seventh Year of the Reign of King Richard the First* (ed. D. M. Stenton, P.R.S., NS, vol. VI; London, 1929), pp. 98, 110, 141, 215. *Auxilium* and *tallagium* were also frequently used alternatively in Normandy at the close of the century (Powicke, *Loss of Normandy,* p. 347, n.1).

[92] *The Great Roll of the Pipe for the Thirty-Fourth Year of the Reign of King Henry the Second* (P.R.S., vol. XXXVIII; London, 1925), *passim,* especially pp. 42, 159, where *de tallagio* is used interchangeably with *de dono.* See also, Stephenson, *Bor. and Town,* pp. 160ff.; Tait, *Med. Eng. Bor.,* p. 343; Maitland, *Township and Borough* (Cambridge, 1898), p. 73; and Stephenson, "The Aids of the English Boroughs," *E.H.R.,* XXXIV (1919), pp. 457–475.

lage" and "aid" and "gift," as the Pipe Rolls use the terms, seems clear; and, since *donum* and *auxilium* make their appearance earlier than *tallagium,* it is in those two taxes that the origins of royal tallage must be sought.

The details of the nature and origins of the twelfth century *donum* and *auxilium* are beyond the scope of this discussion, but certain of their general characteristics are relevant not only to the origins of tallage but also to the constitutional position of the royal demesne. In the first place, they were two different taxes and not simply two different names for the same tax. If tallage owes its origins to both of them, then tallage represents a combination of two different levies. This becomes clear when we examine the earliest Pipe Rolls in which they both appear, many years before tallage begins to take their place. In the three earliest Pipe Rolls of the reign of Henry II, *dona* were paid in the second and fourth years and *auxilia* were paid in the second. In the third and fourth years, there are notices of the completion of various accounts of the *dona* and *auxilia* of preceding years. This evidence presents a mass of detail from which it can be shown that two distinct taxes were being recorded. The following analysis, while not dealing with all the evidence, is sufficient to establish this point:

(1) *Donum* is closely associated with payments arising out of judicial amercements and fines. In no case does the *auxilium burgi* or *auxilium civitatis* seem to have any connection whatever with judicial business. Middlesex and Berkshire, for example, are charged with sums *de dono comitatus et de placitis et murdris.* In Devonshire the payment is made *de murdris et placitis per Henricum de Essex' et de dono comitatus,* while in Gloucestershire the phrase is *de dono comitatus et ciuitatis et de murdris et de placitis,* and in Kent, *de dono comitatus et de murdris.*[93] Conversely, in the second year Norfolk and Suffolk pay the sums of two hundred marks and eighty pounds, respectively, and the rest of the record of the two counties contains only six references to "pleas and murder fines," most of which look like old accounts; in the fourth year, however, Norfolk and Suffolk make no large round-sum payments, by way of *donum* or under any other name, and the record of the two counties contains a long list of new payments due from various hun-

[93] *P.R. 2–3–4 Hen. II,* pp. 5, 34, 47, 49, 67.

dreds, most of which are said to be *pro murdrum*—a total of eleven different hundreds are separately recorded as making payments. So also in Huntingdonshire, Cambridgeshire, and Hertfordshire, *dona* are paid in the second year, and there are no references to payments from hundreds, while of the two murder fines mentioned one is said to be *de veteribus murdris.* Turning to the fourth year, we find that instead of *dona* from these three counties there are separate accounts *de placitis* and *de murdris.*[94] There seems to be no doubt that *donum* was associated with judicial business and that *auxilium* was not. And yet, it would be wrong to conclude that the *donum* was a "consolidated account" or took the place of judicial amercements and fines. In Hampshire, to cite one example, *donum comitatus* was paid in the fourth year, and the following entries are full of payments from hundreds for "pleas and murder fines." [95]

(2) *Auxilium* was an urban tax exclusively at this time; *donum* was usually paid by the county, occasionally by the town, and sometimes by county and town together. (There is one apparent exception to this rule, in the case of Sussex. In the second year Sussex is said to pay an *auxilium comitatus,* but we may confidently ascribe this to a simple mistake, because the *auxilium* which it pays shares all the other characteristics of the *donum,* and because in the fourth year it pays a *donum* which is the same kind of payment as its so-called *auxilium.*[96] The two terms refer to the same kind of tax, and it is the same kind of tax paid by all other counties.)

(3) When a town is said to pay a *donum* it is clearly paying something different from an *auxilium.* Thus, in the second year Lincoln, Shrewsbury, Worcester, and Canterbury pay *donum,* but this is not simply another name for *auxilium,* because in each case the city is recorded as having paid an *auxilium civitatis* in addition. Two different taxes must be intended. In the same year, both York and Gloucester pay an *auxilium civitatis,* and in quite separate entries the sheriff in each case renders an account *de dono comitatus et civitatis.*[97] So also, in the fourth year when we read that Carlisle, Lincoln, York, and Newcastle all paid *donum,*[98] the term is not

[94] *Ibid.,* pp. 6–10, 127–130; 14, 16, 20, 164f., 166, 135.
[95] *Ibid.,* pp. 172ff.
[96] *Ibid.,* pp. 61, 79, 182.
[97] *Ibid.,* pp. 28, 44, 63, 67; 27, 49f.
[98] *Ibid.,* pp. 119, 137, 147, 177.

simply a synonym for *auxilium,* because in the second year we have seen that *dona* were distinguished clearly from *auxilia,* and in the fourth year there is not a single instance of an *auxilium civitatis* currently due. Finally, the distinction between *auxilium* and *donum* is emphasized by the fact that, although towns may join in paying *dona comitatuum et civitatum,* counties never join towns in paying *auxilia.*

(4) In contrast with *auxilium,* which appears as the only term for the tax, *donum* is occasionally called *assisa* (and in one case, as we have seen, *auxilium*), and once it is not even given a name. It is certain that the *assise* which the counties of Norfolk, Suffolk, Buckinghamshire, and Bedfordshire pay in the second year are the same as *dona,* because none of these counties pays a *donum* in addition to its *assisa,* the payments have the same characteristics, and in the fourth year Buckinghamshire and Bedfordshire pay a *donum comitatuum* together instead of what is earlier called an *assisa comitatuum.*[99]

The foregoing analysis does not exhaust the differences between *donum* and *auxilium* as revealed in the first three Pipe Rolls of the reign, but there can be no doubt that two distinct taxes or payments are meant by the two terms. We are not dealing with only one tax which was called *donum* in one connection and *auxilium* in another.

In addition to their differences, the two taxes exhibit certain common features which are characteristic of royal tallage as soon as the latter makes its appearance. The *auxilia* and *dona* of the Pipe Rolls are, generally speaking, round sums. So far as the evidence can show there is no element of consent involved in either tax. It might be argued that the round sums imply negotiation, but they could, of course, equally imply an arbitrary imposition set by higher authority. In either case, they resemble royal tallage, about which the same remarks can be made.

Despite these common characteristics shared by tallage, *donum,* and *auxilium,* we cannot speak of tallage as simply a new name for either or for both. Between tallage and these two taxes there is one great difference. When *auxilium* and *donum* first appear in the financial records, they are levied from the whole realm; when tallage first appears, it is a tax on the royal demesne.

99 *P.R. 2-3-4 Hen. II,* pp. 7, 9f., 23, 139.

The earlier of the two taxes was the *auxilium*. In the only Pipe Roll surviving from the reign of Henry I it appears as a tax falling upon both counties and towns, the realm as a whole. *Auxilia* were collected from most of the larger or wealthier towns in 1130, and there are, in addition, occasional notices of an *auxilium civitatis* or *auxilium burgi* still unpaid from previous years. No *auxilium comitatus* was levied in 1130, but it seems clear that it was paid in 1129, because Wiltshire, Yorkshire, Berkshire, and Middlesex all have unpaid accounts *de preterito auxilio comitatus*.[100] The *donum* first appears in the earliest surviving Pipe Roll of Henry II, and we have already seen that it too fell upon both county and town, as *donum comitatus* and *donum civitatis*, or the like. Despite the occasional terminological variations, noted above, the tax is distinct from *auxilium;* it is the same tax whether it is called *donum, assisa,* or *auxilium* (in one instance), or even entered in the roll without any name.

We are now in a position to draw the conclusions to which this discussion of the evidence concerning *donum* and *auxilium* has led. So far as royal tallage owes its origin to either *donum* or *auxilium* or both, it grew out of taxes which were originally "national" in scope, falling upon the realm as a whole. Tallage was essentially royal (or "public") rather than seignorial, so far as the question of origins is concerned. *Donum* and *auxilium* were, in the middle years of the century, replacing the "antiquated" Danegeld because they were more profitable and flexible, i.e., they did not depend upon a fixed assessment of agricultural area and value. They could be imposed or negotiated as a round sum reflecting ability to pay and including the new commercial wealth of the towns. The growth of tallage was a development by which the incidence of these taxes was restricted from the whole realm to the boroughs and royal demesne. Finally, it was this restriction of the tax to boroughs and royal demesne—this association of the two under a common levy—which "brought the boroughs under the general head of *dominia*."[101] In 1130 the boroughs (to which Domesday Book allots a special position usually

---

[100] *P.R. 31 Hen. I,* 20, 26, 124, 151.

[101] Tait, *Med. Eng. Bor.,* p. 343; Stephenson, *Bor. and Town,* pp. 160ff. A stage in this process of restriction may possibly be seen in the absence of *auxilia comitatuum* in the earliest Pipe Rolls of Henry II.

quite apart from the *Terra Regis*) were not yet considered to be royal demesne, even though the king was the greatest landlord of most boroughs and had control of their administration. From a general tax in its ultimate origins, then, royal tallage by the end of the twelfth century was restricted to those areas where consent was least (or not at all) necessary, royal manors and boroughs which (partly for this reason) became royal.[102]

---

[102] It has been argued that royal tallage must be traced back to an urban tax and that it was rather an extension of this original urban tax, to include royal manors, that produced tallage and is responsible for consolidating the boroughs with the royal demesne. This interpretation is not supported by the original nature of the *donum,* because there were more *dona comitatuum* levied than *dona civitatum,* when the tax first appears. Nor can a special priority for borough taxation be claimed in the case of *auxilium,* which also fell upon the counties as early as it did on towns, long before tallage was taken only from boroughs and the royal demesne.

It might be urged that the *auxilia comitatuum* of Henry I are not the same kind of tax as the *auxilia civitatum* and that only the latter are the original *auxilia* while the county payments are really something else, called by that name only for lack of a better descriptive term. But this is an argument from silence against the only evidence we have, viz., the name of the tax itself. The four references to *auxilia comitatuum* in Henry I's Pipe Roll are not detailed enough to establish, by themselves, the nature of the tax, and there is no evidence suggesting that the taxes which consistently bear the same name are not identical taxes.

Alternatively, it might be urged that Henry II's *donum* was essentially a county tax (even though the boroughs occasionally paid it) and that the county *auxilium* of Henry I is really a *donum,* just like the payment from Sussex is called *donum* in 1158 and *auxilium* two years earlier. This argument, by abandoning *donum* as a possible origin, would then trace tallage back to *auxilium* in order to explain tallage as the extension to the royal demesne of an original borough tax. But this is still an argument almost from silence—the analogy drawn from the case of Sussex is not directly applicable to the earlier Pipe Roll, and it is so exceptional that our interpretation should not have to rest upon it alone. Furthermore, there is some evidence against it. The *donum* of Henry II's second year, so far as the evidence can show, was a new tax. There are some accounts *de dono comitatus,* or the like, which look like they originated in the previous year; but if we are to find a precedent for the payment in the Pipe Roll of Henry I we cannot find it under that name. The three instances in that roll in which the word occurs as a payment to the king all concern debts of individuals or groups, not counties or towns, and they are called simply *dona* or *dona regis.* The payment in that roll which is most nearly analogous to the *donum* of Henry II, must be a round sum paid by counties or towns and connected with the judicial amercements and fines with which the *donum* is so frequently associated. If there is a precedent for the tax in the Pipe Roll of Henry I, then, it is probably not the *auxilium comitatus,* but rather the *forisfactura comitatus* which was paid by four counties or the payments *de minutis judicibus et juratoribus comitatus et hundretorum* or the entries such as that of Yorkshire which states, *Judices et Judicatores Eboraciscir' debent c libras ut ne amplius sint Judices nec Judicatores,*

It is not essential to the interpretation presented here, but it may be conjectured that *auxilium* and *donum* became restricted to the royal boroughs and the royal demesne for the following reasons. The obligations of society were feudal in the reign of Henry II, and the government preferred to exploit the possibilities of scutage and the profits of feudal lordship, rather than to press a right of taxation over powerful barons who could extort concessions. Politically, it was the barons who were strong enough to limit or defeat the work of Henry's government, not the burgesses or tenants of his demesnes. It is therefore not surprising that the feudal monarchy at this time relinquished, vis-a-vis the barons, those rights of taxation (including Danegeld) which had been the legacy of the Anglo-Saxon monarchy, but which came too close to appearing merely tyrannical to the feudal baronage; [103] and at the same time the monarchy was asserting them to the full, vis-a-vis the boroughs, where the complexity or heterogeneity of tenure had left the Anglo-Saxon kings in an ambiguous position. In the process, the demesne right of the king was enhanced, the royal demesne was enlarged and consolidated, and the English monarchy emerged with a near monopoly of the seignorial profits which could be extracted from the urban areas during the period of their most rapid growth. Finally, to complete these conjectures, the word "tallage" came to be used more frequently and finally replaced *auxilium* and *donum,* as a direct result of the transformation of the boroughs into royal demesne. Once they were considered to be directly and wholly under the king, it would be reasonable to dissociate this tax on the royal demesne from any connection (even in name) with that *auxilium* which feudal lords could take from their vassals—but with their vassals' consent. At first a general and descriptive term, tallage would by usage and the definition of rules under which it was levied become a

---

and the like. In other words, the *dona* of Henry II seem to be new; and their only counterpart may be found in the round sums connected with judicial matters which are noticed occasionally in 1130. The evidence will not support an identification of Henry II's *dona* with Henry I's *auxilia comitatuum* (*P.R. 31 Hen. I,* pp. 43, 114, 136; 2, 81, 90, 109; 28, 97, 101, 103, 160; 34. Cp. Stephenson, *Bor. and Town,* pp. 160ff.; Tait, *Med. Eng. Bor.,* p. 343).

[103] "Mutua quidem debet esse dominii et homagii fidelitatis connexio, ita quod quantum homo debet domino ex homagio, tantum illi debet dominus ex dominio praeter solam reverentiam" (Glanvill, IX, 4, in *Select Charters,* p. 193).

precise and technical name for the "prerogative" tax of the thirteenth century monarchy.

Royal tallage never became the same as manorial tallage. It was in origin, and remained throughout its history, to some extent a negotiated revenue. It retained some of its original character as a "gift." It was never quite restricted solely and wholly to lands which were recognized officially as, and possessed the peculiar characteristics of, royal demesne. For all these reasons and also because of its incidence and the administrative system worked out for its assessment and collection, royal tallage was of all the twelfth century taxes the one which had a future before it.[104] It was the first royal revenue based upon all of the wealth of the person taxed, rather than upon his landed wealth alone or upon an artificial unit such as the knight's fee. Finally, it was the first tax whose assessment and collection were wholly in the hands of officials of the crown.

These characteristics of tallage stand out clearly in the thirteenth century, but they may already be illustrated by the evidence of the twelfth. That tallage was in origin not wholly arbitrary is suggested not only by the earliest names under which it was levied, but also by casual statements among the Exchequer records. A prior "did not wish to promise anything" when the king's tallagers came to him.[105] The records, furthermore, are full of neat round sums which

---

[104] Mitchell believed that "the tallage and the dona . . . illustrate the tendency to have service performed in money, but except in this very general sense they did not lead to further development in taxation. In other words, the taxation of property did not grow out of either of these levies" (S. K. Mitchell, *Studies in Taxation under John and Henry III* [Yale Historical Publications, Studies, II; New Haven, 1914], p. 10). Parliamentary taxation of movables certainly is related to the extraordinary feudal aid, and shares with it the element of consent. Furthermore, parliamentary subsidy ultimately replaced tallage of the boroughs and the royal demesne. But does this mean that tallage had no future? Both the extraordinary feudal aid and the later parliamentary subsidy owed much to tallage and in a real sense grew out of tallage. Thus, it was tallage which, of all the twelfth century taxes, really had a future. Chronology favors this view, since *donum* or tallage was well developed before the feudal aid based on movables—even before 1166 and 1189. But the argument does not rest upon *post hoc, ergo propter hoc* reasoning. Rather, it is in the incidence, administration, and the element of negotiation that tallage was the pattern for the transformation of the feudal aid from a tax based on the knight's fee to one based on personal property, extended below the ranks of the tenants-in-chief, and administered according to counties rather than honorial units.

[105] "Prior de Hurle nihil uoluit promittere quando abbas de Theokesbir' et H. archidiaconus Staff' taillagium fecerunt quia dixit quod ecclesia eius cella est et

could not be totals of individual assessments and thus may imply negotiation.[106] And the Dialogue of the Exchequer confirms and describes the process of negotiation in its discussion of the assessment.[107] In the twelfth century this process was restricted primarily to the boroughs, but in the next century royal manors which never achieved borough status were being treated in the same way.[108]

It must be admitted that there was a radical difference between this negotiation and feudal consent. The latter was granted prior to the levy of the aid, while the former was in essence merely the administrative consequence of assessment after the levy had been ordered: negotiation was thus at the king's discretion rather than founded upon the right of the taxed population. If the king's officials could not agree with the men to be tallaged, they always had the alternative of assessing the tallage individually. But legal distinctions must not be drawn so fine that they obscure important political facts or ignore the consequences of administrative practice. It was administrative practice, not adherence to strictly legal rights, which brought the boroughs into the royal demesne. Borough resistance to arbitrary tallage is too well known a chapter of English constitutional history to be repeated here. It did not end until the boroughs were represented regularly in parliament and the collection of tallage was discontinued. Throughout this period, kings never yielded their claim to take arbitrary tallage. It would be difficult indeed to defend a theory of legal consent to parliamentary taxation from boroughs parallel to the consent of the lords and knights derived from feudal consent to the extraordinary aid.[109]

Gaufridus f. Petri est aduocatus ecclesie sue" (*Mem. Roll 1 John,* p. 57). The reason alleged complicates the evidence, but, presumably, if these reasons did not obtain the prior would "promise" something. See also *ibid.,* p. 41.

106 For example, 50 marks, 80 marks, 40 pounds (*P.R. 6 Hen. II,* pp. 24, 29f.); 30 shillings, 40 shillings (*P.R. 34 Hen. II,* pp. 111, 184).

107 Citizens may be assessed *per singula capita,* or the assessors may accept a flat sum *que principe digna videatur* (*Scac. Dial.,* p. 145). The remarks of the Dialogue are illustrated by the Pipe Rolls; e.g., "Burgenses de Dunewiz debent c m. de dono promisso per ipsos in comuni" (*P.R. 34 Hen. II,* p. 61).

108 For example, Basingstoke was assessed at 8 pounds in 1195, 20 marks in 1205; this was prior to John's grant of the farm to the men of the vill in 1210. See Baigent and Millard, *Basingstoke,* pp. 360ff., and Tait, *Med. Eng. Bor.,* p. 218.

109 The element of negotiation with separate communities led Stephenson to compare royal tallage rather with the extraordinary feudal aid than with the continental *taille* ("Taxation and Representation," p. 308). For a discussion which ac-

The transition from tallage to parliamentary taxation of the royal demesne was—for the boroughs at least—a very small change, passing unnoticed by the chroniclers when it happened and largely ignored by modern historians.[110] The reason appears to be that the negotiations which inaugurated parliamentary taxation of the demesne in 1294 had abundant precedent in the negotiations by which tallage had been levied for a century and a half before that time. It was no revolution, then, when the royal demesne was included in parliamentary consent to taxation, for an element of consent had already been operating there in the administrative practice involved in levying tallage.

This discussion is anticipating later developments, however, and there still remain certain features of tallage in the twelfth century which must be noticed. One of these is the fact that tallage, after the reign of Henry II, cannot be conceived as relating solely to the royal demesne, if the distinctions of the twelfth century Exchequer itself are to be taken seriously. It has already been seen how, with the growth of central control of the administration of the royal demesne, and with the development of special administrative machinery to control and exploit the lands which fell in to the crown by escheat and wardship, a distinction was beginning to appear between what has been termed "temporary" and "permanent" royal demesne.[111] Not that the former might not become incorporated in the latter in particular cases, nor that there was in the twelfth century any notion of restraint upon alienation of any royal demesne: this distinction was due to administrative practice, and the corollary theory of an "ancient demesne" had by no means appeared. Still, the distinction was made, and it had important consequences. For example, escheat to the king did not transform the tenants of a former tenant-in-chief into tenants-in-chief.

> This was recognized by the practice of the exchequer under Henry II. . . . It becomes necessary to distinguish between those tenants in chief who are conceived as having always held immediately of the king,

---

counts for parliamentary consent without depending upon the analogy of the feudal aid or the concept of "political consent," see Gaines Post, "*Plena Potestas* and Consent in Medieval Assemblies," *Traditio,* I (1943), 355–408.

[110] Hoyt, "Royal Demesne, Parliamentary Taxation, and the Realm," *Speculum,* XXIII (1948), 58–69, especially pp. 58–61.

[111] See above, p. 102.

and those who hold of the king merely because a mesne lordship has escheated: in other words, between those who hold of the king as of his crown (*ut de corona*) and those who hold of him as of an escheated honour. . . .[112]

Nor were tenants by knight's service of an escheated mesne lordship considered to have become, by reason of the escheat, tenants of the royal demesne. They held their tenements in fee by knight's service; by definition, the king could not hold those tenements in demesne. Escheat or wardship could not change the terms of tenure.[113]

For certain purposes, however, the demesne manors of escheats and wardships were lumped together with the royal demesne, and it is in this sense that they have been called temporary demesne. It is not surprising that one of these purposes was the collection of tallage, since it has already been seen that this tax had its origin in royal rather than feudal or seignorial rights of the monarchy. Tallage was taken not only from the royal demesne but also from those lands which were in the king's hands by escheat, wardship, or vacancy. This distinction is noted regularly in the heading under which tallage accounts for the various counties are enrolled.[114]

Particular attention should be called, in this connection, to ecclesiastical lands in the king's hands because of a vacancy. These lands could by no legal theory be considered to be royal demesne in the full sense of the phrase. But while in the king's hands they were subjected to tallage,[115] even though they were so little a part of the demesne that their liberties could still hamper royal officials who were collecting the tallage.[116]

Before leaving this subject, it is worth noticing that the government used the same new officials, the itinerant justices, in the assessment of tallage as were used in the extension of royal justice.[117] This

---

112 Pollock and Maitland, *Hist. Eng. Law* (2d ed.), I, 282.

113 *Ibid.,* I, 281.

114 "De tallagio dominiorum Regis et terrarum que tunc erant in manu regis" (*P.R. 34 Hen. II, passim*).

115 "Homines de Malmesberia debent iiij l. et xvj s. et viij d. de dono quia abbatia est in manu regis" (*ibid.,* p. 139).

116 "Homines Sancte Marie Ebor' debent xvj s. et viij d. de taillagio. Vic. dicit quod non potest illuc manum extendere propter libertatem suam quam habent" (*Mem. Roll 1 John,* p. 59).

117 The Pipe Roll headings often indicate the justices by name, e.g., *P.R. 34 Hen. II,* p. 99. "Si ciues summam aliquam . . . iustitiariis offerant et ab eis suscipiatur . . ." (*Scac. Dial.,* p. 145). See also, Art. of 1194, c.22, in *Select Charters,* p. 254.

is enough to warn against making too much of distinctions between the "private" and "public" character of the feudal monarchy. The itinerant justices took with them a clerk who kept a tallage roll to be delivered into the Exchequer.[118] For the actual collection of the tallage the sheriff and his regular shire administration were responsible, at least for the rural lands.[119] In case of a dispute, the Exchequer could call in *legales homines* from the locality involved, put them on oath, and establish the facts upon which to base judgment.[120]

The importance of these details of the assessment and collection of tallage is that they illustrate a mature system of taxation. The regular tallage of the royal demesne and lands in the king's hands is typical of the growth of the Angevin central government in all its other phases. The Exchequer is at the center, exercising direct supervision of assessment and the settlement of disputes. It uses the ordinary administrative system of the shires in the more routine business of collection. But where discretion, judicial judgment, or negotiation are involved, either the barons in the Exchequer or the barons and others acting as itinerant justices represent the full scope of royal authority. All this amounts to a centralization of control which is parallel to the growing centralization of the economic exploitation, or general administration, of the royal demesne. Furthermore, the same officials and techniques are found in operation.

---

118 "Thomas scriptor debet respondere de j rotulo de oblatis . . . et de j de taillagio facto per Reginaldum de Cornhull' et socios suos" (*Mem. Roll 1 John*, p. 16). "In rotulo archidiaconi Stafford' et Willelmi de Faleise contenetur quod in itinere suo quando tailliare debuerunt" (*ibid.*, p. 40).

119 *Ibid.*, pp. 13, 23, 49, 51, 53, 56. These references also illustrate the many respites and pardons granted by writs sent to the sheriff. The sheriff used the writ of respite or pardon to account for the total due by the tallage roll handed in by the justices' clerk. Two entries on the Memoranda Roll illustrate one phase of the collection of tallage assessed in Southwark and Guildford, Surrey. The sheriff was unable to collect certain sums from men tallaged in these towns but residing elsewhere, beyond his authority. He was therefore directed to bring in a schedule of their names, places of residence, and the amounts assessed on each. With this information, copied onto the Memoranda Roll, the Exchequer could proceed to distrain for collection of the tallage (*ibid.*, pp. 18–20).

120 Thus, the sheriff of Somerset was directed "quod faciat uenire xxiiij homines de Radecliue a festo sancti Martini in xv dies ad scaccarium ut stent juri de eo quod non fuerunt tailliati quando alia dominica R. fuerunt tailliata" (*ibid.*, p. 10). That they were not able to establish their exemption is indicated by a later entry providing for the payment of their tallage in three installments (ibid., p. 42).

Itinerant justices not only assess tallage, but also restock manors or hold inquests into their condition. Centralization under the Exchequer, then, did not mean differentiation. The business of the Exchequer was growing, as reflected in the growing size of the Pipe Rolls. Specialization would eventually be forced upon the central government; barons *in* the Exchequer would become Barons *of* the Exchequer. But at the end of the twelfth century this was only beginning. A large part of the reason can be seen in every Pipe Roll of the last two decades of the century: the increasing attention and administrative effort being expended upon the exploitation of the royal demesne.

The feudal monarchy in England may be said to have begun the twelfth century with the emphasis in royal policy upon the personal relations in feudalism. Danegeld, the tax on land, was on the decline; the ancient threefold territorial division of England into the law of *Westsexia, Mircena,* and *Denelaga* [121] was obsolete. The king's rights as feudal lord and overlord were stressed: reliefs and other feudal incidents, the services and obligations of the king's vassals, were more important than his revenues as landlord. The possibilities of the royal demesne were left largely unexploited by the Conqueror's sons. Between the monarchy and its demesne lands stood the sheriffs; and the royal demesne as such was considered less valuable than the support which its alienation to the baronage and the Church could purchase.

At the end of the century, the monarchy is still essentially feudal, but with the growth of the central government there is an emphasis upon what may be termed the territorial element in feudalism. The king looks rather to fiefs than to vassals for support. As the territorial basis of scutage and the feudal aid, the revenues collected from the knight's fee are becoming more important than the personal services performed by its tenant. So also, the royal demesne is no longer represented primarily by the farms of two dozen sheriffs, but is becoming a definite entity under the control of the central government. As the law of the king's court was becoming a common law, the demesne lands of the king were becoming a common royal demesne to which had been added the royal boroughs in a great

[121] *Select Charters,* p. 123.

process of simplification. Both the development of the common law and the centralization of the royal demesne were accomplished by the same general administrative reforms of the reign of Henry II. Administrative practice was giving rise to a distinction between lands falling in to the monarchy by feudal right and lands which were more properly the royal demesne of the king. Implicit in this development was the possibility of a distinction between the personal king and the impersonal crown. Finally, the feudal monarchy was rapidly developing upon the lands and towns directly subject to its control a tax based upon wealth rather than upon land or feudal units. Thus, the royal demesne had by the end of the century become a consolidated and profitable basis of the feudal monarchy.

APPENDIX C

Alienation in Cambridgeshire to c.1200

THE following table is based primarily on the data contained in William Farrer, *Feudal Cambridgeshire* (Cambridge, England, 1920), supplemented occasionally by evidence from the Pipe Rolls which he did not use. The first column consists of a list of the manors which appear under the rubric *Terra Regis* in Domesday Book, and the table therefore concerns only what, in the second half of the thirteenth century, were considered to be ancient demesne manors. The manors which Edward held are distinguished by an (E) after their names; an asterisk following the name signifies that the holding belongs to another manor. In the second column, the capital letters, A, B, and C, respectively, indicate that in Domesday Book the manor comprehended all of, more than half of, or less than half of, the hidage of the village from which it took its name. The Domesday hidage is that given T.R.E., rather than T.R.W., because of the frequent arbitrary reductions at the later date found in Cambridgeshire.

The fact of alienation, sometime before or during the twelfth century, is indicated by italics. Doubtful cases have been indicated by a question mark in brackets.

MANOR	CLASS.	HIDAGE	REMARKS
Abington Pigotts *	C	2½v.	At farm, 1189
Babraham *	C	2½v.	At farm, 1166–1200
Chesterton (E)	A	30h.	In *firma comitatus,* 1155
Cheveley (E)	B	8h. 40a.	Alan de Dinan pardoned 16s. danegeld, 1130
Comberton (E)	C	2h. 2½v.	In *f.c.,* 1155; tall., 1189
Exning	B	13h. 2v.	King's demesne in E. pardoned 26s. danegeld, 1162

MANOR	CLASS.	HIDAGE	REMARKS
Fen Drayton	C	2v.	No record, a.1200; no royal demesne here in 13th century
Fordham (E) [?]	B	6h. 2v.	Restocked, 1173 (as escheat?); among *terre date,* 1189
Fulbourn	C	4h.	No record as royal demesne
Great Abington	C	½v.	No record as royal demesne
Great Shelford *	C	3h.	No record as royal demesne; a serjeanty by 1236
Great Wilbraham (E)	C	2h.	*Terre date,* 1155
Haslingfield (E)	C	7h. 1v.	No record as royal demesne
Hinxton * [?]	C	1h. 2v.	No record as royal demesne; but insufficient evidence of alienation
Isleham (E)	B	6h. 40a.	No record as royal demesne
Kingston (E)	C	1h. 3v.	No record as royal demesne
Litlington	B	4h. 3v.	Alienated before 1160
Soham (E)	B	9h. 2v.	In *firma comitatus,* 1155; alienated c.1212
Wood Ditton	B	10h.	Alienated before 1166

Except that three out of the four largest manors were not alienated, no characteristic distinguishing alienation can be discerned (and size cannot be pressed, because of the five next largest manors, all were alienated). Of the nine manors which Edward held, five, and probably six, were alienated.

Although there may be some doubt in particular cases, of the total of nineteen manors on the Domesday *Terra Regis,* two-thirds had been alienated. Of the royal demesne hidage in 1066, totalling approximately 113 hides, roughly fifty-five hides, or one-half the assessed hidage, had been alienated.

APPENDIX D

Alienation as Illustrated by the Northamptonshire Survey

THE following table presents a list of the Domesday *Terra Regis,* arranged by hundreds, and the name of the holder, if specified, in the Northamptonshire Survey of the twelfth century. The capital letters, A, B, and C, respectively, indicate that in Domesday Book the manor comprehended all of, more than half of, or less than half of, the hidage of the village from which it took its name. Where the hidage alone, but no name, is given, there is some reason to believe that the land was in the king's hands at the time of the Survey. The hundreds follow the order given in Appendix B.

DOMESDAY *TERRA REGIS*		NORTHAMPTONSHIRE SURVEY TENANT
Sutton hundred		
1. King's Sutton	A	King
Cleyley hundred		
1. Passenham	A	"1h."
2. Pokesle	B	Fee of the Earl of Leicester
Gravesende hundred		
1. Fawsley	A	King
2. Sokeland		? (No record of, in Survey)
Eadboldesstowe (Abbodestowe) hundred		
1. Whitfield	A	Gilbert de Monte
Foxley (Norton) hundred		
1. Green's Norton	A	"7h. iv."
2. Blakesley	C	"Belonging to the hidage of Norton"
3. Adstone	C	Fee of the Earl of Leicester

DOMESDAY *TERRA REGIS*		NORTHAMPTONSHIRE SURVEY TENANT
Towcester hundred		
1. Towcester	B	Earl of Arundel
Huxloe hundred		
1. Islip	C	Aubrey the Chamberlain
2. Barnwell All Saints	B	Robert de Ferrers
3. Outlier of Finedon		? (No record of, in Survey)
Willybrook hundred		
1. Duddington	A	"1h."
2. King's Cliff	A	"1½h. ½v."
3. Nassington	A	"6h."
4. Apthorp	A	"2h."
5. Tansor	A	Hasculf de St. James and fee of the Earl of Warwick
Navereslund hundred		
1. Finedon	A	King
Nobottle-Grove hundred		
1. Upton	A	King
2. Harleston	C	"3h." (of this ½h. is in Upton, in Domesday Book)
Mawsley and Spelho hundreds		
1. Kingsthorpe	A	"5h. less 1v."
2. Moulton	C	"1½h. 1b."
3. Weston	C	"1h."
4. Brixworth	A	Fee of Courcy and fee of *Salesbyrs*
5. Faxton	A	Fee of Baillol
6. Wold and Walgrave	C	Earl Aubrey and Henry de Tracy
Witchley hundred		
(Not in the Survey)		
Stotfald hundred		
1. Kelmarsh	B	"½h. 1 small v." (the remaining hidage has been alienated to various tenants)
2. Oxendon	B	"1h. 1v." of the soke of Rothwell, and therefore alienated
3. Clipston	C	"1 small v." of the soke of Rothwell and therefore alienated
		"5 small v." of the soke of Geddington, in the king's hands

DOMESDAY *TERRA REGIS*		NORTHAMPTONSHIRE SURVEY TENANT
Stoke hundred		
1. Rockingham	A	"1h."
2. Stoke Albany	C	William Daubeny
3. Wilbarston	C	William Daubeny
Higham hundred		
1. Outlier of Finedon		? (Possibly part of William Peverel's 33h. 2v. 1b. in demesne)
Corby hundred		
1. Gretton	A	All three listed together as 10h.
2. Corby	A	
3. Brigstock	A	
4. Geddington	B	King
5. Stanion	A	"1½v." of the soke of Brigstock
6. Weekley	A	Fee of the Count de Warren' de Morteyn
Rothwell hundred		
1. Rothwell and Orton	A	Eudo de Haschull'
2. Loddington	A	Eudo de Haschull' and William the Constable
3. Clendon	C	"½h." of the soke of Geddington, in the king's hands
4. Draughton	B	Fee of Rothwell (alienated)
5. Arthingworth	C	Peter
6. Desborough	C	Norman (or Reginald)
7. Barford	A	"1h." of the soke of Geddington, in the king's hands
8. Rushton	C	"1½ small v." of the soke of Geddington, in the king's hands
9. Outlier of Finedon		? (No record of, in Survey)
Hamfordshoe hundred		
1. Holcot	B	Fee of William de Courcy
Orlingbury hundred		
1. Cransley	C	Various tenants (the holdings are redistributed
2. Broughton		? (No record of, in Survey)
3. Outlier of Finedon		? (No record of, in Survey)
Wymersley hundred		
1. Hardingstone	A	Fee of King David
Geritone hundred		
(Not in the Survey)		

There are two reasons for believing that where the Northamptonshire Survey gives the hidage but omits the name of the holder, it refers to land in the king's hands. First, the document is "probably connected with the assessment of Danegeld" (Round, *Feudal England,* p. 215); if it was drawn up for the use of the sheriff, as collector of geld, it would be superfluous for him to have the king as holder noted down for those manors of the royal demesne which he already farmed, but it would be necessary for him to have an accurate record of their geld assessment. Second, the entries for Clipston, Clendon, Barford, and Rushton give the hidage but do not name a tenant; in each case, however, they are said to be of the soke of Geddington, which is stated to be the king's.

In the list above, alienation in Northamptonshire is illustrated on the basis of hundredal distribution. Assuming that where the hidage is given, but not the name of a tenant, the king holds the land in demesne, and leaving aside altogether the land of which no record is contained in the Survey, it will be found (by reference to the Domesday hidage given in Appendix B) that of nineteen hundreds: in seven hundreds all royal demesne is alienated, in two hundreds more than half is alienated, in five hundreds less than half is alienated, and in five hundreds no royal demesne is alienated.

It is impossible, in this analysis, to discover any trace of a policy. Geographically, the distribution of the nineteen hundreds reveals no significant pattern; large manors and small manors are both alienated and retained; no effort is suggested (by the A, B, and C classification of manors in the list) to "round off" the lands of the royal demesne by granting away small manors which are only part of a village and by keeping in hand those which include an entire village. It is, in short, impossible to determine why one manor was alienated and another manor was not.

These conclusions are even more strikingly borne out by the following list, in which the manors of the Northamptonshire royal demesne are arranged not by hundreds, but as estates, or as groups forming an administrative or tenurial unit in Domesday Book.

DOMESDAY MANOR AND HUNDRED	TENANT IN SURVEY
1. King's Sutton, Sutton	King
Whitfield, *Eadboldesstowe*	Gilbert de Monte
2. Passenham, Cleyley	"1h."
Pokesle, Cleyley	Fee of Earl of Leicester
3. Fawsley, *Gravesende*	King
Sokeland, *Gravesende*	? (No record)
4. Green's Norton, Foxley	"7h. 1v."

	DOMESDAY MANOR AND HUNDRED	TENANT IN SURVEY
	Blakesley, Foxley	"Belonging to hidage of Green's Norton"
	Adstone, Foxley	Fee of Earl of Leicester
5.	Towcester, Towcester	Earl of Arundel
6.	Brigstock, Corby	"10h. with Gretton and Corby"
	Geddington, Corby	King
	Stanion, Corby	"1½v.," soke of Brigstock
	Islip, Huxloe	Aubrey the Chamberlain
7.	Corby, Corby	"10h. with Gretton and Brigstock"
	Stoke Albany, Stoke	William Daubeny
8.	Gretton, Corby	"10h. with Brigstock and Corby"
	Duddington, Willybrook	"1h."
9.	Barnwell All Saints, Huxloe	Robert de Ferrers
	Tansor, Willybrook	Hasculf de St. James and fee of Earl of Warwick
10.	Finedon, *Navereslund*	King
	Outlier in Huxloe	? (No record)
	Outlier in Higham	? (No record)
	Outlier in Rothwell	? (No record)
	Outlier in Orlingbury	? (No record)
	Outlier in *Geritone*	? (No record)
11.	King's Cliff, Willybrook	"1½h. ½v."
12.	Nassington, Willybrook	"6h."
	Apthorp, Willybrook	"2h."
13.	Upton, Nobottle-Grove	King
	Harleston, Nobottle-Grove	"3h." (of which ½h. is in Upton, in Domesday)
14.	Kingsthorpe, Mawsley	"5h. less 1v."
	Moulton, Mawsley	"1½h. 1b."
	Weston, Mawsley	"1h."
15.	Rothwell, Rothwell	Eudo de Haschull'
	Orton, Rothwell	Eudo de Haschull'
	Loddington, Rothwell	Eudo de Haschull' and William the Constable
	Draughton, Rothwell	Fee of Rothwell
	Clendon, Rothwell	(King, because soke of Geddington)
	Arthingworth, Rothwell	Peter
	Desborough, Rothwell	Norman (or Reginald)
	Oxenden, Stotfald	Soke of Rothwell
	Clipston, Stotfald	Soke of Rothwell, in part; soke of Geddington (thus the King) in part

DOMESDAY MANOR AND HUNDRED	TENANT IN SURVEY
Kelmarsh, Stotfald	Various Tenants
Cransley, Orlingbury	Various Tenants
Broughton, Orlingbury	? (No record)
16. Rockingham, Stoke	"1h."
17. Wilbarston, Stoke	William Daubeny
18. Brixworth, Mawsley	Fee of Courcy and fee of *Salesbyrs*
Holcot, Hamfordshoe	Fee of Courcy
19. Faxton, Mawsley	Fee of Baillol
Wold and Walgrave, Mawsley	Earl Aubrey and Henry de Tracy
20. Weekley, Corby	Fee of Count de Warren' de Morteyn
21. Barford, Rothwell	(King because soke of Geddington)
Rushton, Rothwell	(Same)
22. Hardingstone, Wymersley	Fee of King David

The evidence of this list is essentially negative so far as an effort to establish any policy of alienation is concerned. Certainly, it demonstrates that no single principle guided the granting out of lands from the royal demesne. Such negative evidence has its value. It supports and illustrates the interpretation put forward in the text, that the feudal monarchy called upon its landed wealth to suit its day-by-day needs. It rules out the possibility—so inviting and congenial to the twentieth century mind—that the monarchy would make use of its royal demesne to simplify the feudal structure in order to clarify and exploit more efficiently its feudal rights and revenues. More than a century passed before an effort was made to simplify and regularize the feudal tenure of land, and that effort took the form of legislation governing all land tenure. The opportunity to simplify land tenure by controlling the passage of lands through the king's hands, in by way of escheat and forfeiture and out by way of alienation, was not taken.

These remarks may be illustrated specifically by reference to certain of the above listed manors and manorial groups. Nos. 1, 2, 4, 6, and 7 are instances where Domesday combinations are split up and outlying "appurtenances" are alienated. In only some of the cases are the outliers in hundreds other than those of the capital manors. Nos. 6, 15, and 21 reveal that a manor once belonging to another manor has now become the center of a soke made up of lands lying in three different hundreds. In Domesday Book, these lands belonged to two different combinations with which the new center (Geddington) had no connection in 1086. All the king's land in Stoke hundred, save the one hide at Rockingham (where the Conqueror had built a castle) had been granted to one tenant (nos. 7 and 17), which was accomplished by breaking the connection between Corby and Stoke Albany (lying in different hundreds). This transaction suggests a territorial principle of alienation, but it is contradicted by the record of Pokesle and Adstone (nos. 2 and 4) and Brixworth and Holcot (no. 18).

Finally, it should be remembered that the lists presented in this appendix concern only the alienation of the royal demesne of Domesday Book and throw no light upon the extensive alienation of lands which fell in to the monarchy after 1086. The evidence they provide makes clear that the Norman kings had no notion of an inalienable "ancient demesne" represented by the Domesday *Terra Regis*. Of the twenty-two estates or manorial groups held by the king in 1086 (assuming that the king held the lands for which hidage but no tenant is given): in seven instances all royal demesne is alienated, in one instance more than half is alienated, in five instances less than half is alienated, and in nine instances no royal demesne is alienated.

However, in only three instances is the king, in the Northamptonshire Survey, specifically stated to be holding manors or groups of manors which he held in Domesday Book. Green's Norton, the only manor which the Confessor held in Domesday, is not one of these three, and its land in Adstone has become part of the fee of the Earl of Leicester.

CHAPTER V

Politics and Privileges: The Royal Demesne of John and Henry III, 1199-1272

Such is the unity of all history that any one who endeavours to tell a piece of it must feel that his first sentence tears a seamless web. . . . A statute of limitations must be set; but it must be arbitrary. The web must be rent. . . .[1]

THE first sentence is but the first tear in the seamless web. For both convenience and coherence, the historian must isolate the elements which comprise the whole of his problem. Such a process is arbitrary, of necessity, but the parts selected for separate analysis must be put back into a meaningful relation to one another. The art of history lies in this process of synthesis which follows the arbitrary division and "scientific" analysis. The historian must rend the seamless web of history with a purpose, to draw his interpretation from, and not impose it upon, the evidence.

Chronological chapters in the history of any subject, including the royal demesne in England, are but arbitrary divisions. They serve the historian of institutions, however, in one important regard: they help emphasize development and growth. The royal demesne of the thirteenth century as a whole is a different thing from the royal demesne of the twelfth century as a whole, though the year 1200 marks no abrupt, nor even perceptible, change. The seamless web of history is a changing web, and no greater violence can be

[1] Pollock and Maitland, *Hist. Eng. Law* (2d ed.), I, 1.

done to history than exaggerating its continuity to the point of losing sight of its essence, which is change. For fear of being arbitrary, for fear of making sharp breaks and setting artificial boundaries, the historian may fall into the opposite error of failing to perceive the new. Then he attributes to men of a remote age ideas, distinctions, and institutions of which they were ignorant.

It has already been seen how the royal demesne in the latter half of the twelfth century was beginning to be treated as an entity, how administrative practice and the development of tallage were leading to the consolidation of the royal demesne. By the middle of the thirteenth century this process was complete. The *terrae regis* of the early Anglo-Norman law books,[2] the *regia dominica* of the mid-twelfth century chronicler,[3] the *fundi regii* and *fundi qui corone annominantur* of the Dialogue of the Exchequer,[4] have by the middle of the thirteenth century become the *antiquum dominicum domini regis*,[5] and by the end of the century the idea may be given an additional flourish—a manor or tenement is said to be *de antiquo dominico corone Anglie*[6] or *de antiquo dominico corone nostre*.[7] A survey of administrative and legal developments affecting the royal demesne will show that this terminological or conceptual change reflects new ideas and distinctions which are basic. They are no less substantial, and for the monarchy and the tenants of the royal demesne no less important, than the new ideas reflected in the contemporary appearance of such phrases as *communitas regni* or *le commun de Engleterre*.

That the thirteenth century in England was pre-eminently an age of legal and political definition cannot be doubted. The "first century of Magna Carta," beginning with a strong emphasis on "self-government at the king's command," running through the "age of

[2] *Leg. Hen.*, XIX, 2, in *Select Charters*, p. 125.

[3] Will. Newb., II, 2, in *ibid.*, p. 151.

[4] *Scac. Dial.*, pp. 89, 66, 80, 132. *Fundus* is an obvious classicism; cp. the nearly contemporary *dominia domini regis* of the Inquest of Sheriffs (c.14, in *Select Charters*, p. 177).

[5] *Plac. Abbrev.*, p. 117 (Pleas at Oxford, Easter, 1241).

[6] *Inquisitions and Assessments relating to Feudal Aids: with other Analogous Documents . . . A.D. 1284–1431* (6 vols., P.R.O.; London, 1899–1920), III, 411 (Smithdon hundred, Norfolk).

[7] *Liber Memorandorum Ecclesie de Bernewelle* (ed. J. W. Clark; Cambridge, 1907), p. 188.

Bracton," and ending with the great series of *quo warranto* inquests and trials under the "English Justinian," is a century in which "the main outlines of our medieval law have been drawn for good and all." [8] The history of the royal demesne in this period is no anomaly. What was latent at the end of the twelfth century was clearly defined by the end of the thirteenth. In the process, the importance of the royal demesne was enhanced in two ways. First, the royal demesne became a controversial factor in politics; and second, part of the royal demesne came to be distinguished as ancient demesne and its inhabitants endowed with privileges enforceable in the royal courts.

To account for the royal demesne as a factor in thirteenth century politics, it is necessary to investigate the administration and economic exploitation of the demesne of John and Henry III. Once this has been done, it will be possible to throw new light upon the nature and origin, as well as the constitutional significance, of the privileges of ancient demesne.

REIGN OF JOHN AND MINORITY OF HENRY III

The tendency to withdraw royal manors from the *corpus comitatus* under the sheriff and to assign them to special keepers or farmers continued into the thirteenth century. At the same time, a concerted effort was made by the government under John to increase the farms—both of the counties and of separate manors under individual farmers. This is too well known, however, to call for more than passing notice, in its relation to the royal demesne. It should be remembered that the method, i.e., adding an "increment" to the customary farm, was begun even as far back as the middle years of the reign of Henry II (with regard to manors) and under John "profits" were added to the increments of the farms of both counties and royal manors.

What was new was the aggressive application of this system on a wider and wider scale.[9] Both Richard I and John were continually in need of money, and just as they sold grants of fee farm to boroughs, so also it is under them that royal demesne manors were be-

[8] Pollock and Maitland, *Hist. Eng. Law* (2d ed.), I, 174.

[9] It was this practice which led to the baronial opposition discussed below. See Turner, "Sheriff's Farm," pp. 121ff.

ginning to be let to farm to the men of the vills, on an appreciable scale, though rarely at fee farm.

There are indications that John went beyond the government of Richard. In 1194 the men of Kingston-on-Thames, Surrey, petitioned in vain to have their farm. Under John they were successful —at double the fine and at a higher farm.[10] In Cumberland, the men of four different vills in each instance offered fines and a total of eleven pounds *de cremento* to have their farms in 1201. Their failure was due not to opposition from the government, but rather to their having been outbid by an individual farmer who offered twenty pounds as an increment to the combined farms.[11] The men of Kingsthorpe, Northamptonshire, held their vill at farm, as did the men of Basingstoke, in Hampshire. Both were granted by John.[12] If the memories of the jurors whose returns made up the Hundred Rolls may be trusted, the farms of other vills and sokes by the men or "free sokemen" originated under John.[13] Further instances could be cited,[14] but until the remaining Pipe Rolls of the reign of John are published it would be futile to attempt any final estimate of the frequency or significance of the practice of farming royal manors to the men of those manors. The impression to be derived from the evidence now available is that the practice was still unusual if not actually rare and that it was largely restricted to manors which possessed "*quasi*-burgal" characteristics.

However infrequent or restricted the direct farm of the royal vill to its men may have been, the instances cited above are enough to suggest that there was nothing in the practice inherently opposed

10 See above, Chapter IV, footnotes 69 and 70; also, *Rot. Litt. Claus.*, I, 610.

11 *The Great Roll of the Pipe for the Third Year of the Reign of King John* (ed. D. M. Stenton, P.R.S., NS, vol. XIV; London, 1936), p. 254.

12 *Rot. Litt. Claus.*, I, 609 (Kingsthorpe); and Baigent and Millard, *Basingstoke*, p. 362.

13 *Rot. Hund.*, I, 265 (Caistor), 354 (Grantham).

14 *The Great Roll of the Pipe for the Ninth Year of the Reign of King John* (ed. A. M. Kirkus, P.R.S., NS, vol. XXII; London, 1946), p. 142 (Odiham, Hants); *C.R.R.*, VII, 20 (Brill, Bucks); Thomas Madox, *Firma Burgi or an Historical Essay concerning the Cities Towns and Boroughs of England* (London, 1726), pp. 54f. (examples of the farm of "noncorporate" royal vills and manors, e.g., Rothbury, Jaclinton, Corbridge, Godmanchester, Cookham and Bray); *Rotuli de Oblatis et Finibus . . . Tempore Regis Johannis* (ed. T. D. Hardy, Rec. Com.; n.p., 1835), pp. 54, 66, 238, 249f., 330, 521; *Cl.R. 1227–31*, pp. 21f. (Andover granted at fee farm by John and confirmed by Henry III).

to royal policy. Increased revenue was the primary consideration. The history of the Basingstoke farm bears out the plain implications of the case of the Cumberland vills. Between 1207 and 1256 Basingstoke was in and out of the hands of the men of the manor, depending upon their success in meeting their payments.[15]

An important consequence of this occasional practice of farming directly to the men of a royal manor was the opportunity it provided for communal action and responsibility. Such responsibility reached its highest point—rivaling the full-fledged borough—where the men held at farm the hundred attached to the royal manor. Such was the case at Kingston,[16] Kingsthorpe,[17] Basingstoke,[18] and Andover.[19] Not too much should be made of these "rare instances of the letting of a royal hundred to the men of a royal manor," [20] for they represent the extreme. They are instructive nevertheless, for they show that the men of manors which were not yet boroughs and which were not chartered could, by royal grant, exercise considerable autonomy in judicial matters. There are no surviving rolls of these four hundred courts prior to 1307, and there are no surviving manorial court rolls of other manors farmed to their tenants. It would therefore be useless to speculate about the degree to which farming contributed to corporate or communal action.

Even more difficult to assess is the importance of "subfarming" of royal manors by their men. The very fact that a manor farmed by the sheriff or a private person was in turn leased by him to the tenants is known only when the matter was brought to the attention of the royal courts. The case of the men of Kingston, already noticed, affords an interesting example. In 1194 they had offered thirty marks to have their farm again as they had it by charter from Henry II, but "apparently the offer was refused, for no charter seems to have been granted by Richard I. The charters granted by John make

---

15 Baigent and Millard, *Basingstoke,* pp. 62–68.

16 The hundreds of Kingston and Elmbridge belonged to the manor of Kingston-on-Thames (*C.R.R.,* I, 240, 252; M. H. Mills, ed., *The Pipe Roll for 1295: Surrey Membrane* [Surrey Record Society, No. XXI; Guildford, 1924], p. xlviii).

17 *Rot. Litt. Claus.,* I, 609.

18 Baigent and Millard, *Basingstoke,* p. 67.

19 *Cl.R. 1227–31,* pp. 21f.

20 Cam, *"Manerium cum Hundredo,"* p. 89.

no reference to any earlier charters." [21] The reason is suggested by an inquest taken in 1200, when the jury stated that the men of Kingston held their farm not from the king, but from the sheriff.[22] This reflects upon the claim put forward in 1194 that they had held the vill at farm by a charter of Henry II which had been accidentally burned.

Another subfarm may possibly be detected in the curious entry in the Pipe Roll of the ninth year of John, where the township of Basingstoke is recorded as standing pledge for ten marks of the 1000-mark debt of the late sheriff of Hampshire, *per Willelmum prepositum.*[23] This is not the only, even though a probable, inference which could be drawn from this evidence; but an undoubted case of the subfarm of a royal manor is revealed by the contemporary inquest in which the jurors were asked, among other things, "what and how much the men held at farm of the sheriff" at Brampton, in Huntingdonshire.[24]

It is, of course, impossible to determine how common the subfarm of a manor by its tenants from the "farmer-in-chief" actually was. The round sums which many a royal manor *portat in corpore comitatus*—sums which in some instances reached back to Domesday Book [25]—clearly imply that between the sheriff and the royal manor there often stood a farmer. But this subject is one of those "problems which have so far defied solution," [26] and will probably remain obscure. What is important to notice in the present con-

---

21 Richardson, Introd., *Mem. Roll 1 John,* p. xv, n.5.

22 "Juratores . . . inquisiti per cujus bailliam habuerunt simul eas [hundredum et villa] vel per regis vel per vicecomitis, dixerunt per vicecomitis" (*C.R.R.,* I, 252).

23 Biagent and Millard, *Basingstoke,* p. 64. The reference may be found in *Rot. de Obl. et Fin.,* p. 451, under date of 1207.

24 "Quid et quantum tenuerunt ad firmam de vicecomitibus [antequam] eadem villa veniret in manus Lamberti de Colon' " (*C.R.R.,* VII, 349). This should be compared with Appendix E, no. 23, where there is no reference to the sheriff.

25 For example, Hatfield Regis, Essex: ". . . uicecomes inde recipit lxxx libras et c solidos de gersuma" (*D.B.,* II, fol. 2b); "Et in terris datis. . . . Et Ricardo de Luzi quater xx li. numero in Hadfeld" (*P.R. 2-3-4 Hen. II,* p. 132). Under Richard the amount contributed to the farm of the shire was increased to 90 pounds (*Mem. Roll 1 John,* p. 84). In 1130, the fine paid by the sheriff *pro comitatu habendo* was called *gersoma* (*P.R. 31 Hen. I,* pp. 2, 52). One is tempted to see in the *c solidos de gersuma* of Domesday a payment *pro manerio habendo ad firmam* by the tenants, but see Tait, *Med. Eng. Bor.,* p. 150, n.8.

26 Mills, "Experiments in Exchequer Procedure," *T.R.H.S.,* 4th Ser., VIII (1925), 160.

nection is that the subfarm of a manor provided most of the opportunities, if not all, which a direct farm from the crown might provide for communal action on the part of the tenants of a royal manor (except where a hundred belonged to the manor).

The growing practice of farming royal manors to their tenants, either directly or by subfarming, together with the consequences which that practice entailed, were but the by-products of a more basic and general effort by the government to increase the revenues of the royal demesne. This effort is clearly revealed in all the Exchequer records of the early thirteenth century, and it applied to royal manors both within and outside the county farms of the sheriffs. The addition of increments and profits to the farms of the counties was passed on by the sheriffs to the farms of the hundreds, so that ultimately the hundred bailiffs, or others who held the hundreds, had to recoup themselves "at the expense of the countryside." [27] In the process, a certain amount of extortion or oppression was bound to occur, though it may well have been merely the novelty, the departure from customary and longstanding rates, which occasioned the opposition and resistance enshrined in the twenty-fifth chapter of Magna Carta.

The interesting feature of Chapter 25 of the Great Charter is that it repeats word for word the fourteenth chapter of the Articles of the Barons, except for the addition of "wapentakes and ridings" to the counties and hundreds mentioned by the barons: "Let all counties, hundreds, wapentakes, and ridings be [held] at the ancient farms without any increment, except our demesne manors." [28] This statement is the first unequivocal recognition, in either a public document or a private work, that there was a difference between the king's rights over his counties and hundreds and his rights over his demesne manors—that with regard to the former the force of custom should limit royal will, and that the royal demesne was in a special sense within the scope of arbitrary royal will. Implicit in

[27] Cam, *The Hundred and the Hundred Rolls* (London, 1930), p. 93.

[28] "Omnes comitatus, hundredi, wapentakii, et trethingii, sint ad antiquas firmas absque ullo incremento, exceptis dominicis maneriis nostris" (*Select Charters,* p. 296). The first half of the fourteenth chapter of the Articles of the Barons concerns the holding of pleas of the crown; the second half reads: "et ut comitatus et hundreda sint ad antiquas firmas absque nullo incremento, exceptis dominicis maneriis regis" (*ibid.,* p. 287).

this distinction is the further distinction between the crown and king, i.e., between the king as supreme in the government of the realm, wherein he is limited by custom, and the king as lord of his demesne lands, wherein the rights of his vassals are not affected.[29]

The twenty-fifth chapter of Magna Carta does not mark the entrance of the royal demesne into political controversy. In 1215 the implications were not yet spelled out; but the premises upon which the royal demesne could, and finally did, become a political issue are implied by the distinction drawn by the barons and accepted, unwillingly, by John. The increments and profits introduced by Richard and John were, in essence, nothing more than an intelligent effort to keep the royal income from the counties abreast of the growing wealth of England, just as the heavy fines and increased farms of boroughs and manors were justified—at least in part, because they were sought out by the recipients—by the growing wealth of the towns and royal demesnes. From the king's point of view, the barons' demand was an attempt to shift the burden of supporting the government relatively more onto the royal demesne and to lift the burden relatively from the rest of the realm. The issue thus stated, of course, is an oversimplification to the extent that it ignores the other baronial grievances; but it is nevertheless true that in the baronial program of 1215 there may be found the earliest hint of the doctrine that "the king should live of his own."

The royal position is clearly implied by the omission of Chapter 25 from the reissue of Magna Carta in 1216, as one of the *capitula . . . gravia et dubitabilia*,[30] and by its unqualified omission in the reissues of 1217 and 1225.[31] But this was no doctrinaire stand. As a matter of practical politics, during the minority of Henry III, the

---

[29] W. S. McKechnie, *Magna Carta: A Commentary on the Great Charter of King John* (2d ed., rev.; Glasgow, 1914), p. 320. For some of the broader aspects of this distinction, and of the following discussion, see C. H. McIlwain, *The Growth of Political Thought in the West* (New York, 1932), pp. 374–382; and G. Lapsley, "The Interpretation of the Statute of York," Part II, *E.H.R.*, LVI (1941), 423–437.

[30] *Select Charters*, pp. 338f. The chapter is referred to as a *capitulum . . . de consuetudinibus comitatuum*. This may imply that the royal government in 1216 was not prepared to admit the distinction between one and another category of the components of the farm of the county. But the phraseology should not be pressed; the government was not in a position to draw sharp or fine lines in its effort at conciliation which the reissue of 1216 represents.

[31] *Select Charters*, pp. 342, 350.

royal government was not prepared to force the issue, and although "the clause forbidding profits of the shire was dropped in Henry III's reissue of the Charters, only profits from demesne manors, a quite separate item, appear on the Pipe Rolls at the beginning of his reign . . . [and] up to the eighth year of Henry III, this provision of Magna Carta was observed." [32]

This denial of the baronial claim, together with its tacit acceptance in actual practice, illustrates the period of the minority, "during which the crown and the baronage act together uncritically upon the old feudal assumptions, largely unconscious of divergent interests." [33] So far as the profits of the shires were concerned and the assertion of royal rights which was implicit therein, this period was brought to a sudden end in 1224. The restoration of the profits followed immediately on the papal declaration that Henry was of age and the crisis of 1223, the most notable event of which was the fall of Fawkes de Breauté. It was a point in the general program of enhancement of the royal power in 1224 undertaken by Hubert de Burgh.[34] It was made part of the administrative reform in which many new sheriffs were appointed, and in which was inaugurated "the practice of entrusting the counties as custodies at will, and not at farm . . . so that the sheriffs henceforth returned every detail of their revenue, and the Exchequer might hold them to an itemized account." [35] This again may be ascribed to the policy of Hubert de Burgh, who at the time not only controlled the government but was sheriff of Kent, Norfolk, and Suffolk as well.

Not until eight years after Runnymede, then, did the royal government put into effect its official rejection of Chapter 25 of Magna Carta. The tacit acceptance of the distinction between demesne revenues and the rest of the farms of the shires was a policy at once ambiguous and suggestive. Was there a reason for the government's acquiescence, a broader, more general reason, of which Chapter 25 represented not a contradiction but only a special application with which the government could not agree? A review of the other evidence relating to governmental policy toward the royal demesne

32 Mills, "Exchequer Procedure," pp. 166f.
33 Jolliffe, *Const. Hist.*, p. 266.
34 Mills, "Exchequer Procedure," p. 167.
35 Jolliffe, *Const. Hist.*, pp. 269f.

suggests forcibly that the answer is yes, that the government itself had already begun to draw the same distinction between its rights over the royal demesne and its rights over the realm. It was not this distinction which the government rejected—far from it, for royal policy from the reign of Henry II on had emphasized it—but rather the inference that because its demesne rights were not limited, therefore the farms of shires and hundreds should be restricted to the customary payments.

The history of royal taxation, alienation, and resumption in the first two decades of the thirteenth century provides the commentary necessary to place Chapter 25 in its proper context. Under John, and during the minority of Henry III, the royal demesne, which had become consolidated and had been made the object of intensive exploitation by Henry II and Richard I, emerged for the first time as a crown endowment specially subject to unhampered royal will and annexed to the office, rather than merely belonging to and disposable by the person, of the king.

Scutage and tallage, as levied under John, offer a striking parallel with the farms of the shires and of royal manors. Scutage was being taken with increasing frequency, and in combination with fines set arbitrarily by the royal government.[36] This was an "element of royal and national taxation which is incompatible with purely feudal principles." [37] But although scutage had "a prerogative basis, and there is no evidence of baronial consent," [38] it was directly related to knight's service, its abuse could nullify the feudal contract, and the new system of fines associated with it violated the customary practices which had been established in preceding reigns. Hence the baronial demand in 1215 "that no scutage . . . be taken in the realm, except by the common counsel of the realm," [39] and this was incorporated into Magna Carta, Chapter 12, in practically the same words.[40] The monarchy's assertion of its prerogative right to take

36 A. L. Poole, *Obligations of Society in the XII and XIII Centuries* (Oxford, 1946), pp. 41–44.

37 Pollock and Maitland, *Hist. Eng. Law* (2d ed.), I, 274.

38 Jolliffe, *Const. Hist.* p. 244.

39 "Ne scutagium . . . ponatur in regno, nisi per commune consilium regni" (Articles of the Barons, c.32, in *Select Charters,* p. 288).

40 "Nullum scutagium . . . ponatur in regno nostro, nisi per commune consilium regni nostri" (*ibid.,* p. 294).

scutages without consent is indicated first by the omission of this chapter in the reissue of the Charter in 1216, and then again by Chapter 44 of the second reissue a year later. What is more important, however, is that this assertion of prerogative right is accompanied by the admission that the prerogative is not unlimited or arbitrary, that custom should set the limits within which scutage should be levied, even though consent was not such a limit: "Let scutage be taken henceforth just as it used to be taken in the time of King Henry our grandfather." [41]

Like scutage, tallage under John was being taken not only more frequently but, especially toward the end of the reign, at a higher rate than before [42] and against growing resistance, particularly by the towns. The barons in 1215 had demanded that tallages and the *auxilia civitatum* of London and other cities *quae inde habent libertates* be put on the same basis as scutage, that is, subject to the common counsel of the realm.[43] This demand, probably a bid for the political support of the heavily taxed burgesses, was rejected by John (except alone for aids from the city of London).[44] In the reissues of the Charter during Henry III's minority and in 1225, the subject of tallage was likewise ignored, while even aids from the city of London were omitted.

In short, John successfully prevented any encroachment on his prerogative right to tallage his demesne boroughs without consent, and this has been noticed in the commentaries on the charter.[45] But

---

[41] "Scutagium capiatur de cetero sicut capi consuevit tempore Henrici regis avi nostri" (*ibid.*, p. 343).

[42] It is unrealistic to attempt any statistical determination of the total revenue derived from tallage, because the Pipe Roll accounts do not distinguish (particularly in the case of rural vills) the sums due from tallage from those arising from amercements, and also because of the likelihood that payments were made directly into the chamber without being recorded on the Pipe Rolls. Some indication of the trend may, however, be derived from a comparison of the payments of tallage due from seven towns (Worcester, Northampton, Bristol, Winchester, Hereford, Oxford, and Southampton), all of which are known to have been tallaged in the years 1199, 1205, 1210, and 1214. The approximate totals due from these towns in each of these years were, respectively: 1200, 1375, 3640, and 2040 marks. Mitchell, *Taxation, passim,* collected most of the evidence; for the foregoing figures, see p. 341, n.188.

[43] Articles of the Barons, c.32, in *Select Charters,* p. 288.

[44] "Nullum scutagium . . . nisi per commune consilium regni nostri . . . simili modo fiat de auxiliis de civitate Londoniarum" (Magna Carta, c.12, in *ibid.*, p. 294).

[45] McKechnie, *Magna Carta* (2d ed.), pp. 234–238.

a comparison of Chapter 32 of the Articles of the Barons and Chapter 12 of Magna Carta suggests that a great deal more was at stake for the monarchy and, further, that in this instance it was the monarchy which was insisting upon distinctions and upon a definition of its demesne right which the barons had—however half-heartedly—tried to deny or ignore. It was not the demand for consent alone that was dangerous to the monarchy and rejected by John. It was the implication that "cities which have liberties" were not part of the royal demesne and under the demesne right of the king, but rather should be treated as being on a level with the vassals of the crown—that they were subject to *auxilia posita in regno per commune consilium* rather than subject to *tallagium super dominica per preceptum regis.* Here the monarchy was drawing the distinction, as the barons had with regard to the farms, between the royal demesne and the rest of the realm. There is nothing to indicate that the barons disagreed with this distinction or denied John's prerogative right to tallage his demesne. The point in controversy was where to draw the line: were chartered boroughs within the royal demesne? For the first time the royal definition of its demesne was questioned, and it was questioned on the very ground upon which Henry II had incorporated the boroughs into the royal demesne.

As a political issue between the king and the barons, much importance should not be attributed to the provision on tallage in Magna Carta, but it does mark the entrance of the royal demesne into politics. Further, it would be incorrect to infer from Magna Carta and its reissues, on this subject, that the monarchy in insisting upon the demesne status of the boroughs was adopting an antagonistic policy toward the boroughs. The liberties and free customs of London and all other cities, boroughs, and vills were confirmed not only in 1215 but in each of the succeeding reissues of the Charter. What no Exchequer official, at the end of the reign of John, could have failed to observe was that of all the types of royal taxation employed during the period, and of all possible sources of extraordinary revenue, the levy of a thirteenth of movable goods in 1207 and the two tallages of 1210 and 1214 had been by far the most productive.[46] As political opposition eliminated the former source of

[46] Mitchell, *Taxation,* p. 354.

revenue, by removing all hope of consent, the government had greater reason than ever to emphasize and protect the distinction between the royal demesne and the rest of the realm and to insist upon the demesne status of the urban centers of taxable wealth.

A significant difference between the baronial grievances of 1215 and those of 1258 and 1311 is the complete absence, in the former, of any reference to alienation of the royal demesne. This might seem surprising in view of the fact that Henry II had begun his reign by resuming illegally alienated royal demesne and that the legality of the Donation of Constantine was already a bone of contention between papal and imperial political controversialists and pamphleteers skilled in Roman law. In other words, both specific English precedent and general discussion of the widest political problems of the day were available to Stephen Langton and the barons to help formulate a grievance based on the notion that "the king should live of his own," if such a grievance existed. Furthermore, the idea that the royal demesne should not be alienated, that it belonged to the crown, and that if alienated it must be recovered, was enunciated—perhaps for the first time in so many words—in a nearly contemporary English tract [47] which influenced the greatest legal mind of the next generation. The idea, it is safe to assume, was not wanting; its source and sustenance, however, came from royal policy and administration, as we have seen, and not from baronial opposition. Therefore it is not surprising that the Articles of the Barons contain no hint that the royal demesne should be inalienable.

Here again is evidence that the monarchy took the lead in em-

---

[47] "Debet uero de iure rex omnes terras . . . corone regni huius in integrum cum omni integritate et sine diminutione obseruare et defendere, dispersa et dilapidata et amissa regni iura in pristinum statum et debitum uiribus omnibus reuocare." This statement occurs in the anonymous tract entitled *De iure et de appendiciis corone regni Britannie; et quod sit officium regis,* which may be found in the *Leges Anglorum Saeculo XIII Ineunte Londiniis Collectae,* printed in Liebermann, *Gesetze,* I, 635ff. According to Richardson and Sayles, Bracton used the tract in commenting upon the coronation oath (H. G. Richardson and George Sayles, eds., *Select Cases of Procedure without Writ under Henry III* [Selden Society, vol. LX; London, 1941], p. xxi). See also, P. E. Schramm, *A History of the English Coronation* (tr. L. G. Wickham Legg; Oxford, 1937), pp. 197f.; McIlwain, *Growth of Political Thought,* pp. 379f.; Lapsley, "Statute of York," *E.H.R.,* LVI (1941), 435; and Richardson, "The English Coronation Oath," *Speculum,* XXIV (1949), 61f.

phasizing the difference between the royal demesne and the rest of the realm. It did so in the spirit of the administrative reforms of Henry II and with no desire, or even any understanding, that its policy would eventually foster baronial opposition to national taxation based on that very policy. Restraint on alienation of the royal demesne, on the other hand, was not a self-imposed constitutional limitation which a far-seeing Angevin monarchy, or a provident minority government under Henry III, voluntarily adopted out of theoretical considerations. It grew out of the same general program of tightening control, consolidation, and exploitation of the royal demesne which by the opening years of the thirteenth century had enlarged the demesne, enhanced the demesne right of the king, and increased royal revenues from the demesne. The monarchy had in fact achieved a position where it could live—not of its own alone, for its needs increased faster than its demesne resources—more securely based on what it was coming to consider its permanent endowment.

This policy was not, it must be stressed, a self-imposed limitation; it was the natural corollary of the economic changes of the age, which made a money income more important than feudal services. For this reason, the typical grant of royal demesne in the thirteenth century was a grant at farm, either in fee farm, for a term of years or life, or *quamdiu regi placuerit.* The grant at farm did not alienate the land from the royal demesne. It produced a money income which could be anticipated and counted upon, like the farm of the shire; and, because it was not alienated, demesne lands held at farm might still be subject to tallage.[48] Grants of royal demesne at farm,

[48] The right to take tallage could be included in the grant of a royal manor at farm, or it could be reserved to the king. In the former case the exercise of the right was restricted to those occasions on which the king tallaged his demesnes, and it could be levied only by issuance of a writ of tallage to the sheriff. To whom was tallage due if it was neither granted nor expressly saved to the king? According to Madox, "if such Saving was not expressed, it was to be understood." This seems eventually to have become the doctrine, though not without some hesitation and doubt. In 1325 the Barons of the Exchequer, after reversing their decision, held that *tallagium in locis qui sunt de antiquo Dominico Regis est mere annexum Coronae Angliae, & quod videtur non posse aliquo modo separari a Corona &c., nisi per speciale factum quod expressam facit mentionem inde.* Mich. Communia 19 Edw. II, rot. 33a, quoted by Madox, *Firma Burgi,* pp. 248ff., n.*f.* For the thirteenth century the only evidence I have seen concerns specific disputes from which it would be hazardous to generalize.

then, left the royal government with a direct interest in the condition of the manor and its tenants. Hence, the Exchequer and the central courts were not only willing to protect them, but also interested in preserving their rights. Royal income was at stake: this was true whether the tenants were small freeholders or villeins.

The idea that royal demesne should not be alienated or, if alienated in the past, should be resumed so that it might be restored as part of the crown endowment was at the bottom of the mid-thirteenth century arrentation of serjeanties, as it was later an underlying justification of that part of the *quo warranto* inquests which concerned alienation of royal manors or tenements within royal manors. Both arrentation and *quo warranto* proceedings conformed with the general royal policy of the thirteenth century of converting its demesne rights into cash revenue.[49] This was a royal policy, well under way long before the *communitas regni* ever thought of opposing alienation, and this policy grew naturally out of the administrative developments of the reign of Henry II, one of which was the regular inquiry into purprestures. After all, to a sworn jury it made little difference whether the itinerant justices sought to find out

The question needs investigation, The *Liber Memorandorum de Bernewelle* (pp. 76–82) contains a collection of documents relating to the tallage of Chesterton, Cambridgeshire, which illustrate these statements. To this subject we must return in another connection. Here it must be stressed that (1) royal will and not custom determined whether the king or the farmer received the tallage of a manor granted in fee farm (the Chesterton case was in dispute, with precedent on the king's side, but the issue was decided in the prior's favor *per consideracione curie nostre*—a *tractatum* held before some very important people [*ibid.*, pp. 79f.]); and that (2) the grant of a royal manor at farm did not extinguish the king's rights over the men or the land of the manor (an invasion of the tenants' rights was to *nostri preiudicium manifestum,* and against *ius nostrum* therein [*ibid.*, p. 188]).

[49] "Thomas Faber tenet j. virgatam terre in Upton de dominico domini regis per servicium ducentarum sagittarum, et valet per annum xx. s." ("Placita corone de comitatu Gloucestrie," in *Book of Fees,* II, 1339). This case comes from the year 1221 and illustrates the royal government's policy of valuing serjeanties, in order that they might be rented for money in the event of alienation in the future. The more familiar arrentation of serjeanties by Passelewe was based upon precedents going back at least as far as 1198. See Pollock and Maitland, *Hist. Eng. Law* (2d ed.), I, 334. The serjeanty was a special case: it was royal demesne *(de dominico domini regis),* but it was held by service, not in socage, and so long as it was so held it did not pay tallage. Thus it shared features of land "held in chief in demesne as of fee," and it was not royal demesne in the same sense that lands in custody, in farm, or in socage were royal demesne. It was distinguished by the element of honorable service rather than *viles operationes* or the cash sum which represented agricultural value.

whether any "inhabitants near estates which are assigned to the crown have usurped for themselves any portion of them and include it among their own possessions," [50] or put to them the questions "what does the lord king have in K. and in the vicinity and what has been alienated by the men of K. by any hand. . . . what are the demesnes of the lord king at A. and . . . by what right the tenants hold them." [51]

In either case, it was a matter of common local knowledge: whether illegally occupied or illegally alienated, the king's rights were equally affected, and the machinery of the inquest was equally applicable under the itinerant justices. Why should the king be concerned with who occupied, what was alienated, or how the tenements of his manors were held? Such things might affect the actual value of the manor, and the royal revenue might suffer; but much more important and immediate were the judicial profits involved. The roots of the *quo warranto* trials of Edward I go back to these early inquests *quo jure . . . teneant:* long before alienated jurisdiction concerned the monarchy, it was actively concerned with alienated royal demesne lands.

The consequences of these inquests anticipate the procedure and the profits of the later trials. From the Oblate Rolls of John, for example, it may be learned that

> Adam Salsarius gives the lord king 100 s. for having seizin of Old Salkil with pertinences, which had been seized into the lord king's hand on the occasion that it had been deposed in the king's presence that the said land had been of the king's demesne, and whereof the same Adam showed the king charters which he has from King Richard and the lord king himself.[52]

[50] "Habitantes prope fundos qui corone annominantur aliquam eorum portionem sibi vsurpent et suis possessionibus ascribant" (*Scac. Dial.*, p. 132).

[51] "Quid dominus rex habeat in K. et in visneto et quid alienatum est a hominibus de K. per alicujus manum. . . . Que sint dominica domini regis apud A. et . . . quo jure tenentes illa teneant" (*C.R.R.*, I, 209, 26). These were the questions put to the jurors of Kingston, Aylesbury, and Brill in 1200 and 1204.

[52] *Rot. de Obl. et Fin.*, p. 119. The date is 1201. Adam had a charter from Richard I in 1194, granting him Old Salkil in fee farm (*The Cartae Antiquae: Rolls 1–10* [ed. Lionel Landon, P.R.S., NS, vol. XVII; London, 1939], p. 96). During the Hilary term, earlier in 1201, a jury stated in the king's court that Adam held the land in question by Richard's charter (*C.R.R.*, I, 387f.). The fine of 100 shillings thus probably represents the cost to Adam of securing the charter of John to which the Oblate Roll refers, confirming the charter of Richard.

This entry alludes to the three stages of the proceedings. First, an inquest—this one allegedly in the king's presence—was held to discover what lands were or ought to be royal demesne; second, the land was seized into the king's hands, and the tenant was required to show his right to the land; and finally, this having been done to the satisfaction of the king's justices, possibly the barons of the Exchequer themselves, the tenant was allowed to regain his seizin on payment of a fine, though he always had the option of declining. Such proceedings look arbitrary and suggest that John was indeed "a bad king for his age." [53] And such he would have been if the tenant were a tenant-in-chief holding in fee. But it must be remembered that the king could legally be arbitrary with respect to his demesne; it was the amount of the fine, perhaps, but certainly not the legality of the transaction which reflects upon the royal government in a case such as this one. The object of demesne exploitation had become a cash revenue. This case must be read together with the notices occurring in the Pipe Roll of the same year, where royal vills are leased to the highest bidder.[54] The whole system of farming the royal demesne depended upon the vigilance of the Exchequer. It had to prevent royal lands from slipping away from its control; it had to keep the farms up to the rental value of the lands. The technique adopted was obvious for such an age; frequent "resumptions" of royal lands, followed by fines for reseizin and possibly an increased farm, would guarantee some correspondence between the value of the manor and the actual royal revenue therefrom.

The royal policy is well illustrated by an interesting case in 1204 which suggests that the government was not always wholly arbitrary in judicial matters affecting the royal demesne, even where it might have been, so long as its revenue was not in danger. A Derbyshire jury was put on oath to answer whether Ralph of Matlock held the manor of Matlock by gift of the king's predecessors in fee or by permission of the sheriff. The jury averred that the manor of Matlock *semper fuit dominicum domini regis,* but that it was held by Ralph's great-great-grandfather, great-grandfather, grandfather, and father, although they knew not by whom they had entry. They did know, however, that in the time of Henry II the manor was restocked and

[53] Jolliffe, *Const. Hist.,* p. 248.

[54] See above, footnote 11.

the sheriff had given it to Ralph at a higher farm as a result. This could only refer to a subfarm of the manor, since the sheriff could not give the land in fee. All in all, Ralph's claim to hold the land of the king in fee is put in considerable doubt, not to say denied. And yet, the record continues that *consideratum est quod . . . habeat seisinam suam*. Ralph claimed to hold of the king, but all he could show was a charter from Robert de Ferrers "who gave that land to Roger of Matlock his father for his service." The practical effect of this judgment, then, was to ensure that a royal estate, in the hands of one family for five generations (according to local knowledge), did not slip away from the royal demesne by virtue of a transaction which was probably wholly private and unauthorized by the central government. The manor of Matlock was placed back in the *corpus comitatus* at the increased rate. Finally, it should be noticed that, early in the proceedings leading to this judgment, the government had accepted a fine of twenty marks from Ralph (the manor produced only two pounds yearly) that he might have peace of that manor till judgment were given. This suggests that the government was willing to recognize local arrangements which in strict law might be irregular so long as such leniency was productive in cash revenue and the demesne right of the king was secured for the future.[55]

The cases of Old Salkil and Matlock concern whole manors; but, although the manor or vill was the normal unit of the royal demesne for financial purposes, the government was equally interested in tenements within manors, *quid alienatum est a hominibus per alicujus manum*. There is scattered evidence of this interest which antedates the better-known and wide-scale inquests beginning in 1212.[56] This suggests that such inquiry into alienated tenements was a routine matter which had become a familiar feature of the itinerant justices' work, and such an impression is strengthened by the chronicler's apparent misconception of the great inquest into tenures-in-chief and alienations by tenants-in-chief begun on 1 June

[55] *C.R.R.*, I, 30; *The Great Roll of the Pipe for the Sixth Year of the Reign of King John* (ed. D. M. Stenton, P.R.S., NS, vol. XVIII; London, 1940), p. 170.

[56] For example, "Rex &c. Vic' Lincol' salutem. Precipimus tibi quod reddi facias Abbati de Rufford' i. toftum in Grimesday q' Rogerus de Lesseby dedit eis in liberam elemosinam et unde ipse Abbas dissaisitur fuit quia jurat' fuit esse de dominico nostro et occupatum super nos" (*Rot. Litt. Claus.*, I, 23 [1205]).

1212. According to the chronicler, John ordered his sheriffs to inquire by sworn oath in each hundred

what lands were formerly of the demesne of the kings who were his predecessors and how they left the hands of those kings, and who holds them now, and for what services.[57]

What John's writ directed, however, was that the sheriffs inquire

concerning all fees of knights and all manner of tenements . . . which are held of us in chief . . . by military service or by serjeanty . . . and likewise concerning all tenements which formerly used to be held *of* us or *of* our progenitors, kings of England, which have been given or alienated by marriage, or by service, or in free alms, or in any manner by which less might be held of us in chief. . . .[58]

It is clear that the writ was concerned not with alienation of the royal demesne but with alienation by tenants-in-chief, which was an entirely different matter. The primary object of an inquiry into alienated royal demesne was the recovery or increase of cash revenue; the primary object of the writ was the recovery of lost services due from the king's tenants-in-chief and serjeants. The surprising thing is that the sheriffs themselves "took divergent views as to the exact nature of the information to be supplied by them," [59] and some of them seem to have thought that alienation of the royal demesne was the main subject of inquiry—just as did the chronicler quoted above. The returns of the inquest for Nottingham and Derbyshire are headed: "Inquisicio facta coram Philippo Marco, vice-

[57] "Quae terrae essent de dominico praedecessorum suorum regum antiquitus, et qualiter a manibus regum exierint, et qui eas modo tenent, et pro quibus servitiis" (Ann. Waverl., s.a. 1212, in *Annales Monastici* [ed. H. R. Luard, 5 vols., R.S.; London, 1864–1869], II, 267).

[58] "De omnibus feodis militum et omnimodis tenementis . . . que de nobis tenentur in capite . . . per militare servicium vel per serianteriam . . . et similiter de tenementis omnibus que antiquitus de nobis aut de progenitoribus nostris, regibus Anglie, teneri solent que sunt data vel alienata per maritagium, vel per servicium, vel per elemosinam, vel alio modo quo minus de nobis tenentur in capite" (Exch. K.R.S. ij. 6 [1 June 1212], as printed in *Book of Fees,* I, 52). The italics in the English translation are mine.

[59] *Ibid.,* I, 52. Maxwell-Lyte's view was that "the terms of the writ itself are somewhat ambiguous, and it is *not* surprising to find that the sheriffs took" etc. (italics mine). The stress is clearly on services and feudal or honorable tenures-in-chief. Some other explanation than simple failure to understand the writ seems to be called for.

comite Notinghamie, de dominicis domini regis."[60] Later, the following words were added to the heading by interlining: *et feodis* (after *dominicis*) and *et quo modo ab eo alienata fuerint* (after *regis*). Such changes, together with the conflicting evidence of the chronicler and the writ of 1 June 1212, suggest the possibility that one return was made to two separate inquests or that the writ of June 1 enlarged the scope of a previously ordered inquest into alienated royal demesne. Although this explanation is no more than a reasonable inference, it does avoid the unreasonable alternative which would attribute to both the chronicler and many sheriffs a failure to understand the plain language of the writ.

It is difficult to evaluate men's minds from such partial and scattered evidence, but when these documents are read against the background of the other legal records cited, it seems clear that the generation which lived in the opening years of the thirteenth century had come to expect that the royal government would regularly and as a matter of course investigate and punish illegal alienation of the royal demesne. Such restraint on alienation did not apply to the crown, nor was it a "constitutional limitation"; its sole purpose seems to have been to conserve the endowment of the monarchy and increase the revenue from that endowment.

The financial aspect of resumption of royal demesne comes out strongly in the legal records which are quite probably the consequence of inquests such as that of 1212. For example, in 1213 Thomas de Fekenham was summoned before the king's court *ad respondendum quo warranto* he held Boarstall, a member of the king's manor of Brill, in Buckinghamshire, since the lord king had been given to understand that the said Thomas had no entry there except by the keeper of Brill who held the manor in custody at the king's pleasure. Although Thomas claimed that he held the vill as his right and inheritance, his case was weak, and the trial reached an abrupt end when the men of Brill offered twenty marks to the king that they might have the vill at farm, as they were once allegedly accustomed to have held it as a member of Brill. Thomas countered with an offer of twenty marks that the king should confirm his right, but the men of Brill outbid him and the record ends with the notation that the oblation of twenty-five marks of the men

[60] *Book of Fees,* I, 148.

of Brill was accepted, that they might have Boarstall to farm at an increment of twenty shillings.[61]

A review of these developments antedating Magna Carta is instructive, for it throws light on the general resumption of the royal demesne which Henry III's minority government undertook in the first year of the young king's reign. Stubbs compared the resumption ordered 29 September 1217 with "the similar task undertaken by Henry II at the beginning of his reign," and contrasted Henry II's policy of economy and resumption with John, who "wasted all that he could waste." [62] These parallels and contrasts are misleading, especially in the implication that (with regard to this resumption) the work of William Marshal's administration was somehow baronial rather than monarchical in spirit, "constitutional" rather than willful, and "English" rather than inspired by a love of foreign favorites.

Henry II had challenged the legality of the charters by which Stephen had alienated certain royal manors; important people were involved, and the issue was one of strict law. The government in 1217, on the other hand, ordered all the sheriffs to establish by inquest what were the royal demesnes in each county and, having done so, to take them in hand and hold them till further direction.[63] No right of tenure was questioned, since none was involved. No legal proceedings followed, either, for within the month following the writ of 29 September 1217, the Close Roll is cluttered with orders directing the sheriffs to reseize the previous tenants or others of the royal manors.[64] The difference is vast: Henry II was concerned not with royal demesne, but with manors granted in fee by the king out of the royal demesne, i.e., manors which were no longer royal demesne; in 1217 the government was concerned with royal demesne, i.e., royal manors which had not been granted out in fee but which were held at farm or in custody. The act of 1217 was but the extension to all the royal demesne, throughout all the counties and at one time, of a policy which John and prob-

---

61 *C.R.R.*, VII, 20; and *Rot. de Obl. et Fin.*, p. 521.

62 *Const. Hist.*, II, 26, 585.

63 *Rot. Litt. Claus.*, I, 336.

64 *Ibid.*, I, 333–339.

ably Richard I before him had developed, using the same technique of the inquest *per legales et discretos homines.* The business of 1154 was legal; the business of 1217 was political. The government in 1217 was exercising the natural precaution of placing the custody or farm of royal manors in the hands of politically trustworthy persons. Thus the king's uncle was almost immediately reseized of all the manors he held in farm or custody, while a supporter might be given the farm of a manor *ad se sustinendum in servicio nostro quamdiu nobis placuerit.*[65]

It is clear that the policy of William Marshal in 1217 conformed with the policy established in the reigns of Richard I and John, and was not related at all to Henry II's "resumption" in 1154; that the resumption of 1217 was not the "baronial" or "constitutional" reaction to John's wasting all he could waste, for the manors remained in the sheriffs' hands only three or four weeks, and they had never been alienated in the first place; and that the whole event was governed by political expediency, not by legal or constitutional theory.

By the beginning of the reign of Henry, therefore, the several tendencies in royal policy and in political events were converging —whether they concerned economic exploitation of the demesne, national taxation, local administration, or alienation and resumption—to emphasize the demesne right of the king and to distinguish the area within which that right operated from the rest of the realm.

---

65 *Ibid.,* I, 339. Jolliffe (*Const. Hist.,* pp. 267f.) has called attention to the writ of 9 August 1220 (*Rot. Litt. Claus.,* I, 437) which ordered "the first general enquiry *quo warranto* in English history." The plan seems to have been to investigate the rights of tenants who held royal manors, but "the adventure was not carried through." The only thing new about this was the nationwide scale contemplated, and it did not concern alienated jurisdiction. More important, politically and constitutionally, were the resumption of castles and the "strict interpretation of charters" in which may be found the origins of the later *quo warranto* inquests concerning royal rights and alienated jurisdiction. See F. M. Powicke, *King Henry III and the Lord Edward* (2 vols.; Oxford, 1947), I, 323. If any single writ should be thought of as inaugurating the first *quo warranto* inquest, a better choice would seem to be the letter close to all sheriffs dated 9 April 1223, directing sworn inquests to determine *quas consuetudines et quas libertates dominus J. Rex pater noster habuit . . . de terris et forestis et aliis infra burgum et extra* (*Rot. Litt. Claus.,* I, 569). Inquiry into royal demesne lands had already become a routine responsibility of the itinerant justices (e.g., *Book of Fees,* II, 1352ff.).

THE ROYAL DEMESNE OF HENRY III

The connection between the history of the royal demesne and political events during the reign of Henry III is close. On the one hand, baronial opposition to taxation made demesne revenues all the more important. On the other hand, baronial efforts to control the royal administration made it essential for the monarchy that the royal demesne be kept clear of the often conflicting rights which led to political controversy and, eventually, civil war.

The government's concern over its demesne revenues and administration reached a climax in the years from 1236 to 1242, in a series of developments which were but part of the larger administrative reforms of that period. The details of these reforms are important for the history of the Exchequer and the household, but for the royal demesne their interest lies not in their novelty but in the culmination they provided for the whole trend of administrative policy from the time it becomes apparent in the early years of the reign of Henry II. Most important was the removal of the last royal manors from the control of the sheriffs, which coincided with the general reappointment of most sheriffs in 1236.[66] So little was this a revolution, however, that the farms of the shires remained at the same level, and the profits were practically unaffected.[67] By this date the royal estates still within the *corpus comitatus* had dwindled until, from the sheriffs' point of view, "the demesnes were few and scattered." [68] The removal of the remaining estates merely completed the process of excluding the sheriffs from the economic exploitation of the royal demesne.[69]

The practice of leasing royal manors at a cash farm or placing them in custody, which had steadily been growing more frequent, now became universal, for the immediate result of the replacement of the sheriffs was the assignment of custodians for the manors removed from the county farms. In May, 1236, the king, "by com-

66 Matt. Paris, III, 363, in *Select Charters,* p. 325; *Calendar of the Patent Rolls . . . 1232–1247* (P.R.O.; London, 1906), pp. 141–148.

67 Mills, "Exchequer Procedure," pp. 158f.

68 Powicke, *Henry III,* I, 102.

69 Sheriffs may still be found farming or keeping manors, but not as an official function of the shrievalty (*Cl.R. Hen. III, 1237–42,* pp. 59f., 221; and *P.R. 26 Hen. III,* p. 51).

mon counsel of his lieges," appointed Walter de Burgo and Warner Engayn to take into his hands all royal manors and demesnes except those in Yorkshire, Northumberland, Cumberland, and Lancaster, for which Robert de Crepping was appointed keeper. The *custodes dominicorum,* as the three were styled, were directed "to enquire how much they are worth yearly in demesnes, rents, services, villeinages and other issues and touching alienated lands." [70]

The government took this occasion to tighten up on the farms of manors which had fallen behind, particularly those which had been granted to the men of a manor, and also to resume into the king's hands (at least temporarily) manors and tenements which were farmed or kept in custody by individuals *quamdiu regi placuerit.* This did not affect manors enfeoffed by charter and granted at fee farm.[71] The keepers of the king's demesnes thus fulfilled the same function on the royal demesne which the escheators served with regard to wardships, forfeitures, and escheats. They took charge of a kind of pool of royal manors, supervising the local bailiffs in charge and accounting for their issues at the Exchequer. From this pool the king granted manors, tenements, or "librates" of land to recipients of the royal favor or, more often, to royal officials and servants both great and small.[72]

The transfer of royal manors from the *corpus comitatus* to the custody of special keepers contributed measurably to the decline of the sheriff.[73] In scores of ways, the keepers took over responsibility and exercised the control over local bailiffs which had made the sheriffs important and powerful in their counties. The activities of Walter de Burgo, appointed *custos dominicorum* in 1236, illus-

[70] *Cal. Pat. Rolls, 1232–1247,* pp. 146f., 156. That the sheriffs did not always retire gracefully from the royal manors (and the possibility of some incidental profits or extortion) is indicated by the order to the sheriffs of Cumberland, Yorkshire, Westmoreland, and Northumberland to keep out of all royal manors and allow Robert de Crepping to answer for their issues at the Exchequer, saving the pleas of the crown and the pleas which the sheriffs ought to have. *Rot. Orig.,* I, 2.

[71] Except, of course, where fee farmers had fallen behind in payment (*Cl.R. 1234–1237* (P.R.O.; London, 1908), p. 357; *Cl.R. 1237–1242,* p. 19; *P.R. 26 Hen. III,* pp. 240, 263).

[72] The Close Rolls are full of notices of grants *ad se sustentandum in servicio nostro quamdiu nobis placuerit.* For examples, see *Rot. Litt. Claus.,* I, 349, 415, 610, and *passim;* also, *P.R. 26 Hen. III,* p. 51.

[73] See W. A. Morris, *The Medieval English Sheriff to 1300* (Publications of the Univ. of Manchester, Hist. Ser., No. XLVI; Manchester, 1927).

trate the varied duties of the keepers, which made them liaison officials between the central government and the local officials and people administering or living upon the royal demesne. He was directed to provide shingles for the king's houses; haul timber for the king's castle at Windsor; reduce the rent of a mill of Bloxham, Oxfordshire, for the benefit of a certain widow; receive fourteen oaks and sufficient stakes from John de Nevill for making a wardrobe in the hall at Brill, Buckinghamshire, and for enclosing the chamber and chapel at the same place; construct a mill for the king at Newport, Essex, from oaks to be taken from the wood at Hatfield Regis; hold an inquest into the rights of the Abbot of Cirencester in the king's manors of Cookham and Bray, Berkshire; make an extent of the king's manor of Bampton, Oxfordshire and put Imbert Pugeys in seisin of fifteen librates of land there; hold an inquest to determine the rights of Walter of Merton and his predecessors at Basingstoke, Hampshire, where the latter had a free tenement; and see to the repair of the king's house at Geddington, Northamptonshire.[74]

There are signs that all did not go well with Walter de Burgo's custody, or with that of the other keepers of the king's demesnes. The men of the manors of Feckenham, Lugwardine, and Marden complained that Walter demanded other services and dues than they were accustomed to render; the Abbot of Cirencester had been wrongfully disseized by Walter, he complained, of the pasture and wood to which he had rights in Cookham and Bray; and Walter had been unable to pay his debts, for which distraint had to be made on the chattels of Walter's debtors.[75] Complaints and difficulties accompanied the experiment of transferring the royal demesnes to the care of special keepers. Nor was the Exchequer satisfied, and in 1240 there began a series of inquests into the condition of the king's manors which led to the dismissal of many of the keepers and their bailiffs and their replacement by others or the granting of the manors at farm to the tenants of the manors.[76]

---

[74] *Cl.R. 1237–1242*, pp. 25, 34, 46, 64, 70, 84, 131, 186.

[75] *Ibid.*, pp. 39, 142, 273, 291, 315.

[76] For example, Peter de Tany and Walter of Merton were directed to take the demesne manors of Kent, Essex, Middlesex, and Hertfordshire into the king's hands, replace the bailiffs, and make inquiry into the stock, renders, and other things pertaining to the manors (*ibid.*, p. 220. See also, pp. 186, 307. 367).

The returns of the inquest into the administration of the royal manor of Ospringe, in Kent, have survived.[77] The articles were few but searching. The central government wanted to know: (1) the number and amount of stock and grain or agricultural produce, (2) customs and dues wrongly exacted,[78] (3) an itemized list and the sum totals of various judicial fines and amercements, and (4) an extent of the manor—i.e., the yearly rental value of each source of revenue in the whole manor, and the total value of the manor both stocked and *nudi et sine instauro.* All this having been investigated and recorded on the oaths of the local jury, the commissioners [79] then committed the manor to the custody of three of the tenants of Ospringe, at least two of whom had served on the jury. An interesting sidelight on the negotiations which accompanied such a transaction appears in the record:

> And the jurors say that the manor was delivered to them (the bailiffs) in good condition, as well in enclosed woods under custody as in pastures and stock. And they say that the standing crops which are in the fields are worth much more this year, as it seems and appears, than they were worth in other years, and . . . that they are worth a sixth part more than is usual.[80]

By these gratuitious remarks the jurors were attempting to induce the commissioners to set a lower yearly rental value for the manor than might be indicated by the unusually good crops of the current year.

But the inquest does not yet end. There follows a full record of three complaints of certain of the tenants against the two local bailiffs, together with the bailiffs' replies. In each case, the bailiff admits his deed, but claims that *fecit hoc per judicium curie,* or the like. The judgment or verdict of the court of the manor is the last resort, the bulwark of defense. And these two men were bailiffs

---

[77] Printed in *Book of Fees,* I, 620–623. The tenor of the articles or heads of inquiry may be reconstructed from the statements of the jurors. Ospringe was in the custody of Walter de Burgo.

[78] "De consuetudinibus male levatis" (*ibid.,* I, 620).

[79] The same Peter de Tany and Walter of Merton (see above, footnote 76).

[80] "Et juratores dicunt quod manerium dimittitur eis in bono statu, tam in boscis clausis et custoditis quam in pasturis et stauro. Et dicunt quod bladum quod est in terris valet hoc anno ut videtur et sicut apparet multo melius quam valeret aliis annis, et . . . quod valeat de sexta parte plus quam consuevit" (*Book of Fees,* I, 622).

of Walter de Burgo, who held in custody royal manors in half a dozen counties. That the commissioners considered the bailiffs' defense satisfactory may be inferred from the fact that one of them was among the three men to whom custody was given following the inquest.[81]

It was not enough for the government to know the value of its manors; it was necessary to find responsible parties who would produce the annual revenue corresponding to that value. There were cases where the *custodes* appointed in 1236 merely piled up debts at the Exchequer, and the actual revenues went unaccounted for.[82] The actual policy finally adopted seems to have been one of farming for a fixed sum (rather than placing in custody with all issues accounted for at the Exchequer), for a term of several years, usually five, and renewable if satisfactory. There is some evidence that the government preferred farming to the tenants of the royal manors, but if this was the new rule adopted, it was not without exceptions.[83] As an incident in the process, the sheriffs may have

81 Three aspects of this whole proceeding will be noticed below in another connection: (1) Ospringe was not ancient demesne; (2) even when under an important royal official as *custos dominicorum,* the local bailiffs are bound by and subordinate to the manorial court, which they themselves stress in their own defense; and (3) the authority of the royal government stands behind the manorial court and guarantees the customary rights of (as it invites the grievances of) the tenants of the royal manor. Of course, the possible implications of this evidence should not be stressed too much, because the case comes from Kent, where, a half century after this inquest, it was being claimed that everyone is born free. It will be seen, however, that this kind of inquest is typical of the royal demesne everywhere.

82 A list of the debts remaining from the custody exercised by Warner Engayn is printed in *Book of Fees,* I, 625. By 1242, Warner had run his Exchequer debts up to the startling sum of over 500 pounds.

83 Cheltenham and Brigstock were granted at farm to the bishop-elect of Hereford and the *probi homines* of the manor, respectively, in October, 1240, in each case for a term of five years *et ulterius si nobis placuerit.* See *Cl.R. 1237–1242,* p. 230, where both entries are canceled because in the Fine Roll; Ketton and Benson were also committed to individuals rather than the tenants in the same year (*ibid.,* pp. 185f., 230).

A statement of royal policy in the matter is provided by the following instructive entry in the Originalia Roll of this year:

"Sumerset'—Quia provisum est de consilio regis quod omnia dominica regis tradantur ad firmam decetero hominibus singulorum maneriorum, mandatus est ballivis de Sumerton' quod convocari faciant homines predicti manerii et manerium illud predictis hominibus tradant cum waretto fenis carucis et omnibus aliis instauris que rex habet in eodem manerio, que omnia instaura appreciari faciant per sacramentum proborum et legalium hominum antequam illud predictis hominibus dimiserint, et de precio postea regi certificent per ipsum que (*sic*) rex ad partes illas miserit ad certifican-

been employed to disseize unsatisfactory keepers and effect the transfer of the manor at farm to the tenants or some individual.[84]

As the government was striving to increase its income from the royal demesne, it was also using every means to extract from the Church and the barons whatever extraordinary revenue might be raised. Baronial and episcopal opposition to extraordinary taxes —opposition which could be expressed and made good, because of the necessity of consent—was one of the main reasons for the attention bestowed upon the royal demesne revenue. The connection between extraordinary and ordinary income was not lost upon the barons and bishops. Matthew Paris inserted in his history the record of a refusal by the great council to a request for an aid in 1242. The interest of this document lies in the reasons put forward for declining the grant, for in them may be found the earliest formulation of the idea that the king should live of his own. The barons argued that since the last grant, which had not been spent so far as they knew, the king "had so many escheats . . . that from those escheats alone he ought to derive a large sum of money if it is well conserved. Moreover . . . the itinerant justices have not ceased to itinerate . . . and nearly every vill is heavily amerced." [85] In the eyes of the bishops and barons, the revenues of escheats, vacancies, and judicial profits constituted the normal and ordinary income whereby the king might live of his own. Considering the amount of effort that was spent by the government in exploiting

---

dum homines predictos ad quod forum predictum manerium et instaura predicta rex eis concedet ad firmam tenenda, salvis regi bladis suis que fecit in predicto manerio hoc anno xxiiii seminari que salvo ad opus regis custodiantur.

"Eodem modo scribitur Ballivis de Esenden', Beiford', Fecham, Neuport, Mawurthyn, Acornebur', Lugwurthyn, Abbetorp, Geintinton', Tingden', Clive, Brehull', Brikestok', Torp', Fordinton' " (Public Record Office, Exchequer [L.T.R.] Originalia Roll No. 7, m.5).

Marden, Finedon, and Brigstock were farmed to the tenants (*Cl.R. 1237–1242,* pp. 208, 307, 230), but I do not know what happened in the other instances. The Fine Roll for this year has not survived.

84 "Mandatum est omnibus vicecomitibus Anglie excepto vicecomite Cornubie quod capiant in manu Regis omnes terras quae sunt de potestate Regis" (*Rot. Orig.,* I, 5). I have found no evidence that this order was ever carried out.

85 "Tot habuit escaetas . . . quod solummodo de illis escaetis debet ipse habere grandem pecuniae summam si bene custodiatur. Praeterea . . . non cessaverunt justitiarii itinerantes itinerare . . . et fere omnes villae graviter amerciantur" (Matt. Paris, IV, 186f., in *Select Charters,* p. 361).

the royal demesne, it is surprising to find absent from this argument any reference to the revenues for which farmers and keepers accounted out of the king's manors. The argument is long and detailed, and it can only be surmised that the magnates entertained no great hope that the royal demesne could contribute significantly to the king's living of his own.

The first explicit statement, emanating either from an official source or arising from the relations between the crown and the baronage, that royal demesne was inalienable appears in the form of the oath to be taken by the king's councilors in 1257, on the eve of the Barons' Wars. From what has already been said about royal policy concerning alienation, and the absence of any grievances on the subject among the barons, it should not be a surprise to find a royal source for the first expression of the idea. The councilors were required to swear "that they will allow nothing to be alienated from those things which pertain to the ancient demesne of the crown." [86]

This provision is the culmination of a long process. Its sudden appearance in 1257 marks no revolution, and, if the documentation for this period were fuller, it might not stand out in such bold relief. It is probable that councilors sworn to the king took an oath in approximately the same form earlier than 1240. Sir Maurice Powicke has pointed out that a colorful incident of that year, involving the fall of the household and government official, Simon the Norman, was immediately due to his refusal to seal a writ *contra coronam domini regis*.[87] The whole incident implies that there was at that time a councilors' oath and that a responsible clerk could do something against the king's will which might still be in the interests of the crown and in accordance with that oath. Although the royal demesne was not itself involved in this incident,

[86] "Quod nihil consentient alienari de his quae ad antiquum dominicum coronae pertinent" (J. F. Baldwin, *The King's Council in England during the Middle Ages* [Oxford, 1913], p. 346). There are, of course, earlier references to the inalienability of royal "rights and honors," or the like, but these are connected with the coronation oath of the king and do not specifically concern the royal demesne or the duties of royal councilors. The oath taken by Peter des Roches, Richard Marsh, and Hubert de Burgh before December 1218, not to alienate lands during the minority of Henry III, is a possible, but remote, precedent for the oath of 1257. See Richardson, "The English Coronation Oath," *Speculum,* XXIV (1949), 51–56.

[87] Powicke, *Henry III,* App. E, II, 772–783.

it indicates the growth of the general idea of the inalienability of "things which pertain to . . . the crown."

It can almost be said that with the evolution of the distinction between crown and king, the growth of this idea was inevitable. This is not the proper place to discuss the influence of canon law or Roman law on English law, and yet in this connection it is worth recalling "the canonical principle which forbids the alienation of church goods" and the fact that Bracton was influenced by the "artificial facade" built up by the canon lawyers to explain and rationalize this principle. Bracton, dealing with the specific problem of alienation by ecclesiastics, insisted that this could not be done without the consent of the patron to whom the advowson belonged and generalized his reason (borrowing from the canon lawyers): "Since the consent of all those whom the matter touches will be necessary and must be required." [88] Such statements may be "artificial facades," but the men who trouble to make them are thinking men—political thought flourishes among men who try to rationalize the assumptions of their age, or the prejudices of party, which they find congenial. As soon as the kingship is conceived as possessing rights which go beyond the person of the king, whether it is his heirs or the *communitas regni* who share in those rights, the principle of *quod omnes tangit, ab omnibus comprobetur* may be applied to the crown. Bracton himself did not apply it, but then he was not writing a political treatise on the crown.[89] The important point is that such ideas were becoming defined, were gaining support, and, most important of all, conformed with or expressed theoretically what in fact had been taking place in day-to-day administrative practice.

The royal demesne was not an important factor in the period of the Barons' Wars, but the years 1258–1267 may nevertheless be taken to mark the final emergence of the concept of the ancient demesne of the crown. This is not to say that the phrase appears no earlier; nor would it be true that there was no further elaboration of the idea. But it was in this period that the monarchy made

[88] "Quia omnium illorum consensus quos res tangit erit necessarius et requirendus" (Post, "A Romano-Canonical Maxim, '*Quod Omnes Tangit,*' in Bracton," *Traditio,* IV [1946], 232).

[89] F. Schulz, "Bracton on Kingship," *E.H.R.,* LX (1945), 136–176, especially p. 145.

its policy toward the royal demesne an issue in political controversy; and it was in this period that the baronial opposition shows the first signs of recognizing and accepting legal rules and in the ideas and distinctions which so far had been confined to the royal courts or royal administrative policy.

With regard to alienation of the royal demesne, it was (as might be expected) the monarchy which introduced the subject as a point of contention. During the year 1261, when there was a possibility of a royal reaction and when the two sides were still jockeying for position, Henry III drew up a list of complaints against the baronial council. Among other things, the king alleged: "Item, they permit Edward the king's son to squander what the lord king has given him as an endowment of the crown of England, and which (lands) were conveyed to him so that they should not be separated from the crown of England, as appears by his charters." [90] Of this complaint there was no immediate result, and it may well have been no more than a propaganda flourish at the time. This, however, is just what makes it important: such a point was considered worth including. Like the other complaints, it was designed to appeal to notions which the barons could not disown though they might deny the facts at issue. The royal complaint cannot be dismissed as mere quibbling; it accurately expressed royal policy; and, in the general pacification which brought the war to a close, the idea reappears more fully and carefully stated as the sixth chapter of the Dictum de Kenilworth: "All places, rights, property, and other things pertaining to the royal crown shall be restored to the crown itself and to the lord king by those who detain them in their possession, unless they show that they possess them by reasonable warrant from the lord king himself or his predecessors." [91]

The Dictum de Kenilworth is thus a milestone in the develop-

---

[90] "Item permittunt Edwardum filium regis distrahere que dominus rex ei dedit in augmentum corone Anglie et que ei tradita fuerunt ut non separentur a corona Anglie sicut patet per cartas suas" (N. Denholm-Young, "Documents of the Barons' Wars," in *Collected Papers on Mediaeval Subjects* [Oxford, 1946], p. 128, reprinted from *E.H.R.,* XLVIII [1933], 574). In the French text of these complaints there is no corresponding article.

[91] "Ut omnia loca, jura, res, et alia ad coronam regiam pertinentia, ipsi coronae et domino regi restituantur, per eos qui ea detinent occupata, nisi ostendant se illa per rationabilem warantiam ab ipso domino rege vel a suis antecessoribus possidere" (*Select Charters,* p. 408).

ment of the doctrine of the inalienability of the royal demesne, *loca . . . ad coronam regiam pertinentia.* A comparison of the Dictum with the councilor's oath of 1257 reveals a similar stress on the crown, implying the distinction between land which was in the king's hands as feudal lord and lands which were conceived as being more permanently or fundamentally the king's in virtue of his office.

Although the Dictum de Kenilworth may not have been clearly one of those enactments which were "generally regarded in after ages as parts of the written law," [92] it was a "public" document and an important one, for in it were incorporated the terms of the final settlement of the Barons' Wars. In that settlement was included, for the first time in a public document, a clear statement of royal policy on alienation of the royal demesne.

Even more significant is the difference between the provisions concerning alienation found in the councilors' oath of 1257 and the Dictum de Kenilworth. The oath appears to prohibit altogether any alienation of "things" belonging to the ancient demesne of the crown. Should this be taken to imply that the monarchy recognized a constitutional limitation? Such a view is denied utterly by the Dictum. The crux is not whether ancient demesne, but whether held with "reasonable" warrant. The monarchy was attempting to prevent alienation which was without warrant, i.e., accomplished by its own officials or by rebellious subjects who acted in its name but not in accordance with royal will. The councilors' oath was a bond between king and servant; it restrained the servant, not the king. Hence the difference between such an "intramural" document and one which enunciated publicly a royal policy. This is why no legal rule prohibiting alienation of ancient demesne could develop in the thirteenth century. Pollock and Maitland recognized that the theory of nonalienation, so far as it had developed, was a "strong sentiment—it is rather a sentiment than a rule of law." [93] What they left untouched was the question, whence and why the sentiment? It came from the monarchy, not its opposition; it was a statement of policy aimed at conserving and enhancing royal revenue. Neither Henry III nor his son felt in the least con-

[92] Pollock and Maitland, *Hist. Eng. Law* (2d ed.), I, 180.
[93] *Ibid.*, I, 518.

strained from alienating any particular manor, whether it were held by his predecessors or not.

The monarchy, then, was not building a strait jacket for itself. It was merely stating in general terms the principle upon which it proceeded in the following year to resume lands which had been alienated by others acting in its name. In the general inquest during 1267, which followed the Dictum de Kenilworth, the commissioners were given a specific mandate: "They shall inquire whether any lands of the demesne of the king may have been granted out by reason of this disturbance, and who holds them, and by whom had they been granted, and for what penalty." [94] The lands to be resumed were those alienated irregularly rather than *ab ipso domino rege vel a suis antecessoribus*. Thus the general principle stated in the Dictum appealed to the distinction between crown and king and emphasized the legality (*rationabilem warantiam*) of proper alienation, while the administrative order defined the application of that principle to conditions which were, in the eyes of the monarchy, simply revolutionary and illegal.

Before leaving the period of the Barons' Wars, one more subject requires attention. This is the attitude toward the royal demesne exhibited by the baronial opposition while in power. There is not much direct evidence, but it seems clear nonetheless that when the monarchy was put in commission the government of Simon de Montfort accepted the concept of its royal demesne and demesne right which the royal government had reached at that time. The first indication of this attitude is found in practically the first act of the baronial party in 1258, in the inquests undertaken concerning local administration. The chapter concerning the royal demesne is entitled *De Dominicis domini Regis alienatis sine waranto*,[95] which is simply the routine inquiry, phrased in the same words, long since adopted by the royal government as an article of the general eyre. The absence of any reference to the

[94] "Lein enquerra si nules terres du demeine le Roi soient donez par acheson de cest movement, et ki les tient, et a ki e les sunt donees et pour quel forfet" (*Cronica Maiorum et Vicecomitum Londoniarum* [ed. Thomas Stapleton, Camden Society; London, 1846], p. 97).

[95] P.R.O. Fragments of Hundred Rolls, Box 8, No. 5 (6), printed in E. F. Jacob, *Studies in the Period of Baronial Reform and Rebellion, 1258–1267* (Oxford Studies in Social and Legal History, ed. Paul Vinogradoff, vol. VIII; Oxford, 1925), p. 340.

royal demesne in the Petition of the Barons, the Provisions of Oxford, and the Provisions of Westminster suggests that the barons entertained no grievances in that direction.[96] When fighting actually broke out, the royal demesne seems to have suffered even less than average from the inevitable loss and destruction: "Of depredations upon the royal demesne there is very little record. . . . It was not de Montfort's policy to strip or confiscate a legitimate source of royal wealth or to prevent the king from living of his own." [97] There was no administrative change carried through by the baronial government, so far as the economic exploitation of the demesne lands was concerned.

One of the most interesting records of the early period of the baronial reform movement is connected with the eyre of Hugh Bigod, the justiciar, which "produced the great part of what redress the commonalty received from the baronial government." [98] By order of the king and his chief justiciar, the treasurer and barons of the Exchequer committed the royal manor of Brill to the king's *probi homines* of Brill, to be held in custody at pleasure.[99] This action followed a plea before the king and justiciar at Woodstock,[100] concerning certain complaints of the tenants against the bailiffs and farmers of Brill, which both in its general nature and sequel parallels the inquest and action taken at the royal manor of Ospringe, Kent, in 1240, which has already been discussed. To this trial we must return, but here it is enough to notice that Hugh Bigod associated himself with the royal policy of redress of grievances of manorial tenants and the farming of royal manors to those tenants.

So far as both the negative and positive evidence can reveal, the baronial party took up the royal policy without change. It comes as a surprise, then, when in 1261 Henry III's list of complaints against the baronial council included the following charge, which introduced into political controversy the conditions and rights of the tenants of the royal demesne: "On the other hand, the soke-

---

96 *Select Charters,* pp. 373–394.
97 Jacob, *Studies,* p. 225.
98 Jolliffe, *Const. Hist.,* p. 298.
99 L.T.R. Mem. Roll, 34, 42–43 Hen. III, m.4, quoted by Jacob, *Studies,* p. 13, n.6.
100 Printed *ibid.,* App. II, pp. 344–350.

men (of the king) and the king's own tenants are more aggrieved and treated worse than others of the realm, *pur ceo qils nount defense sil veignent au concles despise,* and they depart without gaining anything." [101] In the rather garbled passage, the king seems to be alleging that if his tenants come before the council, the council despises them, or holds aloof, and they must depart without relief. When it is recalled that one of the first acts of the baronial government was to investigate and redress local grievances, including those of tenants of royal manors such as Brill (noticed above), it would seem that "the charge about socmen was grossly unfair." [102] And yet, two years and a half separate Hugh Bigod's eyre from Henry's complaints of 1261. In the interval many farmers or keepers may have been replaced. It is possible that what really lay behind this complaint was the appointment of new bailiffs, partisans of the baronial cause, and that the council was not in practice keeping a very strict control over them or preventing extortion. But such an explanation cannot be tested by the published documents, and the really important point to notice is the claim for preferential treatment for the king's sokemen: they are aggrieved and treated worse than others of the realm because they do not get relief from the council. Such a statement simply does not make sense, unless the king's sokemen enjoyed a privileged position. The baronial answer to this charge is instructive: the council denied responsibility and referred the king's sokemen to the normal judicial machinery or to the Exchequer, which it claimed had been the customary resort.[103] The council did not deny protection by the central government; it merely denied its own liability. The whole transaction is obscured by the difficulty of identifying *lez soquemans et les*

[101] "Dautre part lez soquemans et les propre tenauntz le Roy pluis soient greues et pluis sount tretez que autrez du reaume pur ceo qils nount defense sil veignent au concles despise et saunz rien esploiter dispartount" (Jacob, "The Complaints of Henry III against the Baronial Council in 1261," *E.H.R.,* XLI [1926], 567). The corresponding article in the Latin text is as follows: "Item sokemanni et alii tenentes domini regis magis grauantur modo et peius quam alii de regno" (Denholm-Young, "Documents," in *Collected Papers,* p. 128, reprinted from *E.H.R.,* XLVIII, 574).

[102] "Complaints," p. 563.

[103] "Le conseil dit et respount qe lez sokemanns le Roy ne vindrent vnques deuant eux a pleint faire si homme lour ad fait tort ceo soit amende deuant les iusticez ou les baronz de leschekere si come il doit estre et sil soient malement tretez soit purueu coment ils serrount defenduz desore enauant" (*ibid.,* p. 567).

propre tenauntz le Roy, and by the fact that the council's reply does not mention the latter. Was the king referring to free sokemen and free tenants only, or was he referring to all tenants, free and otherwise? The main point stands out clearly enough, however, and it was a point which the king felt was widely enough accepted that he might include it among complaints which were essentially political and propagandistic in nature. It is confirmed by the council's reply. Tenants of the king were specially protected by access to the central government and (according to the king) to the council itself; if they were denied this protection, they were being "treated worse than others of the realm." Though the council might try to defend itself, it did not deny the main contention, and it could hardly do so. Only two years before, Hugh Bigod, the baronial justiciar, had adjourned the case of the men of Witley, who claimed to be sokemen of the ancient demesne, to be terminated in the parliament of February 1259.[104]

It seems clear, then, that the attitude and policy of the baronial party while in power was essentially the same as that of the royal government toward the royal demesne. By the end of the reign of Henry III, the monarchy had, by a policy which found no real opposition from the *communitas regni,* transformed the royal demesne in a fundamental way which, in certain respects favorable to both the monarchy and the tenants, set the demesne apart from the rest of the realm.

The administrative and political history of the royal demesne may be summarized, to the point now reached, by the following conclusions. Royal policy encouraged and finally achieved a distinction between that part of the royal demesne which was distinctively royal and thought of as permanently attached to the office of kingship as an endowment and that part of the demesne which fell under the demesne right of the king only as an incident of feudal law.[105] This distinction does not suddenly appear at any one date; it grows out of administrative practice or policy which

104 Richardson and Sayles, *Proc. without Writ,* pp. 91f.

105 This comes out clearly in 1274: "Quot et que dominica maneria rex habet in manu sua in singulis comitatibus, tam scilicet de antiquis dominicis corone quam de escaetis et perquisitis" (c.1 of the Articles of 11 October 1274, in Cam, *Hundred and the Hundred Rolls,* App. I, p. 248).

aimed at increasing the cash revenue of the government and tightening the control of the central government over the royal demesne. A necessary part of this development was the direct intervention of the central government into the economic affairs of the tenants of the royal manors, an intervention which by the end of Henry III's reign had come to imply, and to be accepted as implying, a special protection, a privileged position for the manorial tenants of the king. The royal demesne by the end of this period had become a factor, as yet not important, in political controversy. The baronial acceptance of royal policy is the earliest indication that the royal demesne was coming to be thought of as a significant basis and means by which the king might live of his own, a concept which grew out of baronial opposition to extraordinary taxation during the middle years of the reign, but which, so far as inalienability of the royal demesne is concerned, became a crucial issue only in the fourteenth century.

CHAPTER VI

The Nature and Origins of the Ancient Demesne

Up to this point in our discussion no effort has been made to be any more precise in defining this "permanent" part of the royal demesne—which in some important respects was separate from the rest of the realm, and which had come to be thought of as not to be alienated without "reasonable" warrant—than the evidence relating to administrative and political history might warrant. We have attempted to base our interpretation directly upon the surviving documents and to guard against reading into this aspect of the history of the royal demesne any more precise ideas than are found in the evidence available. Where no ancient demesne is mentioned, we have refrained from speaking of ancient demesne. There are two other reasons for this. First, the constitutional significance of the royal demesne as a whole stands out more clearly when it is treated as a whole. Royal manors are farmed by tenants, whether ancient demesne, like Brill, or not ancient demesne, like Ospringe. Tenants of royal manors are visited, put on oath, protected against their bailiffs, again, whether they live on what are actually ancient demesne manors or not. Second, this survey of the royal demesne as a whole is a necessary preliminary to an analysis of the ancient demesne. A discussion of the genus, royal demesne, may throw some light on its privileged species, the ancient demesne. There remains, then, to be discussed the nature, peculiarities, and origins of these peculiarities of the ancient demesne.

THE MEANING OF *ANTIQUUM DOMINICUM*

We have now to inquire exactly what the phrase meant, and what were the full implications, when documents of the middle and late thirteenth century refer to *antiquum dominicum corone regis,* and the like. The law books or theoretical writings of the period provide no answer. Bracton does not specifically mention "ancient" demesne in his treatise, though he has much to say concerning *dominicum domini regis.*[1] The phrase *antiquum dominicum* occurs in one case which he included in his Note Book, but it refers to manorial demesne within an estate, and not to ancient demesne in the usual meaning of the phrase.[2] The procedural tracts, of course, give no assistance.[3] The tract known as Fleta assumes that the reader already knows the meaning of the phrase,[4] and so also does the counsel's opinion ascribed to Aunger of Ripon and known as *Statutum de Antiquo Dominico.*[5] The nearest to a definition is the statement of Britton that "ancient demesnes are lands which were part of the ancient manors annexed to our Crown," [6] and this statement leaves unanswered the main question. Nevertheless, it can be said without hesitation that *antiquum dominicum* had a precise meaning, and for it the law courts were responsible. Later lawyers and judges might quibble as to whether lands or manors held by Edward and not by William, or held by Edward and William but alienated before 1086, or held by William but not by Edward, were or were not ancient demesne.[7] By

1 *De Legibus et Consuetudinibus Angliae* (ed. G. E. Woodbine, 4 vols.; New Haven, 1915–1942), II, 29, 37f.; III, 108f., 131f., 295.

2 *Bracton's Note Book* (ed. F. W. Maitland, 3 vols.; London, 1887), II, 244. See below, footnotes 36 and 79.

3 G. E. Woodbine, ed., *Four Thirteenth Century Law Tracts* (New Haven, 1910).

4 Pollock and Maitland, *Hist. Eng. Law* (2d ed.), I, 384, n.1.

5 *Year Books of the Reign of King Edward the First Years XX and XXI* (ed. A. J. Horwood; London, 1866), pp. xviiif.

6 *Britton: An English Translation and Notes* (ed. and tr. F. M. Nichols, Legal Classics Series; Washington, 1901), p. 344.

7 "Mes ascunes gens entendent que les terres qui furent les demenes le Roy St. Edward sont auncien demene, e autres dient fors les terres que le Conquerour conquist, que furent en la seissin St. Edward le jour quil mourust sont anciene demene" (*Y.B. 15 Edw. II,* p. 455); "Les demesnes qui fuerent en la maine Seint E. sont aunciens demesne, mesque ils fuerent aliens a estraunge mains quant le liver de Domesday se fist" (Fitzherbert, Abr. Monstraver. 4, from Y.B. Trin. 49 Edw. III, pl. 8). These

the second half of the thirteenth century, however, there is no doubt that a manor was considered to be *de antiquo dominico* if it was listed in Domesday Book, under the rubric *Terra Regis*. On the other hand, it must be insisted that there is no evidence to show that such listing, as held by the king either T.R.E. or T.R.W., was "absolutely required to prove the manor ancient demesne." [8] This is merely an inversion of the rule: all manors listed were ancient demesne, but failure to be listed did not in every case keep a manor from being considered ancient demesne.[9] Eventually, Domesday Book became the exclusive mode of proof of ancient demesne condition, but this is not true of the thirteenth century as a whole.[10]

The general rule followed in the second half of the thirteenth century, then, is that all manors listed under the *Terra Regis* rubric in Domesday Book were considered by the courts to be ancient demesne, while a manor not so listed was presumed not to be unless

---

statements are quoted by Vinogradoff, *Villainage*, p. 90, n.3 and n.4. Vinogradoff seems to have been stretching his evidence, at least so far as the thirteenth century is concerned, when he said that "1066 and not 1086 is the decisive year for the legal formation of this class of manors," and again, "the entry as *Terra Regis*, at least *T.R.E.*, is absolutely required to prove a manor ancient demesne." He also stressed that "the important point evidently was that the Norman king's right in this case bridged over the Conquest" (*ibid.*, p. 90 and n.4).

In the first place, the case he cited in support of these views (*ibid.*, App. V, pp. 422ff.) does not bear out the emphasis on 1066 as the decisive date, or the necessity of William's claim bridging the Conquest: "Mildenehalla dedit Rex Edwardus Sancto Edmundo et post tenuit Stigandus sub Sancto Edmundo in vita Regis Edwardi" (De Banco Roll, Mich., 15 Edw. II, m.271). It was held by both kings, but it "bridged the Conquest" as a manor held by Stigand of the Abbot of St. Edmund's, and formed part of William's *Terra Regis* as an escheat in the custody of William Denvers. The manor was judged to be ancient demesne. In the second place, nothing in Domesday Book would indicate that Edward held, on the day he was alive and dead, the manors of Havering, Hatfield Regis, Newport, or Writtle, in Essex, or Hitchin, in Hertfordshire, or King's Ripton, in Huntingdonshire. But they are listed under *Terra Regis* (except King's Ripton) and were never doubted to be ancient demesne, once the phrase came into use.

[8] *Ibid.*, p. 90, n.4.

[9] As Maitland observed, "No one . . . could discover from that record that the manor of King's Ripton was ancient demesne; probably it is there reckoned as a member of an adjoining manor, still its lord when at war with his refractory tenants raised no question as to its quality" (*Hist. Eng. Law* [2d ed.], I, 399, n.1). Vinogradoff treated both King's Ripton and Havering as ancient demesne, although they both fail to meet his "absolute" requirement.

[10] *Ibid.*, I, 399, n.1.

proof to the contrary were forthcoming or the point went uncontested. This general rule is suggestive in two ways. In the first place, the royal courts were enforcing a rule which contradicted feudal law in the sense that a manor granted in fee and inheritance two centuries earlier could be called the demesne of the grantor, his "ancient" demesne, and in some ways his demesne right could still be exercised. This was an assertion which only the king could make and enforce; it could come from no feudal right of lordship, and no feudal lord but the lord king asserted it. In the second place, the rule, if taken literally, simply denied reality: the king's *ancient* demesne would presumably mean that part of the royal demesne which he had long possessed, for example, since the Conquest. But the effect of the rule was the reverse: the *ancient* demesne was actually something much larger than the royal demesne. It consisted, in small measure, of manors in the king's hands, but much more so it was made up of manors which had long been alienated, either in fee farm or in demesne as of fee, for never again after 1087 was the royal demesne so large as it was under William the Conqueror. Thus, conceivably, a manor alienated two centuries earlier was ancient demesne, while one which had escheated to the crown and had remained in the king's hands since 1088 was not ancient demesne.

Such a rule would be easily explained, or easily accepted, if it be assumed that "the manors of St. Edward" or the manors held by the Conqueror were *always,* from 1066, or at least 1086, onwards, considered to be ancient demesne—i.e., considered to be distinguished, as an entity, from the rest of the royal demesne, whether called ancient demesne by name or not, and even though there might be much elaboration of the peculiarities of ancient demesne.[11] We have already found reason to doubt that any such distinction antedates the reign of Henry II. There are other difficulties which must be met before such an assumption may be accepted.

First, there is the rule about consulting Domesday Book, with respect to ancient demesne. The appearance and adoption of this rule can be dated approximately, and its exclusive use was not

[11] This assumption underlies Vinogradoff's whole treatment of ancient demesne. In addition to references cited above, see *The Growth of the Manor* (3rd ed., rev.; London, 1920), pp. 354ff.

only late in developing, but the practice of consulting Domesday at all was late. In the judicial records of the reign of John and of the early years of Henry III, there is much litigation concerning royal manors or the tenants within them, litigation which in the reign of Edward I would often lead to an inspection of Domesday Book because the manors involved were such as would be called, under Edward I, manors of the ancient demesne. And yet, Domesday Book is never consulted. So far as I know, the earliest published case concerned with privileges of ancient demesne, in which a litigant put himself upon "the book called Domesday" in order to prove that a given tenement or manor was or was not either royal demesne, formerly royal demesne, or ancient demesne, is the case of the men of Witley who claimed to be sokemen of ancient demesne, already noticed.[12] This case was held before the justiciar Hugh Bigod in 1258 and adjourned by him to the Candlemas parliament of 1259. But the rule was by no means established by 1258. The Witley case seems to be an exception. In the same eyre of Hugh Bigod, a case between two tenants of the king's manor of Aylesbury, in Buckinghamshire, turned on the point of whether Aylesbury were ancient demesne. The defendant claimed that it was, and the testimony of the jury of twelve settled the case in his favor.[13] In a

12 Peter of Savoy, the defendant, says that the men of Witley "can have no action against him as sokemen of ancient demesne etc., because he says that the manor of Witley never was the king's demesne of the crown. . . . And as to the truth of this, he puts himself on the book called Domesday" (Richardson and Sayles, *Proc. without Writ,* pp. 91f.)

An earlier unpublished case, on a Yorkshire Eyre Roll of Thurkelby's circuit in 1251, recites the record of a case two years earlier in which the tenants of a manor put themselves on Domesday in an unsuccessful effort to prove ancient demesne (P.R.O., Assize Roll No. 1046, m.22). This is the earliest instance I am aware of; one would expect the first references to Domesday in this connection to appear in the records of the central courts, and it is interesting that the record recited in this Yorkshire Eyre Roll is alleged to be contained in a Curia Regis Roll which no longer survives. I have searched the surviving rolls of the Justices of the Bench and of the court held Coram Rege, of the period before 1250, and have found no other instance. In 1250 a case hinged on whether the manor of Chalgrove, Oxfordshire, were ancient demesne, and the sheriff was directed to hold an inquest *in pleno comitatu* to determine the issue; the inquest was held and the result recorded on the plea roll (P.R.O., Curia Regis Roll No. 137, m.14). I owe the reference to the Yorkshire Eyre Roll to the kindness of Mr. E. W. Denham, of the Public Record Office.

13 "Et Willelmus . . . dicit quod manerium de Ayllesbir' est antiquum dominicum Domini Regis de corona . . . Et xii jurati super sacramentum suum hoc idem testantur" (*Plac. Abbrev.,* p. 148).

still earlier case, the sheriff is directed to hold an inquest as to whether a manor is ancient demesne.[14]

The implications of these legal records are fully borne out by the Close Roll entries dealing with tallage. In writ after writ, the sheriff is directed to see that the tenant of a manor had his reasonable tallage if the manor were of the ancient demesne and were accustomed to being tallaged.[15] Both of these facts could have been established without much difficulty by the Exchequer, which had both Domesday Book and the Pipe Rolls and other records at its disposal. The only inference possible is that the customary or routine method was to refer such questions to a local jury. Even so late as 1270, the Exchequer was using local juries to determine the fact of ancient demesne; [16] but after the accession of Edward I, and particularly after 1274, the normal method of determining ancient demesne was by reference to Domesday Book.[17] It is tempting to connect this development with the second and fourth articles of the great inquest of 1274, by which the government inquired into alienated manors and tenements of the ancient demesne and by what warrant such lands were held. The best defense against the allegation of a jury would be the calling of Domesday to witness, and the superiority of the record over the inquest would be quickly established.[18]

---

14 "Ideo preceptum est vicecomiti ad inquirendum si predictum manerium est antiquum dominicum Regis" (*ibid.*, p. 119). On the following page, however, the sheriff is said to have been ordered to inquire *per sacramentum* whether the same manor *fuit dominicum alicujus Regis.*

15 For example, "Quia rex dominica sua per angliam ad presens facit talliari, mandatum est vicecomiti Hunt' quod, si manerium de Herford fuerit antiquum dominicum regis vel predecessorum suorum, regum Anglie, et hactenus talliari consueverit in tallagiis dominicorum regis, tunc priori de Hunt' racionabilem tallagium suum habere faciat . . ." (*Cl.R. 1264–1268* [P.R.O.; London, 1937], p. 476). This instance is from the year 1268.

16 *Cl.R. 1268–1272* (P.R.O.; London, 1938), pp. 193f.

17 For example, "scrutato Domesdei non est antiquum dominicum" (*Plac. Abbrev.*, p. 185); "non sunt tenentes in antiquo dominico per Domesdei" (*ibid.*, p. 188); "scrutato libro de Domesday" (*ibid.*, p. 191); "per librum de Domesdei" (*ibid.*, p. 194); "ponit se super Domesday" (*ibid.*, p. 197); "per Domesdei," "scrutato libro de Domesdei" (*ibid.*, p. 198); "per librum de Domesdei" (*ibid.*, p. 207); "profert librum de Domesday sub sigillo scaccarii" (*ibid.*, p. 222); "per Domesdei" (*ibid.*, p. 228). All but one of these cases are later than 1274.

18 "In quo waranto versus Simonem de Monte Acuto pro manerio de Chedesey quod supponitur esse de antiquo dominico &c. Scrutato libro de Domesdey non reperitur esse. Ideo dictus Simon sine die" (*ibid.*, p. 198 [Easter, 1280]).

Be that as it may, the main point to notice is that inspection of Domesday Book does not seem to become the normal way to establish ancient demesne condition until the reign of Edward I, though it goes back at least to 1250. Now the fact that this practical equivalence of the Domesday *Terra Regis* and what was called *antiquum dominicum* becomes regularized well after, and finally replaces, the system of ordering the sheriff to hold a local inquest to determine the same fact invites further inquiry. If the ancient demesne from the beginning were the manors of St. Edward, why was not Domesday Book from the beginning the only test? Domesday Book was cited in law suits from at least the beginning of the twelfth century; as will be seen in a moment, practically from the beginning of judicial records in England there are cases which turn on the single point, whether or not royal demesne or, later, whether or not ancient demesne. If there always had been an ancient demesne (even though not called by that name) which corresponded with the Domesday *Terra Regis,* why did it take over half a century for the law courts to learn to use the record itself to establish the fact at issue?

These considerations raise some doubt as to the validity of the received doctrine on ancient demesne, but it must be allowed that by themselves they do not prove anything. One fact that seems to have been overlooked by every previous discussion of the ancient demesne may lead to a more definite conclusion. This is the late appearance of the phrase *antiquum dominicum* itself. The conditions, issues at trial, or peculiarities found in the legal and other evidence concerning manors which in 1300 are called ancient demesne are recognizable (even though differently expressed, perhaps) in evidence relating to the same manors shortly after 1200. Probably for this reason, it has been assumed that those manors were "ancient" demesne in 1200, even though they are not so termed. Strictly, the evidence would allow them only to be called *dominicum regis.*[19]

Turning to the Close Rolls, we can trace the phrase *antiquum dominicum* back through the writs of tallage by which sheriffs were directed to allow tenants of royal manors to have tallage when the

[19] For example, Vinogradoff, *Villainage,* p. 96 and n.1, where a rule noted in the margin of Bracton's Note Book concerning a *manerium quod solet esse de dominico domini Regis* is interpreted as applying to any "tenement in ancient demesne."

king tallaged his demesnes. The further back these writs are traced, the more apparent it becomes that *antiquum dominicum* is only an alternative way of describing a manor. In the last years of Henry III, the phrase is usual; in the 1250's it occurs as often as some other descriptive phrase; but in the 1240's it is only exceptionally and rarely employed.[20] Thus, in 1255, Robert de Brus is allowed his tallage of Writtle and Hatfield, *si eadem maneria fuerint antiqua dominica regis;* [21] in 1252, he has his tallage of the same manors *si fuerint dominicum regis vel predecessorum suorum regum Anglie.*[22] So also, the Abbot of Stoneleigh had his tallage from the manor of Stoneleigh, *si aliquando fuerit dominicum regis vel predecessorum suorum,*[23] in 1255, while in 1252 he had it *si manerium de Stanleg' fuerit antiquum dominicum regis.*[24] So also, Aylesbury is styled *antiquum dominicum regis vel predecessorum suorum,* in 1255,[25] and *aliquando dominicum regis vel predecessorum suorum,* in 1252,[26] while the same idea is expressed when the roll says of Uxbridge, *quod antiquitus fuit dominicum predecessorum regis regum Anglie.*[27]

These citations suggest that the essence of *antiquum* was the same as *aliquando* or *antiquitus* when it modified *dominicum:* the point to be stressed was whether or not the manor was formerly in the royal demesne, and with regard to earlier usage, the adverbial form is almost invariably used in preference to the adjectival expression of the idea. Of the manors of St. Edward or the Domesday *Terra Regis* there is not the slightest hint.

The legal records confirm the impression gained from the Close Rolls. References to ancient demesne grow rarer, the earlier the records. The only difference is that the phrase appears about a

---

20 I have found the phrase only once in the Close Rolls prior to 1251. It occurs as *anticum dominicum* in a writ of tallage dated 1 April 1242 (*Cl.R. 1237–1242,* p. 408).

21 *Cl.R. 1254–1256* (P.R.O.; London, 1931), p. 57.

22 *Cl.R. 1251–1253* (P.R.O.; London, 1927), p. 168.

23 *Cl.R. 1254–1256,* pp. 64f.

24 *Cl.R. 1251–1253,* p. 165.

25 *Cl.R. 1254–1256,* p. 108.

26 *Cl.R. 1251–1253,* p. 134.

27 *Cl.R. 1253–1254* (P.R.O.; London, 1929), p. 14.

decade earlier in the plea rolls than in the Chancery enrolments. The itinerant justices holding pleas of the crown at Exeter in 1248–1249 were told by the jurors that Diptford, in Devonshire, *fuit de antiquo dominico domini regis,*[28] while in Leicestershire, in 1247, the jurors presented that Great Bowden *fuit antiquitus dominicum regis.*[29] In each case the itinerant justices wanted to know the value of the manor and by what warrant it was held. In 1244, Newbury, Berkshire, was called *vetus dominicum regis;*[30] in a plea before the archbishop of York and the king's council in 1242, Wytemore under Lyme was called *antiquum dominicum domini regis* on one rotulet of the record, while on another the question was whether it were ever *dominicum alicujus regis.*[31] From the roll of the itinerant justices holding pleas and assizes at Exeter in 1238 comes a very early mention of *antiquum dominicum.* In one case a tenement is alleged to have been *antiquum dominicum domini regis,* while in another case on the same roll a vill is said to be *dominicum domini regis.*[32] Three years later, the roll of the justices at Reading is full of references to *antiquum dominicum,* but there are occasional variations, such as *antiquum manerium et dominicum regis* or *villenagium domini regis,* which clearly mean the same thing.[33] Before the 1240's the phrase is extremely rare. Even in the case cited from 1238, the word *antiquum* has been interlined and may be a later addition to the record. Earlier still, the same meaning is expressed in a variety of ways, some reminiscent of the later *antiquum dominicum.* For example, Milborne Port, Somerset, is called *antiquitus dominicum domini regis,* in 1212. This recalls the usage of the chronicler and of the writ of 1 June 1212 concerning the great inquest of that year: *quae terrae essent de dominico praedecessorum suorum regum antiquitus,* and *de tenementis omnibus que antiquitus de nobis aut de progenitoribus . . . teneri solent,* although the latter, as has been seen, did not refer to the royal demesne.[34] The

28 *Book of Fees,* II, 1426.
29 *Ibid.,* II, 1393.
30 *Ibid.,* II, 1154.
31 *Plac. Abbrev.,* pp. 119f.
32 P.R.O., Ass. Roll No. 174, membranes 3 and 15. See Appendix E, nos. 15 and 16.
33 P.R.O., Ass. Roll No. 37, mm. 24 and 22d. See Appendix E, nos. 18 and 19.
34 *Book of Fees,* I, 152. See above, pp. 151f.

normal usage of this earlier period, however, is simply *dominicum regis,* though occasional variations, such as *manerium corone,* occur.[35]

In both the legal and administrative records, then, the ancient demesne conceived as the Domesday *Terra Regis* makes a late appearance. In the middle of the century, first in the plea rolls and then in the Chancery enrolments, the phrase itself begins to appear, though it is only one of several ways of describing a manor.[36] The essential meaning of the phrase is suggested by the adverbial form in which the idea is sometimes expressed: a manor which is *antiquum dominicum* is one which was formerly *(antiquitus, aliquando)* part of the royal demesne, or formerly in the king's hands. Finally, this evidence indicates that the government takes an interest in lands or manors so described because the point is raised in its law courts, because such manors are subject to tallage, and because itinerant justices hold inquests into alienated royal demesne.

THE THEORY OF SURVIVAL

It may be objected that the evidence so far presented avoids the heart of the problem, that the essential characteristic of ancient demesne was not the name but the tenure peculiar to it and the privileges connected therewith. This objection must be met before any final estimate of the constitutional significance of the ancient demesne can be attempted, for it is ancient demesne tenure—the legal conditions within ancient demesne manors—which have been portrayed as the connecting link between the Conquest and the matured legal doctrine of Edward I's day. Vinogradoff stated the

---

[35] *Book of Fees,* II, 1324ff.

[36] The very earliest occurrences of the phrase *antiquum dominicum* refer not to manors at all, but rather to the demesne of the manor, in the narrow sense. A distinction is drawn between the old demesne and new land added to the demesne (from the villeins' land or from essarts). Thus, a concord about tithes between the Templars and the monks of Sele disposes of the tithes *de antiquo dominio* (*sic*) of Shipley, Sussex, in 1181 (Lees, *Records of the Templars,* p. 230); the Worcester Cartulary records the work which the peasants must accomplish *de antiquo dominico* of a manor (Vinogradoff, *Villainage,* p. 182, n.2, quoting the Cartulary, l.c.); and in 1228 a tenement is claimed not to be *de antiquo dominico eiusdem manerii* by the plaintiff in support of his plea that, although the manor *fuit de dominico domini regis,* his father was enfeoffed with a free tenement and therefore the assize should be taken (*Bracton's Note Book,* II, 244).

currently accepted view that ancient demesne tenure had a pre-Conquest origin, despite procedural or terminological changes which created or defined the privileges of that tenure in later years:

> Ancient demesne socage was connected in principle with the condition of things in Saxon times, immediately before the Conquest. The courts had to impose limitations in order to control evidence; the whole institution was in a way created by limitation, because it restricted itself to the T.R.E. of Domesday as the only acceptable test of Saxon condition. But notwithstanding all these features imposed by the requirements of procedure, ancient demesne drew its origin distinctly from pre-Conquest conditions. . . . Although there is no doubt that this tenure grew up and developed several of its peculiarities after the Conquest, it had to fall back on Saxon times for its substance, which may be described in few words—legal protection of the peasantry. The influence of Norman lawyers was exercised in shaping out certain actionable rights.[37]

The privileges of ancient demesne have been set forth in detail by Vinogradoff and Maitland [38] and need not concern us here, except as they might bear on the origins or constitutional significance of the ancient demesne. The real point at issue is the essence, or "substance," of ancient demesne tenure, "legal protection of the peasantry."

It may be said at once that the concept of rights which are made actionable by writs may be logical, but it is not historical. The growth of law in England, as elsewhere, was largely procedural in its beginnings. The historical development of the common law was the creation of rights out of writs governing procedure. We shall have to notice carefully, then, whether there are any signs of legal protection of tenants of "the manors of St. Edward" which are not due to, or which precede (as Vinogradoff believed), the specific procedural remedies peculiar to ancient demesne.

In the second place, the concept of limitation is the crux of Vinogradoff's argument. There are two aspects of this argument, and with one (the most important one for a discussion of the social and legal conditions within ancient demesne manors) we cannot

---

[37] Vinogradoff, *Villainage in England,* p. 123; quotation used by permission of the Clarendon Press, Oxford.

[38] *Ibid.,* pp. 89–126; Pollock and Maitland, *Hist. Eng. Law* (2d ed.), I, 383–406.

here be concerned. This is the general condition of the Anglo-Saxon peasantry which was allegedly preserved upon, and limited to, the ancient demesne—the "stock of freedom" on the ancient demesne in the thirteenth and fourteenth centuries "which speaks of Saxon tradition." [39] With the second aspect, however, we are directly concerned: the reasons, the nature, and the results of the limitation of ancient demesne to the *Terra Regis* of Domesday Book. Part of the answer to this problem has already emerged from the foregoing review of the term *antiquum dominicum* as it appears in thirteenth century documents. What Vinogradoff does not seem to have noticed is that, so far from limitation (except in the strictest legal sense of that word), the Domesday rule effected a substantial enlargement of the area comprehended by ancient demesne. This fact alone is enough to suggest that the monarchy need not be portrayed in the anomalous terms of conservatism based on moral responsibility as the guarantor of ancient demesne privileges. It will be important to notice, then, whether there was any relation between the development of ancient demesne privileges (and their "limitation" to the Domesday *Terra Regis*) and the royal policy of consolidation, exploitation, and control of the royal demesne—a policy hardly conservative—which has already been discussed.

Before turning to the legal records which throw light upon the conditions and privileges of tenants on royal manors, the statements of Glanvill and Bracton on the subject may be compared. In the first place, there is no doubt that Bracton was aware of certain privileges and peculiarities *de dominico domini regis et de condicione personarum tenentium de dominico*.[40] His statements on the subject are clear. They all concern status and tenure, or else they treat of exceptions to writs because of status or mode of tenure. So far as his actual words go, Bracton makes no specific reference to *antiquum dominicum:* he speaks only of the demesne of the lord king, the royal demesne. He makes no reference whatever to Domesday Book as having anything to do with the *dominicum regis* on which these peculiarities occur, although there is a reference to the Conquest in that connection. This reference is vital. Bracton says,

[39] *Villainage,* p. 137.

[40] *De Leg. et Cons.,* fol. 7; other references to the royal demesne occur on foll. 4b, 7b, 200, 208b, 209, 272 (ed. Woodbine, II, 29, 37f.; III, 108f., 131f., 295).

when speaking of the assize of novel disseisin, that free men holding in villeinage *recuperare non poterunt ut liberum tenementum cum sit villenagium, et cadit assisa.*[41] Then he goes on to say that in addition to free men holding in villeinage,

> Est etiam aliud genus villenagii quod tenetur de domino rege a conquestu Angliae quod dicitur socagium villanum, et quod est villenagium sed tamen privilegiatum. Habent itaque tenentes de dominicis domini regis tale privilegium quod a gleba amoveri non debent quamdiu velint et possent debitum facere servitium. . . . Et huiusmodi villani sokemanni proprie dicuntur glebae ascriptitii. Villana autem faciunt servitia sed certa et determinata.[42]

Leaving aside for the moment his reference to the Conquest, it is clear that his main point is that these villein sokemen are excluded from the assize (although his description of their condition leads him astray from this main point), and he does not need to stress this in so many words, for he had just finished making the point on a preceding folio. He has just said that a free man holding in free socage of the king's demesne by feoffment

> recuperabit per assisam eo non obstante quod faciat talia servitia, quia tenet libere. Si autem in socagio sicut de dominico domini regis, licet servitia certa sint, obstabit exceptio villenagii quia talis sokemannus liberum tenementum non habet quia tenet nomine alieno,[43]

and still earlier, speaking of personal status of tenants of the royal demesne, Bracton had covered the same points:

> Fuerunt etiam in conquestu liberi homines qui libere tenuerunt tenementa sua per libera servitia, vel liberas consuetudines, et cum per potentiores eiecti essent, postmodum reversi receperunt eadem tenementa sua tenenda in villenagio, faciendo inde opera servilia, sed certa et nominata. Qui quidem dicuntur glebae ascripticii, et nihilominus liberi, quia licet faciant opera servilia, tamen non faciunt ea ratione personarum sed ratione tenementorum. Et ideo assisam novae disseisinae non habebunt, quia tenementum est villenagium, quamvis privilegiatum, sed nec assisam mortis antecessoris, sed tantum parvum breve de recto secundum consuetudinem manerii.[44]

---

[41] *Ibid.*, fol. 208b (ed. Woodbine, III, 131).

[42] *Ibid.*, fol. 209 (ed. Woodbine, III, 132).

[43] *Ibid.*, fol. 200 (ed. Woodbine, III, 108).

[44] *Ibid.*, fol. 7 (ed. Woodbine, II, 37).

When all these statements are read together, and in context without separating the descriptive and speculative from the legal exposition,[45] it becomes clear that Bracton never speaks of the privileges of villein sokemen of the royal demesne except with regard to actions or remedies from which they are excluded or the writs and plaints [46] by which their privileges are made good. And yet Bracton, like the villeins of Henry de Tracy of Tavistock, *qui nunquam fuerunt in manu Domini Regis nec antecessorum suorum et loquebantur de tempore Regis Eadwardi,*[47] also spoke of the Conquest when explaining the origin of villein sokemen's privileges. In short, Bracton's allusions to the Conquest are but a rationalization or theoretical justification of the law as he knew it and stated it. Appeals to custom, to the past, especially to well-known and important events, are the stock in trade of medieval rationalization of the present. Is Bracton to be taken seriously as a historian, or is he to be understood as justifying a new thing by an appeal to the past?

Vinogradoff, who with a somewhat uneasy faith relied upon the historicity of Bracton's statements,[48] himself pointed out that villein sokemen are to be found outside the royal demesne.[49] But Bracton does not mention them. Is his authority on events which were remote by a century and a half to be given greater weight than on conditions of his own time? It may, however, be allowed that this argument does no more than raise a doubt.

More important and decisive is the fact that the villein sokemen who Bracton alleges *tenent de domino rege a conquestu* are unknown to Glanvill. Of privileges to be found on royal demesne, there is not a word in Glanvill, and, needless to say, he never mentions ancient demesne. Although he treats at some length of villeins, he never mentions villein sokemen; [50] although he discusses the as-

---

45 For example, Vinogradoff, *Villainage,* pp. 89, n.2, 95, n.2, 109, 115, n.1, 121.

46 The little writ of right close; also, *unde si tales cum aliis querantur non dabitur eis privilegium,* this concerning the *adventitii* who hold by convention and enjoy certainty of services and tenure only *tantum sua conventione,* in contrast to villein sokemen (Bracton, fol. 209 [ed. Woodbine, III, 132]); and *vel aliud breve formatum* (fol. 272 [ed. Woodbine, III, 295]).

47 A marginal note by Bracton (seemingly) in his *Note Book,* III, 250.

48 *Villainage,* pp. 121f., 136.

49 *Ibid.,* pp. 197–203.

50 *De Legibus,* Book V (ed. Woodbine, pp. 83–87).

sizes, he does not exclude villein sokemen from them, as does Bracton.[51] It is true that Glanvill mentions free sokemen, just as Bracton does, and Maitland believed that "the free sokemen whom he has in view . . . are to be found chiefly on the ancient demesne of the crown." [52] Even if this were true, it merely emphasizes the fact that Glanvill had opportunities to mention the villein sokemen, even casually (in connection with villeinage, in connection with writs, and in contrast with free sokemen), but he did not.[53]

It may be objected that Glanvill's treatise is a short, technical manual, dealing primarily with the new assizes, and that there is no reason to find in his work any remarks corresponding with Bracton's. This objection can be met without hesitation, and with assurance. Glanvill discussed the question of the partibility of the estates of free sokemen, and we are assured by the very highest authority that Bracton "had Glanvill's text before him" and "uses almost the selfsame words" in his treatment of the same subject and, further, that "after Glanvill's day there was no further change in the law" on that matter.[54] Turning to the relevant passages,[55] we find *almost* the same words in Bracton, but not quite—and the difference is crucial. That there has been no change in the law concerning free sokemen is clear from the close parallel of thought and even the words used. But Bracton has added a sentence, and it is an obvious addition to the discussion of Glanvill: "Si autem fuerit socagium villanum, tunc consuetudo loci erit observanda." It should be noted that this is the only addition Bracton has to offer to Glanvill's discussion. In Bracton's eyes, Glanvill's treatment was quite satisfactory for his own day, save for the need to mention a class of sokemen whom Glanvill did not seem to know.

Confining ourselves to the evidence, the best explanation would seem to be that the class of villein sokemen of which Bracton has much to say, but which Glanvill did not mention, was a new class. It was a class which may have been forming on royal manors in

[51] *Ibid.*, XIII, 11, 12 (ed. Woodbine, pp. 161ff.).

[52] *Hist. Eng. Law* (2d ed.), II, 269.

[53] *De Legibus* (ed. Woodbine), pp. 101f., 104, 107, 109.

[54] Pollock and Maitland, *Hist. Eng. Law* (2d ed.), II, 269f., 270, n.1; see also, Glanvill, *De Legibus* (ed. Woodbine), p. 227.

[55] Glanvill, VII, 3, and Bracton, fol. 76; the two passages are printed side by side in *Hist. Eng. Law* (2d ed.), II, 270, n.1.

Glanvill's time—this much may be granted. But it was not significant enough to mention in a context which invited some reference, in a context which led Bracton to make his only change in Glanvill's discussion of partibility.

It may be admitted that this argument is negative, based upon silence rather than assertion, and negative evidence may often be explained away satisfactorily. The burden of proof, however, has been shifted to those who would derive ancient demesne condition from "pre-Conquest conditions." Why did not Glanvill mention villein sokemen if he knew they existed? Now the interesting thing is that the historians who treat ancient demesne as "a remnant of the condition of things before the Conquest," [56] a survival of privileged villeinage to be found upon the very numerous, large, well-populated, and widespread manors of the Domesday *Terra Regis* —these historians are as silent about Glanvill as he is about the ancient demesne which they (but apparently not he) thought existed in his day.

Vinogradoff does seem to have recognized the need for some twelfth century evidence which would show continuity between the Conquest and the thirteenth century records. He was able to find only two sources which seemed to have a bearing on his subject, however, and both of his attempts were unfortunate. In the first place, he appealed to the passage in the Dialogue of the Exchequer which gives an account of the formation of villeinage.[57] But here there is no mention of villein sokemen, or even of the royal demesne, as Vinogradoff admitted. On the other hand, as we have seen, the Dialogue frequently mentions financial administration and administrative reforms which touched the royal demesne, but it never takes the opportunity to mention any distinction between "ancient" and other royal demesne, or any privileges or peculiarities affecting tenants of royal manors. Of villein sokemen, of course, it speaks not at all.

Vinogradoff's second effort to bring some twelfth century evidence to bear on the survival of Anglo-Saxon conditions on an alleged ancient demesne was even more unfortunate. This concerns the enfranchisement of fugitive villeins who remain upon privi-

56 Vinogradoff, *Villainage*, p. 124.

57 *Scac. Dial.*, pp. 100f.

leged soil for a year and a day. What was this privileged soil? According to Sir Edward Coke, to whom Vinogradoff refers, "If a villeine remaine in the ancient demeane of the King a year and a day without claime or seizure of the Lord, the Lord cannot have a Writ of Nativo habendo, or seize him so long as he remains and continues there . . . and herewith agree old bookes. . . ." [58] The "old bookes" which Coke cites agree with this statement, except that they speak of "our demesnes" or "demesne lands" [59] or "demesnes of the king" [60] and do not mention in this connection any "ancient demesne," and also except for one "old booke," Glanvill. Turning to the fifth chapter of the fifth book of Glanvill's treatise, which Coke cites, we find a straightforward generalization which is specific and detailed:

> Pluribus autem modis perduci potest ad libertatem aliquis in vilenagio positus. . . . Item si quis nativus quiete per unum annum et unum diem in aliqua villa privilegiata manserit, ita quod in eorum communam scilicet gildam tamquam civis receptus fuerit, eo ipso a vilenagio liberabitur.[61]

In Glanvill, there is no mention of royal manors, only *villa privilegiata* which possess gilds and receive strangers into them as "citizens." It is clear that Glanvill applied the rule only to chartered boroughs. Between Glanvill and the later thirteenth century law tracts, a change has occurred: the privilege has been extended to the demesnes of the king. We can date this change more narrowly by reference to Bracton, who in treating this rule refers to fugitive villeins who might be *manentes in civitate aliqua vel villa privilegiata vel dominico domini regis per unum annum et unum diem sine clamio*.[62] Bracton's distinction makes it clear that Glanvill's *villa privilegiata* cannot refer to royal manors or even royal demesne, as such, although most privileged towns would of course get their privileges from the king and (at least later) be considered to be an important part of the royal demesne.

---

[58] *The First Part of the Institutes of the Laws of England or a Commentarie upon Littleton* (2d ed.; London, 1629), p. 137b.

[59] Britton, I, 32 (ed. F. M. Nichols, L.C.S., pp. 165, 172).

[60] *The Mirror of Justices* (ed. W. J. Whittaker, Selden Society, vol. VII; London, 1895), p. 78.

[61] Ed. Woodbine, pp. 86f.

[62] *De Leg. et Cons.*, fol. 190b (ed. Woodbine, III, 85).

With somewhat less assurance, we can narrow the gap within which the extension of this privilege to all the royal demesne took place. A collection of laws which Liebermann dated c.1210, the so-called *Willelmi Articuli Londoniis Retracti,* includes the following provision: "Item si serui permanserint sine callumpnia per annum et diem in ciuitatibus nostris uel in burgis nostris muro uallatis uel in castellis nostris, a die illa liberi homines efficiuntur, et liberi a iugo seruitutis suae sint in perpetuum." [63] The change from this statement of the rule, restricting the privilege to urban areas, to its wider application on the whole of the royal demesne comes at least as early as the year 1238, for in that year the king ordered the sheriff of Shropshire to proceed with a case concerning a fugitive villein, unless the latter had remained unclaimed in the royal demesne of Worfield for a year and a day:

> Precipimus tibi quod, nisi Alex' de Wyghunhull', quem Hughelina Mustell' clamat nativum suum in comitatu tuo per breve nostrum, manserit in dominico nostro de Wurefeld' per unum annum et unum diem et sine calumpnia, non remaneat loquela predicta in comitatu tuo eo quod mansit in dominico nostro per minus tempus.[64]

All this evidence points in the same direction. The rule of a year and a day, the privilege which Sir Edward Coke applied to the ancient demesne, is never mentioned by thirteenth century sources in connection with ancient demesne; it is never mentioned by twelfth century sources with reference to any but privileged urban areas; and sometime between the composition of Glanvill's and Bracton's treatises—perhaps in the last years of John or the early years of Henry III—the privilege is extended to the whole royal demesne, urban and rural. This is just the period, as we have seen, when the consolidation, exploitation, and control of the royal demesne by the central government were leading to the idea that royal demesne should not be alienated, to the distinction between crown and king and between a "permanent" and "casual" demesne, and to the enhancement and extension of the king's demesne right.

Now let us return to Vinogradoff's brief treatment of the rule of a year and a day. He states: "A villain was freed also, as is well

[63] *Gesetze,* I, 491.

[64] *Cl.R. 1237–1242,* p. 104.

known, by remaining for a year and a day on the privileged soil of a crown manor or a chartered town." [65] In addition to citing Coke (as noted above), he refers to two writs, one of Henry I and one of Henry II, both in favor of the Abbot of Abingdon and preserved in the Abingdon chronicle. These references (and the passage in the Dialogue of the Exchequer already discussed) are the only evidence antedating the thirteenth century which he adduces in support of the theory that ancient-demesne privileges survived from pre-Conquest conditions.

It will be noticed that Vinogradoff did not quote Glanvill, whose authority contradicts rather than supports his reference to "a crown manor," as we have seen. Now it must be determined whether the writs he does cite support Glanvill or Vinogradoff. These two writs are early forms of what is called, in one manuscript of Glanvill, the *breve de nativis et fugitivis* and is later known as the *breve de nativo habendo*. Glanvill gives the writ in full:

> Rex vicecomiti salutem. Praecipio tibi quod iuste et sine dilatione facias habere M. R. nativum suum et fugitivum suum cum omnibus catallis suis et cum tota sequela sua ubicumque inventus fuerit in ballia tua, nisi sit in dominico meo qui fugit de terra sua post primam coronationem meam. Et prohibeo ne quis eum iniuste detineat super forisfacturam meam.[66]

The writ of Henry II is to the same effect: "Praecipio vobis quod . . . faciatis habere Rogero abbati de Abbendonia omnes nativos et fugativos suos . . . ubicumque fuerint in bailliis vestris, nisi sint in dominio meo. . . ." [67] In the first place, it seems clear enough that neither of these writs concerns the year-and-a-day rule. The writ orders the sheriff to return to the claimant his fugitive villein, wherever he may be found, except if he be on the royal demesne. This exception may well be what led to the extension of the rule from privileged vills to the royal demesne as a whole, but it must be remembered that Glanvill, who knows and quotes the writ, does not connect it at all with his specific statement of the year-and-a-day rule. In the second place, it is clear that neither of these writs

[65] *Villainage,* p. 86.

[66] *De Legibus,* XII, 11 (ed. Woodbine, p. 153).

[67] *Chronicon Monasterii de Abingdon* (ed. Joseph Stevenson, 2 vols., R.S.; London, 1858), II, 235, quoted by Bigelow, *Plac. Ang.-Norm.,* p. 220.

draws any distinction between the royal demesne of Domesday Book and any other royal manors, which is the essence of Vinogradoff's theory of survival. Therefore, if there were some privilege implied by the phrase *nisi sit in dominico meo,* it has a royal and not a pre-Conquest origin, so far as this evidence can show. In the third place, neither of these writs either states or suggests that a fugitive villein who fled to the royal demesne might become free.

All three of these considerations apply equally to the writ of Henry I: "Praecipio vobis ut sine aliqua mora faciatis habere Faritio abbati de Abbendona omnes homines suos, qui de terra sua exierunt de Walingeford propter herberiam curiae meae, vel propter alias res . . . ubicumque sint." [68]

The interest of this document lies in the reason put forward for the men's leaving the abbot's land. But before we accept this curious phrase, *propter herberiam curiae meae,* as proof that fugitive villeins remaining unclaimed for a year and a day on a royal manor became free (of course this writ says nothing of the kind), it is well to look at some evidence bearing on the relations of the abbot Faritius with his men. Faritius seems to have had his troubles. The writ which we quote here, and which Vinogradoff relied on, was but one of three writs, all of them dated c.1107, in favor of the abbot on the subject of his fugitives.[69] The first is a general writ to all sheriffs, and the second concerns a fugitive who is supposed to have settled on the land of Robert de Ferrars in Oxfordshire. Now are we to suppose that, because the abbot's villein preferred conditions upon Robert's lands, residence thereon unclaimed for a year and a day would make him free? Certainly not from this evidence. Even though *herberiam* should mean "harboring" in the sense of the protection of a royal manor, that does not imply the harboring of villeins who would be free in a year and a day. And particularly may this be doubted of the abbot's men, who are *homines sui* and not *nativi et fugativi,* and who have left the abbot's land in Wallingford, one of the earliest chartered boroughs in England.[70] Finally, it must be noticed that the three writs concerning Faritius' men who have fled form part of a small collection of writs dealing with difficulties the abbot and his

[68] *Chron. Mon. Abingd.,* II, 82, quoted *ibid.,* pp. 95f.

[69] *Ibid.,* pp. 94ff.

[70] Tait, *Med. Eng. Bor.,* p. 172.

men encountered with the king's foresters,[71] one of whom is a certain Ared or Aretus *falconarius.* Some of the writs are addressed to Ared and the king's foresters; others are witnessed *per Aretum falconarium,* including the one we have quoted above. All in all, it would appear at least as likely that the abbot's men were encroaching upon the king's forest—*propter herberiam curiae meae* [72]—as that they were attracted by some privilege to be found on a royal manor.

To sum up this evidence, then, none of these writs mentions or even encourages the belief that in the twelfth century the year-and-a-day rule was in effect with regard to royal manors, or that there was any distinction between "ancient demesne" and other royal demesne, or that there was any "privileged soil" on a crown manor which might make a villein free under any circumstances. It may be concluded, then, that the evidence on which Vinogradoff relied supports Glanvill's statement but not his own theory of ancient demesne privileges.

There is another argument which would attempt to support the theory of survival in accounting for ancient demesne privileges. This is the argument that the king was "the best of landlords" and that "on the ancient demesne the sokemen multiply; they appear where Domesday knew them not." [73] Maitland observed that the Hundred Rolls again and again show sokemen, both free and villein, upon the manors of the Domesday *Terra Regis,*[74] although Domesday Book itself might never mention them there. The

---

[71] *Chron. Mon. Abingd.,* II, 29f., 78, 81ff., 87, 94f., 113.

[72] Bigelow's Glossary gives "harbouring" as the meaning of *herberia* (*Placita Anglo-Normannica,* p. 323); the *Medieval Latin Word List from British and Irish Sources* (ed. J. H. Baxter and Charles Johnson; London, 1934), p. 202, gives "garden" as the meaning. In a context of forests and foresters, something near the meaning of the *Word List* seems preferable.

This writ presents several difficulties, but their removal would not strengthen Vinogradoff's interpretation, and need not be dealt with here. I am indebted to the kindness of Mr. A. Tompkinson of the University of Manchester for the suggestion that *propter herberiam curiae meae* means "because of the billeting of my household," i.e., that the fugitives were trying to escape the obligation of lodging royal officials, and he justly observes that this interpretation "makes the writ even more irrelevant to the question of ancient demesne privilege." *Herbergaria* or *herbergagium* meant "right of lodging" in the twelfth century (*Word List,* p. 202).

[73] Maitland, *D.B. and Bey.,* p. 66.

[74] *Hist. Eng. Law* (2d ed.), I, 392.

Domesday evidence has already been surveyed, in another connection, and we have found good reason to doubt how good a landlord the king was. We have also found that sokemen, or free men of the soke, of a royal manor could have good reason to flee from, rather than flourish upon, the royal demesne.[75]

THE RISE OF SOKEMEN ON THE ANCIENT DEMESNE

How to account for the sokemen of the ancient demesne of the thirteenth century? Bracton's guidance provides the best approach to the answer. Although all classes are found within the king's demesne manors, free men holding by knight's service or free socage, newcomers holding by convention, and pure villeins, the typical and most numerous class is that of the villein sokeman.[76] Are they essentially sokemen who, having become "manorialized" after the Conquest, are transformed into villeins possessing remnants of a better condition surviving from Saxon times on the ancient demesne of a conservative king? Or are they essentially villeins who, having direct access to the financial and judicial system of an innovating and aggressive monarchy, are so benefited by that access that their condition improves to the point where they are a special class of villeins who have so much certainty of tenure and so many privileges that they resemble sokemen? A close reading of all that Bracton has to say, against the background of the legal records of the first half of the thirteenth century, points clearly to the latter alternative.

Bracton's position is unequivocal: the villein sokemen are *villani et tenuerunt in villano socagio de dominico domini regis,* and their tenure *est etiam aliud genus villenagii . . . est villenagium sed tamen privilegiatum.*[77] Privilege is so typical of these villeins that Bracton stresses the fact that there were, in addition, pure villeins on the king's demesnes, *servi sive nativi . . . qui usque in hodiernum diem* still have uncertain services to perform.[78] In one obscure passage, Bracton seems to be equating (or relating in some way) the distinction between pure and privileged villeinage with the distinc-

[75] See above, pp. 75–80.

[76] *De Leg. et Cons.*, foll. 7, 7b (ed. Woodbine, II, 37f.).

[77] *Ibid.,* foll. 4b, 209 (ed. Woodbine, II, 29; III, 132).

[78] *Ibid.,* fol. 7 (ed. Woodbine, II, 37).

tion between a demesne manor of the king and the demesne land of that manor:

> Item est manerium domini regis et dominicum in manerio, et sic plura genera hominum in manerio, vel quia ab initio vel quia mutato villenagio. Sunt enim in manerio domini regis milites et liberi tenentes per servitium militare et in libero socagio. Sunt etiam adventitii qui tenent eodem modo per conventionem sicut et villani sokemanni, sed tales non habent privilegium sicut alii villani sokemanni, nisi tantum conventionem.[79]

Whether the manorial demesne had anything to do with it or not, this is an exhaustive list, and some important points emerge from Bracton's statement. Villeinage is the only unfree tenure: some villeinage has been so from the beginning, without modification and without privileges; another kind has been transformed into privileged villeinage because of the certainty of the villein sokemen's tenure and services. And then there are the newcomers to the manor who by convention have obtained the status of villein sokemen and participate in their privileges to the extent their conventions or covenants provide. In this account, change and novelty characterize the privileged villeinage of the royal manors—it is *mutatum villenagium* and may be shared by *adventitii* who hold not by custom of the manor but *per conventionem*.[80]

---

[79] *Ibid.*, fol. 209 (ed. Woodbine, III, 132). The distinction between the manorial demesne and the rest of the manor could be a useful point to make in pleading, and this may be what Bracton had in mind. See above, footnote 36, for a case hinging on this issue which Bracton included in his Note Book. An assize of mort d'ancestor was brought by Roger of Hales against the Abbot of Hales, who says that the tenement *fuit de dominico domini regis ubi nulla talis assisa iacet.* Roger does not deny this, but claims the land as a free tenement which, even though within a royal manor, is under the common law, as Bracton says. Roger's argument is that his father was enfeoffed by a certain Agnes; and the Abbot claims that Agnes *neminem potuit inde feoffare,* which she could not, of course, if the land had been part of the manorial demesne. Only the Abbot could enfeoff a tenant with land from his demesne. Roger says that the land *non est de antiquo dominico eiusdem manerii.* He is not denying that the land is "ancient" demesne, but rather trying to support his claim to hold a free tenement. The record continues: *Et quia Rogerus dicit quod pater suus feoffatus fuit de eadem terra, procedat assisa.* For other cases where ancient demesne, or *dominicum regis,* is not denied, but a free tenement is alleged, see Appendix E, nos. 15, 19, 24, and 26.

[80] Britton may have had this passage in mind when he wrote that "sokemanries are lands and tenements which are not held by knight service or by grand or petty

When we turn to the legal records, we find that again they bear out—either directly or in their implications—what Bracton has to say. The earliest plea rolls reveal villeins on the king's manors, villeins who are in some ways quite privileged; but there is no word of villein sokemen or any distinction between one and another kind of royal demesne. The plea rolls of the middle and later thirteenth century begin to mention "sokemen of the king's ancient demesne," and, while they have the same privileges noticed earlier, these are elaborated and defined in more specific terms. The general impression to be derived from a reading of all the legal records available parallels the impression derived from evidence relating to administration and economic exploitation. What is simply *dominicum regis* in the earlier records becomes *antiquum dominicum* in the later; so also the later records begin to mention a distinction between pure villeins and sokemen of the ancient demesne (these latter being the same as Bracton's villein sokemen, distinguished by him and the plea rolls alike from free sokemen).

From the earliest surviving records, it is clear that no assize could be taken concerning lands of the king's villeins; their legal protection did not entail access to the common-law writs. Thus in 1202, two villeins of the manor of Ewell, in Surrey, were in dispute over a tenement, and one of them brought an assize of mort d'ancestor in the king's court. The prior of Merton interceded as one of the defendants, and, having established himself as lord of the manor holding by charter in free alms of the king,

> dicit quod totum manerium illud fuit dominium domini regis Henrici, et omnes qui terras tenent in eo fuerunt villani domini regis et sunt modo villani prioris, sicut prius fuerunt villani domini regis; et dicit quod nunquam solebat fieri assisa vel jurata de terris ejusdem manerii, sicut nec dominicis domini regis, set secundum consuetudinem maneriorum domini regis solebat fieri inter villanos jurata in manerio ipso et non coram justiciariis.[81]

The demandant cannot contradict this, and the judgment is that the assize will not proceed. Like all other villeins, the villeins of the royal demesne are not under the common law but under the custom

serjeanties, but by simple services, as lands enfranchised by us or our predecessors of our ancient demesnes" (Britton, III, 2 [ed. F. M. Nichols, L.C.S., p. 343]).

81 *C.R.R.*, I, 110f.

of the manor. And yet these are no ordinary villeins, for the custom of the manor as determined by a sworn jury of villeins shall settle their disputes—the will of the lord is subordinated to the witness of sworn villeins. Ewell was actually one of the manors which St. Edward held, but this does not enter into the case. What the prior has to establish is that the manor was formerly the demesne of a king. No one *loquebatur de tempore Regis Edwardi,* though here was a case where some one could have; it is *de tempore Regis Henrici*—a king who could innovate and knew how to use a sworn jury—that the prior speaks. Even though the manor had been alienated, the prior does not merely claim the litigants as his villeins and claim his court. He mentions the customs of the king's manors as the alternative to the common law courts. Finally, it may be noted that the demandant in this case later recovered his land in the prior's court at Ewell, and the fact is recorded on the roll of the king's court.[82] This betokens an interest in the king's former villeins which other plea rolls bear out.

That villeinage and not the fact of royal demesne excluded the Ewell case from the royal court is indicated by a plea concerning services for a tenement in Havering, Essex, which was begun and terminated in the king's court at Westminster in 1199 by a writ of right. During the proceedings a local inquest was ordered to determine the service due and whether the tenement were free, which it was.[83] A little later, the king's court entertained a plea concerning a tenement in Cobham, Kent. Some very interesting allegations are made. The sheriff intervened and *petiit inde curiam de Cobham, que est manerium in dominico domini regis et ubi nullum duellum debet esse.* The defendant denied that Cobham was the king's demesne, because it had been the demesne of the Bishop of Bayeux in the time of Henry I, as an escheat in the king's hands, and the king had granted the manor to Geoffrey de Quatre Mares, whose heirs still held the manor in demesne. None of these statements can the demandant contradict, so the king's court retains jurisdiction of the case.

In addition to all this, however, the defendant makes a statement which throws light on the origins of the privileges of the royal

---

[82] *Ibid.,* III, 267f.

[83] *Ibid.,* I, 77; see also, *ibid.,* VI, 68.

demesne. He says that *Cobham non est dominicum regis, set consuetudines dominicorum domini regis debent fieri placitate de tenementis in predicta villa, quia . . . fuit in escaeta domini regis.*[84] This statement is part of the defendant's plea which the demandant cannot contradict. Cobham is not a "manor of St. Edward" and thus cannot derive its *consuetudines dominicorum* from "pre-Conquest conditions" preserved upon the Domesday *Terra Regis* by a conservative monarchy. It acquired them by passing through the king's hands. Again, royal demesne and not ancient demesne is the criterion, and the royal court which has cognizance of the case (because the tenement, presumably, was free) is asked to recognize the customs of the royal demesne. From the meager report, it is impossible to determine what alternative to the duel the sheriff had to offer, but it is clear that the defendant thought of the customs of the king's demesnes as preferable to the alternative the sheriff had in mind and that the central court could take cognizance of those customs.

The essence of the legal protection provided for villeins of the royal demesne was the willingness of the central courts to supervise and intervene in the litigation and justice provided by manorial courts of what the royal justices recognized as *dominicum regis.* This did not mean, strictly, that villeins had any right of appeal to the royal courts; rather, it meant that the courts, like the central government in administrative and financial matters, were willing to intervene and investigate the local affairs of manors which came within the demesne right of the king. The tenants of such manors, of course, benefited from this attitude, as can be shown from various legal records. These all come from the rolls of the central courts or the courts of the itinerant justices. It must be stressed, however, that this intervention or supervision did not extend the common law to the villeins of the king. They were excluded from the assizes because they were villeins or their tenements were held in villeinage. Again and again this point comes out:

Terra illa est vilenagium domini regis, et non vult respondere per hanc assisam, nisi curia consideraverit . . . nunquam de hujusmodi terra capta fuit assisa, ut milites de comitatu testantur; . . . . Alicia

[84] *C.R.R.,* III, 333.

defendit jus suum et dicit quod terra illa est vilenagium domini regis . . . et non videtur ei quod inde debeat respondere. . . . Assisa non jacet quia tenementum illud est de villenagio Domini Regis & ipsi sunt villani Domini Regis & ideo preceptum est vicecomiti quod teneat eis justicium secundum consuetudinem ville de Esingwald.[85]

These excerpts are all from the reign of John. The following come from the first half of the reign of Henry III and illustrate the same points, though it can be noticed that there is a growing tendency to equate "villeins of the king" with "villeinage of the king," and both with "the demesne of the king." Villein status or villein tenure thus gives way to the conception of the king's demesne as an entity from which the common law assizes are excluded, and when this point is reached the little writ of right close and the "ancient" demesne of the king on which it runs begin to appear in the documents.

Dicunt quod tenent terras suas in villenagio de domino rege, nec possunt sine domino rege placitare, quia villa sua habet usuagium suum. Et curia hoc testatur.[86]

Et ipsi veniunt et dicunt quod sunt de soca de Haulton', ubi nullum precipe mitti debet, quia est dominicum domini regis: et Gilibertus hoc cognovit. Et ideo sine die.[87]

Dicunt quod sunt de dominico domini Regis et testatum est quod sunt villani domini Regis et ideo alii inde sine die. Et placitent in manerio secundum consuetudinem manerii.[88]

Dicit quod assisa non debet inde fieri quia terra illa est de pertinenciis manerii domini Regis de Kinton' ubi nulla assisa mortis antecessoris jacet. Et ideo sine die, et ipsa perquirat se alio modo.[89]

Dicit quod terra illa est de dominico domini Regis ut socagium

---

[85] *Ibid.*, VI, 288 (also, *ibid.*, VI, 294, and *Plac. Abbrev.*, p. 85); *C.R.R.*, VI, 68 (also, *Plac. Abbrev.*, p. 75); and *Plac. Abbrev.*, p. 70 (Yorkshire, rot 8d).

[86] *C.R.R.*, VIII, 58 (Hunts, 1219). This is a somewhat grandiose way of putting their case, but the villeins are introducing no new concept here. Even though their privileges led Bracton to call villeins of the royal demesne "villein sokemen," he still calls such pleading as the above an *exceptio villenagii* (fol. 200 [ed. Woodbine, III, 108]).

[87] *C.R.R.*, VIII, 202f. (Hants, 1220); also, *ibid.*, VIII, 201.

[88] *Rolls of the Justices in Eyre . . . for Lincolnshire 1218–9 and Worcestershire 1221* (ed. D. M. Stenton, Selden Society, vol. LIII; London, 1934), pp. 449f.

[89] *Rolls of the Justices in Eyre . . . for Gloucestershire, Warwickshire and Staffordshire, 1221, 1222* (ed. D. M. Stenton, Selden Society, vol. LIX; London, 1940), p. 297. Note the court's suggestion that, though the assize fails, the demandant may get justice *alio modo*.

suum, et ipse illam tenet in socagio de domino Rege et nulla assisa iacet in manerio illo et ipsa hoc non potuit dedicere. Et ideo sine die et secundum consuetudinem manerii deducatur.[90]

Dicunt quod assisa non debet inde fieri quia Bensington est de antiquo dominico regis ubi nullum breve nove disseis' currit & Rad' non potest dedicere & ideo in misericordia. . . . Antiquum dominicum Domini Regis de corona in quo non placitatur per aliquod breve nisi tamen per parvum breve de recto clausum . . . perquirat sibi per aliud breve si voluerit.[91]

The royal courts would not entertain an assize concerning villein lands, even lands of the king's villeins. What distinguished villeins of the royal demesne from all other villeins was that the itinerant or other royal justices were willing to intervene to see justice done in a manor of the royal demesne, just as they might be directed by the government to hold an inquest concerning a tenant's right to hold a tenement of a royal manor. These were but two sides of the same general principle: the king's justice, the justice of the king's court, was not excluded from his own manors by anyone else's demesne right, and such justice could be turned to a profit, whether it arose out of a dispute *inter villanos* or derived from an article of inquiry of the general eyre. From the rolls of the justices in eyre at Gloucester comes a typical instance of the intervention of the royal justices in the judicial affairs of a royal manor:

Et ideo non jacet assisa in manerio illo eo quod est vilenagium domini Regis. Et testatum est ipsi Robertus et Radulfus habuerunt inde seisinam per judicium curie de manerio illo. Et ideo homines de curia illa faciant recordum illud per quod Gilibertus amisit seisinam. Post venerunt Robertus et Radulfus et retraxerunt se . . . et ideo omnes sine die et unusquisque habeat seisinam prius habuit.[92]

Similar instances could be cited at some length.[93] It should be noticed that the royal courts usually effected this intervention *per*

[90] *Lincolnshire and Worcestershire Eyre,* pp. 532f.

[91] *Plac. Abbrev.,* pp. 117 (Oxf. rot. 10d; 1241) and 148 (Bucks rot. 13d; 1258). Bracton collected several cases illustrating the same points. The assize fails because: *de dominico Domini Regis* (*Note Book,* II, 244); *non debent extra manerium illud placitare,* though this does not apply to the free tenement (*ibid.,* II, 500f.); *uillenagio Domini Regis . . . quam non potest neque lucrari neque perdere sine Domino Rege* (*ibid.,* III, 247f.); and *dominicum Domini Regis et uillenagium* (*ibid.,* III, 428).

[92] *Gloucestershire, Warwickshire and Staffordshire Eyre,* pp. 37f.

[93] *Lincolnshire and Worcestershire Eyre,* pp. 468ff., 477f.; Richardson and Sayles,

consensum partium [94] or by bringing the parties into an agreement (*concordati sunt*).[95] The royal courts, in such cases, did not deliver judgment; but with judicial discretion and the prestige of royal justice behind them they brought about a settlement, with or without subsequent action by the court of the manor. One last case may be quoted to illustrate this basic point. The defendant in an assize of novel disseisin pleads that the tenement is part of the king's demesne, and the jury bears witness that it was villeinage and that the defendant did not disseize the demandant. Nevertheless, the judges (who by this time had two good reasons to quash the writ) inquire further and discover that the bailiff had arbitrarily taken the tenement into the king's hand: "Et ideo per consilium curie habeat (the demandant) seisinam suam et dominus Rex si voluerit deducat eum per consuetudinem manerii." [96] The custom of the manor, by counsel (not judgment) of the court, overrides the king's will as expressed by his servant's act upon the royal demesne.

All of these cases cited are early ones, the majority before 1225. They deal with legal protection of villein tenure upon the royal demesne. A review of the legal evidence relating to services and customs performed by the villeins reveals the same protection afforded by the intervention of the royal courts, the possibility of access to the highest source of justice in the realm.[97] This was often accomplished by bringing a common law assize, which, if quashed, would at least invite the correction of an abuse or the settlement of a dispute.

Eventually, protection of tenure and services was afforded by the two writs which are connected in the law books from Bracton's time on with villein sokemen or with the ancient demesne, the little writ of right close and the *monstraverunt*.[98] Enough has been said already, however, to show that legal protection of the royal demesne

Proc. without Writ, pp. 49, 90f.; *Plac. Abbrev.,* p. 117. All but one of these and the above cases are before 1250.

[94] *Lincolnshire and Worcestershire Eyre,* pp. 496f.

[95] *Ibid.,* p. 486. See Appendix E, nos. 9 and 13.

[96] *Ibid.,* pp. 530f.

[97] For example, see the following: *C.R.R.,* VI, 326f., 374; *Plac. Abbrev.,* pp. 25, 86ff.; *Bracton's Note Book,* III, 250f.; and Richardson and Sayles, *Proc. without Writ,* p. 106.

[98] W. S. Holdsworth, *A History of English Law* (7 vols.; vols. I–III, 3d ed., rev.; London, 1922–1925), III, 265f., 661. Bracton does not mention the *monstraverunt.*

peasantry antedates either writ. The little writ close appears in the 1220's at the earliest, and the *monstraverunt* (which is no more than a formalized petition or plaint) appears as a writ of course only at the end of the thirteenth century.[99] Long before that and long before "villein sokemen" or "ancient demesne" are known, the legal protection of the villeins of the royal demesne was growing up as the result of their access to the highest courts of the realm, the courts of their lord king, and particularly the courts held by his itinerant justices. All of the evidence relating to the origins of what are later called the privileges of ancient demesne is closely connected with the growing judicial and administrative activity associated with the reforms of Henry II as they come into fuller light during the reigns of his two sons and his grandson.

Having surveyed this evidence and touched upon some of its more important implications, we may revert to the theory that alleges those privileges, or the legal protection of the peasantry, to be a survival of Saxon conditions upon the *Terra Regis* of Domesday Book. Keeping in mind how the protection of the royal peasantry was actually enforced by the central government and its agents, at the beginning of the thirteenth century, is it plausible (for we have seen that there is no evidence) that Stephen or Matilda, Henry I and his ministers, or William Rufus and Ranulf Flambard would be able, even if they desired, to afford this protection, or to preserve Anglo-Saxon conditions among the peasants on the manors of St. Edward? Is it not much more likely that the itinerant justices who became so active from the reign of Henry II on brought royal justice to the royal demesne, just as they brought to it the assessment of tallage, inquests into the alienation and tenure of manors and tenements, and inquests into its economic administration?

In the surviving records which document the social and legal conditions found upon the royal demesne toward the beginning of the

---

99 Pollock and Maitland, *Hist. Eng. Law* (2d ed.), I, 389, n.1; Poole, *Obligations*, p. 26; Richardson and Sayles, *Proc. without Writ*, pp. xcv, c, n.6; *Lincolnshire and Worcestershire Eyre*, pp. 477f. In 1238 before the itinerant justices at Exeter, *villani Alicie de Moun de Axemenistre in misericordia quia non secuti sunt breve suum de consuetudinibus et serviciis versus ipsam Aliciam*. P.R.O., Ass. Roll No. 174, m.22. Alice de Mohun held both the hundred and manor of Axminster. This could (possibly) be an early reference to the *monstraverunt*, or it could refer to the kind of writ from which the *monstraverunt* eventually evolved as a writ of course.

thirteenth century, all the evidences of privileges enjoyed by the peasantry are connected with royal enforcement of local custom, both by the central courts and by the itinerant justices; there is no hint of Domesday Book, nor of ancient demesne, nor of pre-Conquest conditions, nor of villein sokemen. What ultimately become ancient demesne privileges seem to grow out of events and institutions which are new and changing or are distinctively royal rather than old or popular. Even "the tradition which ascribes to the Conqueror a law in favour of the tillers of the soil" [100] fails to support the theory of survival which would explain ancient demesne privileges. This tradition is embodied in a twelfth century collection of laws, the *Leis Willelme,* and at first glance it seems to be an early statement of what can be recognized as ancient demesne privileges, for it purports to be a command of the Conqueror that cultivators of the soil shall not be vexed for more than their just customs or dispossessed so long as they perform their just services. This calls to mind Bracton's phrases, *a gleba amoveri non debent quamdiu velint debitum facere servitium* and *servitia certa et determinata:* "Cil qui cultivent la terre ne deit l'um travailer, se de lour droite cense noun; ne leist a seignurage departir les cultivurs de lur terre, pur tant cum il pussent le dreit seirvise faire." [101]

There are three reasons for rejecting at least the face value of this statement as it might apply to the present problem. First, although the authorities disagree as to any particular date or period for the compilation, there seems to be little doubt that it is a twelfth century document.[102] Its reference to rent conforms with what is known about the general trend toward commutation of services in the twelfth century,[103] which reflected a decline of the demand for labor, which would consequently tend to increase the need for protection against ejectment. Second, this provision "strongly betrays the influence of Roman law" and thus cannot be directly associated with either William or eleventh-century England.[104] And third, the pro-

[100] Maitland, *D.B. and Bey.,* p. 66; Vinogradoff, *Villainage,* p. 135.

[101] *Leis Willelme,* c.29, in Liebermann, *Gesetze,* I, 512.

[102] A. J. Robertson, ed., *The Laws of the Kings of England from Edmund to Henry I* (Cambridge, 1925), p. 227.

[103] Postan, "Labour Services," pp. 169–193.

[104] Robertson, *Laws of the Kings of England,* p. 227.

vision applies to private, not royal, lands, as the next three chapters of the collection make clear.

Is there an explanation of the origins of ancient demesne privileges, and of the ancient demesne itself, which does not rely upon theory alone, which does not portray the monarchy in anomalous terms of benevolent conservatism, and which does conform with the evidence relating to the administration and economic exploitation of the royal demesne—evidence which pictures the monarchy as aggressively asserting and expanding its demesne right as one aspect of the general growth of Angevin royal power? We believe there is.

We have already seen how the monarchy, beginning in the middle years of the reign of Henry II, inquired into purprestures, held recurrent inquests into alienated royal demesne, and tallaged the boroughs as part of its demesne. All three activities were part of a general program of enlargement, consolidation, and enhancement of the demesne right of the monarchy. All three were part of the effort of the monarchy to convert its demesne right into a cash revenue. This program was partly based upon, and contributed to the further growth of, the idea that royal demesne should not be alienated—that is, the endowment of the crown, in contrast to the lands in the king's hands through escheat or wardship or vacancy, though even over these latter the king asserted his full demesne right while they were in his hands so far as revenues were concerned. The monarchy was therefore interested in knowing what its demesnes actually were; its itinerant justices asked the local juries what lands *antiquitus* were in the king's hands and how much were they worth and how and by what warrant they were now held. So also, the Exchequer clerks in the early years of the reign of Henry III were compiling the same information from the financial records available. The Red Book of the Exchequer contains "constantly recurring notices of tallages, escheats, and *Terrae Datae*" and lists of manors headed *Haec maneria fuerunt hoc anno in manu Regis* or *Haec maneria fuerunt talliata hoc anno tanquam dominica*.[105]

Now the monarchy was not actuated by mere antiquarian zeal. It wanted to know what lands were *in manibus predecessorum nostrorum* for a purpose. Using the typical Angevin device of the sworn

[105] *Red Book Exch.*, II, ccxiii. These notices and lists were omitted from the printed Red Book.

jury to determine the facts, it could then recover or reassert what rights over the lands it could justify. One of these rights was the protection of the peasantry of manors which were once the king's. This sprang directly from the judicial profits involved, no matter what role the element of benevolence might play. The men of Braunton, in Devonshire, who *reddunt compotum de x libris, ut Robertus de Sachoill eis non distringat ad faciendum ei alias consuetudines quam Regi facere consueverunt dum fuerunt in manu sua,*[106] were not the object of the solicitude of a charitable monarchy, regardless of what its ideals of kingship or justice might be. Ten pounds were ten pounds, and intervention in the case might lead to other judicial profits as well. The whole growth of the common law was designed to bring the monarchy into direct relations with all free men of the realm, to bring royal justice to the protection of all free tenements in England—for a fee. The monarchy did not draw the line between the free and unfree willingly: the royal courts notoriously favored freedom, assumed a man free till claimed as and proved to be a villein, and with regard to the villeins of the royal demesne they brought royal justice to bear upon villeinage, though not under common law forms. The question was, what *was* the royal demesne.

As we have seen, for judicial purposes the royal courts were willing to interfere in the affairs of villeins not only of royal manors but of manors which had been *in manibus predecessorum nostrorum.* The demesne right was not extinguished by alienation, even to a church in free alms. This was a right of justice: it meant protection of just rights, and not the conferring of favors. During the course of the twelfth century the lot of the peasantry in England generally improved, and the main feature of this improvement was the commutation of labor services for cash rents. In the thirteenth century, the demand for labor increased and lords generally tried to increase the services of their villeins and enlarge their manorial demesnes.[107] The legal records of the age are full of disputes over *consuetudines et servicia* due from the peasantry. The monarchy escaped most of

---

[106] P.R. 13 John, Devonshire, quoted by Madox, *The History and Antiquities of the Exchequer* (2 vols.; London, 1769), I, 411, n.*u*.

[107] Postan, "Labour Services," pp. 191ff.; Douglas, *Feudal Documents . . . of Bury St. Edmunds,* pp. cxxxiii, clxixf.

these difficulties, however, for it had adopted a program of farming royal manors to the highest bidder. It could count on a fixed cash income from its royal demesne, and it could raise the farms periodically to keep them in some relation to the growing wealth of the realm. For a fee, the royal courts were therefore quite willing to protect whatever peasantry they could protect. Such protection of the peasants against increased services and rents would not affect the royal income from its royal demesne adversely. In fact, it would tend to increase its income, for tallage could be reserved to the crown in the grant of a royal manor. In a sense, tallage was the excess profit which the government extracted over and above the normal income of its demesne. The more wealthy the peasants, the higher the tallage which could be charged. Hence it was to the monarchy's financial advantage to protect the tenure and the status of whatever peasants it tallaged.

Such is the interpretation which we would give to the evidence surveyed in this and the two preceding chapters. We are encouraged so to interpret the evidence not only because of the utter absence of any talk of Domesday Book, Anglo-Saxon conditions, or "ancient" demesne in the documents before the mid-thirteenth century, but also because there are occasional statements which lead us directly to this interpretation.

When the men of Brampton, in Huntingdonshire, were given the farm of their manor in 1199, the royal government was immediately and consequently interested in the men's ability to pay the farm and remain prosperous so that they could be tallaged. No royal writ says this in so many words, but is not this the real meaning of Geoffrey fitz Peter's order to the sheriff to protect those men? The justiciar tells the sheriff that the men have been granted their farm and adds:

> Et ideo tibi precipimus quod predictos homines de Branton' custodias protegas manuteneas nec permittas quod aliquis eis grauamen uel injuriam faciat super aliquo quod ad uillam illam pertineat nec manum apponat ad redditus uel terras uel prata que sunt de dominico domini R.[108]

We have already seen how the men of a royal manor (Ospringe, in Kent) might be protected against the bailiffs of a royal keeper, and

[108] *Mem. Roll 1 John,* p. 37.

we may revert now with profit to the trial of the bailiffs of Brill in 1258. The bailiffs were having their difficulties in raising their farm and resorted to various petty extortions.[109] The men of Brill were loud and specific in their complaints, but they make two generalizations in summing up their case. The truth of these statements is irrelevant; what is important is that they contain ideas to which the men of Brill thought the government would be receptive. The outcome of the case indicates that the government was. These statements can be reduced to the formula, "protection of the royal peasantry equals royal revenue":

> Et unde universi dicunt quod per predictas iniurias, extortiones et rapinas ita gravati sunt et . . . depaupertati, quod vix restat aliquis qui de firma sua domino regi de terra sua debita possit respondere. . . . Ipsi [ballivi] distringunt predictos tenentes ad acquietandum predicta exennia, licet ipsi tenentes non possint habere respectum de firma terrarum suarum reddenda.[110]

Protection of the peasantry cannot be dissociated from royal revenue. This is true even when royal demesne had been alienated. The peasants were protected from tallage at will by their lords, but they were still subject to a royal right of tallage. This illustrates what we have distinguished as the "royal" rather than "seignorial" character of royal tallage. It was considered to inhere in the crown and was not necessarily alienated with the manor; lords had to secure a special writ to take their tallage and could do so only when the king tallaged his demesnes. Again this source of revenue entailed a privileged place for the tenants of royal manors or manors which had been alienated. They were to be exempt from many of the common amercements and fines which fell upon the geldable of the county or hundred.

All of these rights, which meant revenue for the monarchy and protection and privilege for tenants of royal manors, the central government tried to extend as far and over as many manors as possible. This, as we have seen, led to the idea of inalienability which lies behind resumption of crown lands and *quo warranto* inquests. Between the beginning of the reign of Henry II and the close of that of Henry III, there had been, as a result of this gen-

---

[109] Jacob, *Studies,* p. 45.

[110] *Ibid.,* App. II, pp. 347f.

eral policy, a tremendous expansion of the demesne right of the king—it had come to include all lands which had once been royal demesne. Royal intervention, for a fee or at a profit, into the affairs of the peasantry was prevented only where a manor had not ever been in the hands of a preceding king: "Dominus Rex non uult se de eis intromittere ex quo nunquam fuerunt in manu sua nec antecessorum suorum."[111] The logical end of such a rule was to consider lands which were *antiquitus* royal demesne the *antiquum dominicum corone,* and to prove it by reference to the Domesday *Terra Regis.* An aggressive monarchy, and royal courts striving to extend their jurisdiction which produced royal revenue, were quite capable of extending the royal demesne rights to include the whole of the Conqueror's lands. What lands were once *in manibus predecessorum,* after all, depended upon the limit of legal memory, and, since time runs not against a king, 1086 or the Conquest itself could be made that limit. More important, the record contained in Domesday Book was a surer method of proof than the memory of the countryside. This does not mean that by the end of Henry III's reign the whole of the Domesday *Terra Regis* was considered to be actually royal demesne and that it should be resumed into the king's hands. The inalienability of the ancient demesne was and remained a "strong sentiment" and no more, but it was on such a sentiment that the monarchy could assert certain rights over the ancient demesne and could for certain purposes treat the ancient demesne as subject to demesne right. One of the consequences was a privileged position for tenants of the ancient demesne because royal revenue profited from their privileges:

> Tu prefatos tenentes [de antiquo dominico] grauiter distringis ad contribuendum cuidam amerciamento . . . in ipsorum dampnum non modicum et grauamen et nostri preiudicium manifestum, presertim cum ipsi sicut nec ceteri qui sunt de antiquo dominico corone nostre ad huiusmodi contribuciones non teneantur, sed talliari debeant cum burgos nostros in regno nostro . . . nolumus quod ius nostrum in hac parte perimetur.[112]

---

[111] *Bracton's Note Book,* III, 250f.
[112] *Lib. Mem. de Bern.,* pp. 188f.

We may conclude, then, by saying that the ancient demesne was the creation of the Angevin monarchy and that the privileges of the tenants of ancient demesne were an incident of the expansion of the demesne right of the monarchy which created those privileges to enhance its cash revenue: *nolumus quod ius nostrum in hac parte perimetur* and, we might add, *sed increscetur*.

APPENDIX E

Select Cases concerning the Royal Demesne

THE cases printed below are intended to supplement the evidence for, and to illustrate further, the conclusions stated in Chapter VI. These cases also indicate some of the lines of development of what later generations will call "the law of ancient demesne," a development with which the present work is not directly concerned.

Letters or words which have been omitted or which are illegible, in the original, have been supplied in square brackets; these readings may be regarded as certain, so far as their meaning is concerned. Words printed in italics within square brackets are conjectural.

1. C.R.R. 85, m.34d. Pleas before the Justices of the Bench, Michaelmas, 8–9 Henry III (1224).

Bercsir'.—Nicholaus Blundus et Agnes uxor ejus per attornatum suum petunt versus Reginaldum de Mora et Elenam uxorem ejus terciam partem trium acrarum terre cum pertinentiis in Bray ut jus et rationabilem portionem ipsius Agnetis que eam contingit etc. Et Reginaldus et Elena veniunt et dicunt quod terra illa est de dominico domini regis et vilenagio suo. Et ideo sine die; et Nicholaus et Agnes perquirant breve de recto secundum consuetudinem manerii si voluerint.

The main interest of this case is that it contains a very early reference to "the little writ of right close according to the custom of the manor," which, according to repeated statements in the later plea rolls, is "the only writ which runs in the lord king's demesne."

2. Ass. Roll No. 54, m.5d. Pleas and Assizes at Dunstable, 12 Henry III (1227).

Assisa venit recognitura si [1] Willelmus de Merlawe et Emma uxor ejus injuste et sine judicio disseisiverunt Radulfum [2] filium Willelmi

[1] *si* interlined.

[2] *Willelmum* struck through before *Radulfum.*

de libero tenemento suo in Bruhell' post ultimum etc. Et Willelmus et Emma veniunt et dicunt quod assisa non debet inde fieri quia terra illa est soccagium de manerio domini regis de Briwhill' ubi nulla assisa fieri potest. Et Radulfus hoc cognoscit. Et ideo sine die; et perquirat se secundum consuetudinem manerii si voluerit.

This case is typical of the majority of the cases concerning the royal demesne recorded on the plea rolls of the central and itinerant courts. The common law assize is defeated by the defendants' statement, which the plaintiff cannot deny, that the tenement is not free. In this case, the tenement is "socage of the lord king's manor of Brill," but the same point (that the tenement is not free, and therefore not under the common law) may be made in a variety of ways. It is important to notice that the clause *ubi nulla assisa fieri potest* can only be understood to refer to *soccagium,* and not to *manerium* or *Briwhill',* since a free tenement within a royal manor was adjudicable at common law, as will appear below. The plaintiff, in this case, is advised to sue in the manorial court of the royal manor, a normal feature of the cases recorded in the plea rolls.

3. C.R.R. 99, m.6d. Pleas before the Justices of the Bench, Michaelmas, 12–13 Henry III (1228).

Suht'.—Matillis de Basingestok' petit versus Johannem de Basingestok' dimidiam virgatam terre cum pertinenciis in Basingestok' ut jus suum etc. Et Johannes venit et dicit quod terra illa est de dominico domini regis et non debet extra manerium placitare; et hoc idem testatum est pro curia. Et ideo eant ad curiam et per consuetudinem illius deducantur.

The clause, *non debet extra manerium placitare,* is equivalent in this case to *ubi nulla assisa fieri potest* in the preceding case; so also, the "custom of the manor" and *consuetudo illius* (*curie*) are equivalent in the two cases, and both may be contrasted with the custom of the central and itinerant courts, the *consuetudo regni* or common law which applies to free tenements.

4. Ass. Roll No. 62, m.12d. Pleas and Assizes at Newport in the county of Buckingham, 16 Henry III (1231–1232).

Assisa venit recognitura si Willelmus Gray et Rogerus Gray injuste etc. disseisiverunt Willelmum le Porter de libero tenemento suo in Buck' post primam etc.; et unde queritur quod disseisiverunt eum de quodam prato. Et Willelmus et Rogerus veniunt et nichil dicunt quare assisa remaneat.

Juratores dicunt quod predicti Willelmus et Rogerus disseisiverunt eum de quadam parte prati sui quod tenet de Radulfo Harang. Et ideo consideratum est quod Willelmus le Porter recuperavit seisinam suam; et Willelmus Gray et Rogerus in misericordia.

Dampna xij. denarii. (*In margin,* misericordia, *struck through; and above it,* alibi.)

In this case, and others on the same roll concerning tenements in Buckingham, no objection to the assize is made by the defendants. Compare nos. 17 and 27, below.

5. C.R.R. 113, m.33d. Pleas before the Justices of the Bench, Michaelmas, 17–18 Henry III (1233).

Essex'.—Willelmus persona de Estwick' petit versus Hubertum filium Wydonis xviij. acras terre et dimidiam et j. acram et tres rodas prati cum pertinentiis in Hatfeuld, et versus Edricum le Bule v. acras terre et j. mesuagium cum pertinentiis in eadem villa, et versus alios plures etc.

Et super hoc venit prior de Hatfeuld et dicit quod tenet manerium de Hatfeuld de ballio domini regis et ad voluntatem domini regis pro c. libris per annum; et dicit quod terra illa est de predicto manerio; et petit curiam suam, quia nullum tale placitum placitari debet extra manerium illud.

Et predictus Hubertus et alii, quesiti quod servicium faciunt de terris quas tenent, dicunt quod reddunt certam summam denariorum et preterea messuras aruras et triturationes et alia servicia; et dicunt quod dant merchetum pro filiabus suis maritandis etc. Et predictus Willelmus petit terram illam tenendam pro v. solidis et x. denariis. Et ideo hic sine die; et prior teneat ei justiciam secundum consuetudinem manerii.

Since the plaintiff has not claimed the lands as free tenements and the defendants admit that they hold by unfree tenure, the prior's claim is allowed.

6. C.R.R. 115B, m.8. Pleas before the King, 18–19 Henry III (1234–1235).

Essex'.—Preceptum fuit ballivis de Haveringe quod essent coram domino rege ad respondendum quare non tenuerunt Johanni filio Ernisii plenum rectum de quinquaginta acris terre et sex acris prati in Haveringe etc., et quod venire facerent coram domino rege sex de discretioribus hominibus curie de Havering' ad respondendum inde etc.; et unde idem Johannes questus fuit quod diu secutus fuit placitum illud nec potuit inde justiciam habere etc., et unde nunc queritur quod cum presens esset in curia et jus suum ostenderet et narrationem suam faceret petendo terram illam et pratum versus Ricardum de Waude, ipse Ricardus noluit ei respondere ad narrationem suam, nec potentiores curie, qui sunt parentes ipsius Ricardi, hoc ei non permiserunt nec voluerunt ipsum distringere ad respondendum.

Et Warinus de Romford' Ricardus de Ulmis Symon de Abenache Willelmus de Mercdich junior de Wudeham Eadmundus de Gardin' et Willelmus filius Willelmi de Uphaveringe veniunt et dicunt quod nunquam fuit eidem Johanni justicia denegata in prefata curia; et proferunt recordum in quo continetur quod idem Johannes multotiens se essoniavit et distulit negocium suum et ad ultimum diem non venit nec se essoniavit, et unde consideratum fuit quod Ricardus inde sine die et Johannes in misericordia. Et ipse hoc cognoscit, et dicit quod fuit in curia domini regis ad perquirendum sibi de justicia etc. Et quia dicit quod loquela fuit in comitatu, ideo eat ad comitatum si voluerit vel perquirat sibi per aliud breve.

This interesting case illustrates the judicial supervision exercised by the king and his council (see above, p. 167f.) over the manorial courts of the royal demesne, and thus provides a glimpse of the kind of grievance which could induce a tenant in a royal manor to appeal to the highest court of justice in the realm. The wording of the reference to the "record" is ambiguous. The phrase *in quo continetur* suggests that a document, perhaps founded upon the manorial court roll of Havering, was produced in the Curia Regis. On the other hand, I owe to the kindness of Mr. L. C. Hector, of the Public Record Office, the observation that although *profero* is the normal word employed at this time for the production of written evidence, the passage as a whole suggests the same kind of procedure by which the "record" of the county court was proved in the Curia Regis by the oral testimony of four (or six) knights of the court. The tenement involved was free, presumably, for the plaintiff is told to pursue his case in the county court; and yet the suit had been adjudicated in the manorial court. Compare this case with nos. 7, 9, 15, and 28.

7. C.R.R. 115B, m.10d. Pleas before the King, 18–19 Henry III (1234–1235).

[*Es*]*sex'*.—Petrus de Rumford' summonitus fuit ad warantizandum Ade de Lincoln' dimidiam virgatam terre cum pertinentiis in Haveringe quam tenet et de eo tenere clamat et unde cartam suam habet, ut dicit, etc.; et unde dicit quod Philippus filius Laurentii clamat terram illam versus eum in curia de Havering' per breve de recto, et quod idem Petrus illam ei debet warantizare.

Et Petrus venit et cognoscit cartam et donum et ei warantizat. Et Philippus venit et petit terram illam versus eum ut jus suum; et unde dicit quod predictus Laurentius pater suus fuit feoffatus per predictum Petrum; [et] dicit quod idem Petrus dedit terram illam eidem Laurentio, et ipse fuit inde seisitus et obiit inde seisitus; [et d]um fuit infra etatem venit idem Petrus et dedit terram illam isti Ade; et petit seisinam [Lau]rentii patris sui, et dicit quod jus terre illius descendit eidem Philippo.

[Et Pet]rus venit et defendit jus suum nunc et alias etc.; [et] dicit quod nichil juris descendere potuit isti [Philip]po de predicto Laurentio, quia antequam idem Laurentius mortuus esset venit ipse et dedit terram illam cuidam [J]ohanni fratri suo, et [*idem*] Johannes illam postea vendidit isti Ade; et ponit se in quandam juratam [secundum] consuetudinem manerii de Haveringe ad recognoscendum utrum ipse Philippus majus jus habeat in terra illa sicut [*in illa*] que ei descendit de Laurentio patre suo et unde idem Laurentius obiit seisitus ut de feodo, an [id]em Petrus sicut in illa de qua idem Laurentius ante mortem suam se demisit et vendidit Johanni fratri suo, ut idem Petrus dicit. Et fiat jurata per tales qui neutram partem aliqua affinitate attingant. Et preceptum est ballivis de Haveringe quod quamcito convictum fuerit et discussum de jure quod faciant judicium secundum quod de jure facere debent secundum consuetudinem manerii.

This is a complicated case, raising questions which were still open over a century later. The litigation between Philip and Adam seems to have concerned customary land and to have been in the manorial court of Havering. When Adam vouched Peter to warranty the case came to the king's court, which alone could deal with the warranty. Peter defended the title, and an issue was reached which was to be tried by a jury whose nature, however, unfortunately, is obscure. In any case, the manorial court was ordered to proceed to judgment according to the custom of the manor as soon as a verdict had been given. It is notable that both parties had charters from Peter (who was possibly the lord). A century later there was some question whether a charter, or a writ of warranty in the king's court, might not convert customary into freehold land. See *Year Books of the Reign of King Edward the Third Year XVI* (ed. L. O. Pike; London, 1900), II, 560ff. For this explanation I am indebted to Professor T. F. T. Plucknett, who was kind enough to discuss this and other cases with me.

8. C.R.R. 116B, m.5. Pleas before the King, quindene of St. John the Baptist, 20 Henry III (1236).

Hunt'.—Preceptum fuit vicecomiti quod per sacramentum proborum et legalium hominum diligenter inquireret que servitia et quas consuetudines homines de Alcmundebyr' [3] facere consueverunt temporibus Henrici regis avi domini regis, Ricardi regis avunculi domini regis, et domini Johannis regis patris domini regis, antequam manerium illud deveniret ad manus comitis David etc.

Et inquisitio venit per Johannem de Fukeswurth' Oliverum Maufe Robertum de Baiocis Willelmum Mowyn Walterum de Beynvill' Willelmum Cardun Willelmum de Offord Ricardum de Gedding' Stephanum de Catewurth' Robertum de Upton' Walterum filium Willelmi de Grafham et Thomam filium Maugeri de Cattewurth' que talis est. Quod homines de Alcmundebur' tenuerunt manerium de Alcmundebur' tempore Henrici regis, avi domini regis qui nunc est, per xx. libras; et dominus rex talliavit homines predicti manerii quando talliavit alia dominica sua. Dicunt etiam quod dicti homines tenuerunt dictum manerium tempore Ricardi regis avunculi regis eodem modo donec Ricardus rex dedit manerium illud Johanni le Lou. Et dicunt quod idem Johannes statim cepit totum dominicum in manum suam et illud excoluit propriis carucis, et posuit dictos homines ad consuetudines necessarias infra manerium et extra, et [4] ad talliandum quando dominus rex talliavit maneria sua; et tunc temporis reddidit quelibet virgata terre duos solidos per annum de firma, et dederunt herieta et amerciamenta surgentia de placitis. Dicunt etiam quod dicti homines tenuerunt dictum manerium tempore domini Johannis regis [5] predicto modo, donec dicti homines impetraverunt a domino rege Johanne ad tenendum dictum manerium de Alcmundebur' per annum per xxx. libras et ad talliandum ut prius. Et dicti homines ita tenuerunt dictum manerium donec dominus rex Johannes dedit dictum manerium comiti David hereditarie.

Et dicti homines de Alcmundebur', quesiti si fuerunt villani Henrici regis avi regis et Ricardi regis avunculi regis et Johannis regis patris domini regis, dicunt quod sunt villani et quod vocabantur bundemanni regum,[6] et pro voluntate ipsorum aliquando positi fuerunt ad denarios et aliquando ad servitia, et dederunt herieta mercheta et amerciamenta de placitis emergentia.

---

3 *Alcnundebyr'* in original.

4 *ut* in original.

5 *qui nunc est* struck through after *regis.*

6 *villani et quod vocabantur bundemanni regum* interlined.

Et ideo consideratum est [7] quod Stephanus de Segrave, qui nunc habet manerium illud, habeat talem seisinam de predictis manerio et hominibus qualem predicti reges habuerunt tempore quo manerium illud fuit in manibus eorum, et quod pro voluntate sua ponat ipsos ad denarios vel ad operationes et [8] alia servitia sicut predicti reges facere potuerunt temporibus suis; [9] et predicti homines in misericordia.

This case illustrates the principle, fundamental in the development of the law of ancient demesne, that alienation of a royal manor should not change the status of the tenants of the manor—even though they are villeins. It is interesting to note that these villeins, "who were called kings' bondsmen," are said to have held their manor of Alconbury (at farm, presumably) in the time of Henry II.

9. Ass. Roll No. 864, m.2. Pleas and Assizes in the county of Surrey, 19–20 Henry III (1236).

Herbertus filius Elye peciit in comitatu versus Johannem de Fay dimidiam hidam terre cum pertinenciis in Denhurst ut jus suum etc. Ita quod predictus Johannes respondit quod non potuit terram illam lucrari vel perdere quia nichil clamavit in terra illa nisi nomine custodie, quia seisiverat terram ipsam in manum suam post mortem cuiusdam Anselli quousque rectus heres ejus veniret et faceret ei quod de jure facere deberet pro terra illa; et preterea terra ipsa est de dominico domini regis de Bromlegh'. Et super hoc consideravit comitatus quod magna assisa jacuit inter eos. Et ideo ad judicium de comitatu. (*In margin,* ad judicium, *struck through.*)

Postea concordati sunt et Johannes de Fay dat xx. solidos pro licencia concordandi. (*In margin,* xx. solidi.)

See above, p. 199.

10. Ass. Roll No. 864, m.5. Pleas and Assizes in the county of Surrey, 19–20 Henry III (1236).

Assisa venit recognitura si Osbertus filius Mathei et Bundus de Sartrino injuste etc. disseisiverunt Reginaldum le Marbrer de libero tenemento suo in Bermundes' post etc. Et Osbertus venit et dicit quod assisa non debet inde fieri quia manerium de Bermundes' fuit dominicum domini regis et monachi de Bermundes' illud tenent sicut Willelmus rex illud tenuit et in manerio illo non currit aliqua assisa neque de morte antecessoris neque de nova disseisina, et hoc convictum fuit alias coram W. de London' et sociis suis per inquisicionem comitatus. Et

[7] *est* interlined.

[8] *operationes et* interlined over a caret mark.

[9] *sicut predicti reges facere potuerunt temporibus suis* interlined over a caret mark.

ideo Osbertus et Bundus inde sine die et Reginaldus in misericordia; pauper est et perquirat sibi etc. (*In margin,* misericordia.)

The reference to King William may possibly be taken as an allusion to the Conquest, and if so, this would be one of the earliest references in the plea rolls associating the legal peculiarities of the royal demesne with the event which later became a test of ancient demesne (see above, p. 172f.), although it is the testimony of the county court, and not Domesday Book, which is decisive in determining the issue. Actually, Bermondsey Priory, founded between 1082 and 1089, received its land at Bermondsey from William Rufus (Dom David Knowles, *The Monastic Order in England,* Cambridge, 1949, p. 152). The words *illud tenent sicut Willelmus rex illud tenuit* are reminiscent of the language of a charter, and it is possible that such a document was produced at the *inquisicio comitatus;* however, I have not found a Bermondsey charter incorporating them.

11. Ass. Roll No. 775, m.5. Pleas and Assizes in the county of Hampshire, 20 Henry III (1236).

Assisa venit recognitura si Gaufridus de Exton' et Othinus de Holewey injuste etc. disseisiverunt Luciam que fuit uxor Ricardi de La Bere de libero tenemento in Rammeden' post primam etc. Et testatum est per comitatum quod tenementum istud, de quo assisa ista arramiata est, fuit socagium domini regis, et dominus rex dedit manerium de Rammeden' domino Wintoniensi episcopo habendum et tenendum eodem modo quo dominus rex illud tenuit; in quo socagio nullum breve de assisa mortis [antecessoris] nec nove disseisine currit. Et ideo consideratum est[10] quod assisa remaneat; et Lucia in misericordia pro falso clamio; et perquirat sibi etc.

12. Ass. Roll No. 775, m.8d. Pleas and Assizes in the county of Hampshire, 20 Henry III (1236).

Assisa venit recognitura si Emericus de Sacy' injuste etc. disseisivit Gaufridum de Sancto Victore de communa pasture sue in Berton' que pertinet etc. in eadem villa post etc. Et Emericus venit et nichil dicit quare assisa remaneat.

Juratores dicunt quod avus ipsius Gaufridi fuit villanus et tempore suo fuit villanus domini regis et mansit apud Berton' alibi quam in tenemento unde assisa aramiata est, et ipse habuit quendam filium Willelmum qui, quando pater suus fuit mortuus, transfretavit et ivit ad abbaciam de Sancto Victore in Francia et ibi servivit abbati et conventui ejusdem domus in tantum quod abbas et conventus Sancti Vic-

[10] *est* interlined.

toris dederunt ei quandam terram quam habuerunt tunc in Berton' et eum inde feofaverunt, et idem Willelmus habuit communam pasture cum domino rege in quadam pastura que vocatur Oxedon' et alibi in quadam mora ad xij. boves, et idem Willelmus nunquam fuit factus liber per dominum regem et natus fuit in socagio domini regis; dicunt etiam [quod] Gaufridus fuit filius predicti Willelmi et quod ipse [tenet] terram unde Willelmus pater suus fuit feofatus et habet predictam [11] communam pasture et inde est in seisina. Et ideo consideratum est quod Eymericus inde sine die; et Gaufridus in misericordia pro falso clamio per plegium Roberti de Sutton et Ricardi Bissop de Berton'. (*In margin,* custodiatur, *struck through; and below it,* misericordia.)

13. Ass. Roll No. 775, m.10d. Pleas and Assizes in the county of Hampshire, 20 Henry III (1236).

Johannes Kipping et Ela uxor ejus per atornatum suum petunt versus abbatem de Waverl' xl. acras terre cum pertinenciis in Wik' ut jus ipsius Ele.

Et abbas per atornatum suum venit et defendit jus ipsius Ele, et dicit quod non debet ei ad hoc breve respondere quia terra illa est de socagio domini regis eo quod Wike est membrum de Aulton' ubi nullum breve currit nisi breve de recto; et petit judicium. Et Johannes et Ela non possunt hoc dedicere.

Concordanti sunt per licenciam.

The reference to *breve de recto* should be compared with the same phrase in no. 7. Here it clearly means the little writ of right close. Although the court of the itinerant justices cannot entertain the case, at law, it is nevertheless available to the two parties for reaching a settlement of the dispute, *per licenciam*. See above, p. 199.

14. Ass. Roll No. 775, m.10d. Pleas and Assizes in the county of Hampshire, 20 Henry III (1236).

Walkelinus Erkebaud peciit versus Johannem Barfot dimidiam virgatam terre cum pertinenciis in Andevr' ut jus suum in curia de Andevr' per parvum breve; et postea impetravit quoddam pone, quod loquela illa que fuit in comitatu inter eos de eadem terra poneretur coram justiciariis ad primam assisam etc. Et quia loquela illa non fuit in comitatu quando pone illud fuit [12] impetratum, consideratum est quod Walkelinus nichil capiat per hoc breve et sit in misericordia pro falso clamio per plegium Johannis Scrapin de Andevr' et Thome Snel de eadem.

---

[11] *predictam* repeated in original.

[12] *fuit* interlined over a caret mark.

15. Ass. Roll No. 174, m.3. Pleas and Assizes at Exeter, 22 Henry III (1238).

Robertus de Blakeford et Avicia uxor ejus per attornatum ipsius Avicie petunt versus Thomam de Luscote, quem Rogerus de Winkelegh' decanus Exon' vocavit ad warantum et qui ei warantizavit, unum ferlingum terre cum pertinenciis in Branton', et versus Ricardum Bernus dimidium ferlingum terre cum pertinenciis in eadem villa, ut jus ipsius Avicie, unde quidam Philippus Chacebef pater ipsius Avicie fuit seisitus in dominico suo ut de feodo et jure tempore Henrici regis qui nunc est, capiendo inde expleta ad valenciam dimidie marce etc.; et de eodem Philippo descendit jus terrarum illarum isti Avicie ut filie et heredi; et quod tale sit jus suum offert etc.

Et Thomas et Ricardus veniunt et defendunt [13] jus ipsius Avicie et seisinam predicti Philippi et totum, et ponunt se in magnam assisam domini regis et petunt recognicionem fieri utrum ipsi majus jus habeant in terra an predicti Robertus et Avicia. Et Robertus et Avicia dicunt quod magna assisa non debet inde fieri quia predicta terra fuit antiquum [14] dominicum domini regis et dominus rex eam dedit predicto Philippo qui inde fuit seisitus ut predictum est.

Et Thomas et Ricardus bene concedunt quod predicta terra fuit dominicum domini regis, set bene defendunt quod predictus Philippus nunquam fuit seisitus de eadem terra ut de feodo et jure, et petunt quod secundum consuetudinem manerii de Branton' inquiratur per sacramentum xij. etc. de eodem manerio utrum ipsi majus jus [15] habeant in terra illa ut in illa quam clamant tenere [16] in socagium, an predicti Robertus et Avicia ut in illa unde predictus Philippus fuit seisitus in dominico suo ut de feodo et jure ut predictum est.

Et ideo preceptum est vicecomiti quod faciat venire omnes sub[s]criptos qui electi sunt de consensu partium ad recognoscendum etc., scilicet Osbertum [17] de Alvivecote (juratus) [18] Adam [17,19] de Baddecote (juratus) Dobel' [17] de la Forda Willelmum [17] de Salesbiri (juratus) Joelem [17] de la Waita (juratus) Rogerum [17] de Alvivecote Maugerum [17,20]

---

13 *et defendunt* interlined.

14 *antiquum* interlined over a caret mark.

15 *jus* interlined.

16 *tenere* interlined.

17 A dot is placed over this name in original.

18 *juratus* is interlined above all names after which it has been printed in parentheses.

19 Before this name, *Willelmum de Baddewrth* has been struck through.

20 *Maugerus* in original.

de Binnewrthi Willelmum [17,21] Snellard (juratus) Adam [17,22] de Brigedon' Osbertum [17,23] de Balesdon' et Willelmum [17] de la Heia (juratus), preterea [24] Robertum de Pidekewel (juratus) Nicholaum de Fililegh (juratus) Willelmum Fauvel (juratus) Henricum de Dune (juratus) Philippum Luvet (juratus) et Thomam de Lovese (juratus). Qui dicunt super sacramentum suum quod predictus Philippus Chacebef nullum jus habuit in terra quam predicti Robertus et Avicia petunt versus predictum Thomam de Luscote nisi per intrusionem, et quod tam idem Thomas quam predictus Ricardus Bernus majus jus habent tenendi predictas terras in socagium quam predicti Robertus et Avicia tenendi eas in dominico.

Et ideo consideratum est quod Thomas et Ricardus et heredes eorum teneant in pace in perpetuum; et Robertus in misericordia per plegium Herberti de Pynu et Martini de Fisacre. (*In margin,* misericordia, *struck through.*)

The plaintiffs' pleading in this case is highly interesting and unusual. Robert and Avicia claim the tenements as their free inheritance alleging that their ancestor was seized "in his demesne as of fee and right." When the defendants, as might be expected, put themselves upon the grand assize, Robert and Avicia then plead ancient demesne while still claiming the land as a free tenement. But the plaintiffs are not alone in being inconsistent or contradictory; for the itinerant justices, having entertained the plea of ancient demesne, to bar the grand assize, and having accepted the defendants' admission to the same effect, then receive a verdict and deliver judgment which is, in effect, *secundum consuetudinem manerii.* Strictly speaking, we may well suspect that the fourteenth century lawyers would have considered this bad law. The case would normally have been sent back to the manorial court once royal (or ancient) demesne had been claimed and admitted; as to the plaintiffs' claim to the free tenement, the verdict of the county would be the usual method, at this time, of determining whether the land were under the common law. This case is a good example of how royal justices used their discretion in enforcing justice on the royal demesne. They were presumably willing to retain jurisdiction over the case so long as the plaintiffs

---

[21] Before this name, *Robertum Fabrum de Aysse* has been struck through.

[22] Before this name, *Johannem de la Fursa* has been struck through.

[23] *Osbertus* in original.

[24] *et* struck through before *preterea;* the original has *super* after *preterea,* but this word is meaningless here, and it is probable that the scribe neglected to strike it out when the additional names were inserted.

were ready to merge their claim to a free tenement with the issue of the better right to the land. It should, finally, be noted that this is the earliest case (to my knowledge) in which the phrase *antiquum dominicum* appears. See above, p. 179, and also the next case, from the same roll.

16. Ass. Roll No. 174, m.15. Pleas and Assizes at Exeter, 22 Henry III (1238).

Assisa venit recognitura si Galfridus de Okeston' Rogerus Leurich Ricardus Srech Reginaldus Beasho Rogerus Faber Rogerus de Herdecumb' Ricardus Cardon Robertus de Kyppedon' Johannes de la Hill' Galfridus de la Hill' Radulfus le Drak' Eylafus de Ermesdon' Osbertus de Hevetre Edwardus de Hevetre Willelmus de Hevetr' Radulfus Ters et Rogerus de Hevetr' injuste etc. disseisiverunt Willelmum Pipard de libero tenemento suo in Blak'don' post primam coronacionem etc. Et Galfridus et omnes alii veniunt et dicunt quod tenementum, unde assisa ista aramiata est, est in Hevedtre que est dominicum domini regis et inde petunt assisam. Set quia omnes juratores inutiles sunt, et quia assisa non potest capi ante recessum justiciariorum, ponitur in respectum usque ad adventum aliorum justiciariorum. Et vicecomes habet breve. Post venit Willelmus et concedit quod perambulacio fiat inter terram domini regis de Hevedtre et terram suam de Blakedon' si hoc placuerit domino regi. Et ideo loquendum inde cum domino rege.

Et Willelmus Pipard' ponit loco suo Johannem filium Andree. (*In margin,* Loquendum cum domino rege.)

17. Ass. Roll No. 55, m.2. Pleas and Assizes in the county of Buckingham, Hilary, 25 Henry III (1241).

Assisa venit recognitura si Willelmus Grei frater Agnetis filie Willelmi fuit seisitus in dominico suo etc. de u[no] mesuagio cum pertinenciis in Bukingh' die quo obiit et si obiit post ultimum reditum etc. et si etc.; quod mesuagium Rogerus Wikkesoule et Letoria uxor ejus tenent.

Qui veniunt et vocant inde [25] ad warantum Willelmum le Porter de Bukingh', qui venit et eis [26] warantizat et vocat inde ad warantum Willelmum de Breuse. Et quia adhuc non discutitur utrum assisa mortis antecessoris currat in villa Buking', et predictus Willelmus est infra etatem, expectetur adventus aliorum justiciariorum etc. (*In margin,* Bukingh'.)

Compare no. 4, above, and no. 27, below.

[25] *inde* repeated in original.

[26] *ei* in original.

18. Ass. Roll No. 37, m.22d. Pleas and Assizes at Reading, Michaelmas, 25–26 Henry III (1241).

Galfridus Coleman et Alicia uxor ejus summoniti fuerunt ad respondendum Holdeyarde de Wyndesor' de placito quod teneant ei convencionem factam inter eos de quatuor acris terre cum pertinenciis in Wyndes'; et unde queritur quod cum ipsi Galfridus et Alicia dimisissent ei predictas quatuor acras ad firman ad terminum decem annorum, ipsi detinuerunt ei per duos annos unam acram de predictis quatuor acris, unde deteriorata est et dampnum habet ad valenciam etc.

Et Galfridus pro se et Alicia cuius loco etc. venit et dicit [27] quod non debent ad hoc breve respondere quia terra illa est villenagium domini regis et ipse est villanus domini regis nec potest inde respondere sine domino rege. Et ideo Galfridus inde sine die, et Holdeyarda nichil capiat per breve istud et sit in misericordia pro falso clamio. Pauper est.

19. Ass. Roll No. 37, m.24. Pleas and Assizes at Reading, Michaelmas, 25–26 Henry III (1241).

Assisa venit recognitura si abbas de Bello Loco injuste etc. disseisivit Adam filium Roberti de libero tenemento suo in Farendon' post primam transfretacionem etc.

Et abbas venit et dicit quod assisa non debet inde fieri quia dicit quod Farendon' est antiquum dominicum regis et nullum breve debet esse in Farindon' nisi parvum breve quod debet habere justiciam secundum conseutudinem manerii. Et quia totus comitatus recordatur quod Farindon' est antiquum manerium et dominicum regis et quod non possunt homines de manerio illo, nisi feoffati fuerint per cartas, aliquod breve impetrare nec per aliquod breve implacitare nisi per parvum breve, ideo abbas inde sine die et alius in misericordia. Pauper est. (*In margin, against the whole entry, a large, long X.*)

Note that the county court, not Domesday Book, is consulted to establish ancient demesne (or that "Faringdon is an ancient manor and demesne of the king," as the county puts it). A distinction seems to be drawn between the men of the manor who must use the little writ and those who are enfeoffed by charter and can sue at the common law; this statement should be compared with nos. 7, 12, 24, and 26.

20. Ass. Roll No. 37, m.24d. Pleas and Assizes at Reading, Michaelmas, 25–26 Henry III (1241).

Petrus filius Henrici petit versus Fulconem filium Warini unum molendinum et unam virgatam terre cum pertinenciis in Waneting' ut jus

[27] *ven' et dicunt* in original.

suum etc.; et unde quidam Willelmus antecessor ipsius Petri fuit seisitus in dominico suo ut de feodo et jure tempore domini regis qui nunc est, capiendo inde expleta ad valenciam dimidie marce etc. Et quia idem Willelmus obiit sine herede de se, descendit jus terre illius et molendini cuidam Henrico ut fratri et heredi; et de ipso Henrico isti Petro qui nunc petit ut filio et heredi; et quod tale sit jus suum offert etc.

Et Fulco per attornatum suum venit et defendit jus suum quando et ubi etc.; et dicit quod predicta terra et molendinum sunt de antiquo dominico domini regis, et dicit quod nullum placitum debet placitari de huiusmodi tenemento nisi in ipso manerio. Post venit et dicit quod predictus Petrus villanus est, et salva sibi libertate predicti manerii, defendit jus ipsius Petri et seisinam antecessoris sui et totum; et dicit quod promptus est ponere se in magnam assisam domini regis vel in juratam xij. proborum et legalium hominum de ipso manerio, et bene wult quod recognicio fiat utrum ipse majus jus habeat tenendi predictam terram et molendinum cum pertinenciis in dominico an idem Petrus tenendi ea de eo. Et quia comitatus recordatur quod manerium de Waneting' fuit antiqum dominicum domini regis et quod huiusmodi placita solent terminari in ipso manerio per xij. de predicto manerio secundum consuetudinem ipsius manerii, ideo de consilio curie preceptum est vicecomiti quod in propria persona accedat ad ipsum manerium et ibi eligere faciat xij. de legalibus hominibus de predicto manerio ad recognoscendum super sacramentum suum in forma magne assise utrum predictus Fulco majus jus habeat tenendi predictam terram et molendinum in dominico an idem Petrus tenendi ea de eo etc.

This case should be compared with no. 15, where judgment was delivered by the itinerant justices after the local jury had given its verdict. Here, presumably, the jury will appear before the sheriff in the manorial court, where judgment will be delivered. It should be noticed that the itinerant justices dispose of this case "by counsel of the court" (rather than the more usual *de consideracione curie* or *consideratum est* which signified judgment of the issue involved).

21. C.R.R. 121, m.33d. Pleas before the King, 25 Henry III (1241).

Suht'.—Amira que fuit uxor Ade de Gurdon' summonita fuit ad ostendendum quo waranto tenet unam carrucatam terre cum pertinenciis in Tych'sted', que est de antiquo dominico predecessorum domini regis regum Anglie etc. Et Amira venit et defendit etc.; et petit inde visum. Habeat. Dies datus est ei a die sancti Michaelis in xv. dies; et interim etc.

This is the earliest case I have found in the surviving Curia Regis Rolls in which the phrase *antiquum dominicum* occurs. In the other cases of *quo waranto* in this roll the phrase is *dominicum domini regis,* or the like.

22. C.R.R. 124, m.21d. Pleas before the Justices of the Bench, Michaelmas, 26–27 Henry III (1242).

Norf'.—Michael filius Rogeri de Stokton' per attornatum suum petit versus Willelmum filium Rogeri de Stokton' terciam partem 1. acrarum terre et unius mesuagii cum pertinentiis in Elingham et Stokton' [28] ut rationabilem partem suam que eum contigit de hereditate que fuit Rogeri de Stokton', patris predictorum Michaelis et Willelmi et Hugonis et Henrici de Stokton', cuius heredes ipsi sunt etc. Et sciendum quod Hugo et Henricus fratres predicti Michaelis [29] non secuntur.

Et Willelmus venit et defendit jus suum; et dicit quod non debet ei ad hoc breve respondere, quia dicit quod manerium de Stokton' et Elingh' antiquitus fuit dominicum manerium domini regis, et ubi nullus implacitatur nisi per breve clausum. Post venit predictus Willelmus et defendit jus suum etc.; et bene dicit quod predicta terra non est partibilis, nec umquam fuit partita tempore alicuius antecessórum suorum; et quod ita sit ponit se super patriam, et Michael similiter. Et ideo preceptum est vicecomiti quod venire faciat coram justiciariis ad primam etc. xij. etc. per quos etc. et qui nec etc. ad recognoscendum etc. si predicta terra partibilis sit et si umquam fuit partita vel non. Quia tam etc.

23. C.R.R. 125, m.3. Pleas before the King's Council, Trinity, 26 Henry III (1242).

Huntingdon'.—Preceptum fuit vicecomiti quod venire faceret coram Rogero de Thurkelby et sociis suis quos secum duceret associandos die Veneris proxima post festum sancte Trinitatis apud Huntingdon' xij. tam milites quam alios etc. qui nec etc. ad recogno[s]cendum super sacramentum suum que dominica antecessores domini regis reges Anglie habuerunt in manerio de Brampton', et qui illa tenent, et per quem et per quod servicium et a quo tempore illa tenuerunt, et similiter que villenagia dicti antecessores domini regis in eodem manerio habuerunt,[30] et qui illa tenent et per quas consuetudines; et ad recognoscendum etc. si homines predicti manerii huteysum levaverunt super ballivos vicecomitis ibidem missos in auxilium cum ballivis Henrici de Hasting' ad talliandum predictos homines per preceptum domini regis, et averia

[28] *et Stokton'* interlined over a caret mark.

[29] *fratres predicti Michaelis* interlined.

[30] *habuerunt* interlined.

sua capta per predictos ballivos eo quod non permiserunt se talliari contra preceptum domini regis violenter eis abstulerunt, et quosdam eorum verberaverunt et quosdam illorum cum huteyso vi et armis secuti fuerunt usque Huntingdon' contra pacem etc.

Et vicecomes fecit venire ad diem illum inquisicionem que capta fuit per Radulfum de Bereford' Henricum de Fukewurth' Robertum Leonard Rogerum de Cantelupo de Cestreton' Henricum de Faffington' Radulfum de Quassingburn' Willelmum de Lullington' Mauricium de Weston' Willelmum de Baiocis Richerum de Tillebrok' Willelmum filium Thome de Mulleswurth', qui veniunt et dicunt super sacramentum suum quod Henricus rex, avus domini regis Henrici regis qui nunc est, tenuit in dominico suo duas carucatas terre in manerio de Brampton' cum uno mesuagio et boscis et pratis molendinis et placitis, et easdem duas carucatas terre ganiavit propriis carucis suis, et ex alia parte viginti et octo virgatas terre in eodem manerio quas homines ejusdem manerii tenuerunt [31] de eo in villenagio. Dicunt eciam quod, quando dominus Henricus [32] rex tenuit predictas duas carucatas terre in dominico suo cum boscis molendinis placitis et pratis eisdem carucatis terre pertinentibus, tenuerunt homines de Brampton' predictas viginti octo virgatas terre cum pratis eisdem virgatis pertinentibus in villenagio aliquando ad denarios aliquando per consuetudines villanas ad voluntatem ipsius Henrici regis; et quando tenuerunt ad denarios, dederunt pro qualibet virgata terre v. solidos pro omnibus serviciis, et quando fecerunt consuetudines, fecerunt aruras sarcluras averagia et cariagia de cibo et venacione; et dederunt heryettum et merchettum toto tempore suo. Processu temporis dimisit idem Henricus rex predictas duas carucatas terre et mesuagium et pratum pertinencia ad illas duas carucatas et predictas viginti octo virgatas terre et pratum pertinens ad eas pro xx. libris per annum ad firmam, set nesciunt quantum prati pertinebat ad predictas duas carucatas vel quantum prati pertinebat ad predictas virgatas; et retinuit in manu sua boscum molendinum et placita ejusdem manerii. Et post mortem ipsius Henrici regis reddiderunt predicti homines de Brampton' Ricardo regi [33] viginti libras pro predictis terris et pratis, exceptis boscis molendinis et placitis que retinuit in manu sua; et sic tenuerunt usque reditum suum de Allemannia. Et tunc dedit predictum manerium cuidam Lamberto de Colonna,[34] qui cepit viginti libras per annum de predictis hominibus pro predicto

---

[31] *tenuerint* in original.

[32] *Henricus* interlined.

[33] *Ricardo regi* interlined.

[34] *Colonna* written, as a contemporary correction, over *Telon.*

manerio per tres annos et dimidium; et retinuit sibi boscum molendinum et placita. Et postea exigebat ab eis plures alias consuetudines; et quia illas facere noluerunt, venit ad dominum Ricardum regem et reddidit ei predictum manerium et cepit de camera sua viginti libras. Et tunc acrevit idem Ricardus rex firmam suam de x. libris, ita quod toto tempore suo reddiderunt triginta libras; et retinuit in manu sua boscum molendinum et placita. Et post obitum ipsius Ricardi regis seisi[v]it dominus Johannes rex predictum manerium in manu sua; et tunc accreverunt firmam suam de viginti libris, ita quod reddiderunt quinquaginta libras pro predicto manerio et molendino; et retinuit in manu sua boscum et placita. Et non possunt inquirere nec scire quod tempore ejusdem Johannis regis dederunt merchettum vel heryettum; set bene credunt quod hoc fuit ex permissione ipsius regis et non per aliquam convencionem quam fecerat eis per predictas quinquaginta libras; set talliavit eos quando talliavit cetera dominica sua. Dicunt eciam quod predictus Johannes rex dedit predictum manerium comiti David, qui illud tenuit toto tempore suo in eodem statu in quo dominus rex illud tenuit.

Dicunt eciam quod ballivi vicecomitis venerunt apud Brampton' ad faciendum ipsum Henricum habere talliagium de eis per preceptum domini regis; et quia nolluerunt intrare ad dandum talliagium, ipsi ballivi ceperunt averia sua; et tunc venerunt homines ejusdem ville et prosecuti fuerunt eos cum huteyso et clamore usque Huntingdon' et abstulerunt eis predicta averia cum hachiis et baculis; set nessciunt nomina eorum, quia major pars [35] ville de Brampton' ibi fuit. Dicunt eciam quod non est aliquis liber homo in eodem manerio nisi Willelmus filius Radulfi, qui tenet terram suam per sex solidos per annum et respondit infra corpus comitatus.

Et ideo consideratum est quod predictus Henricus remaneat in pace et [36] in eadem seisina predicti manerii in qua predecessores domini regis fuerunt dum manerium illud fuit in manibus suis; et inde faciat pro voluntate sua, sicut predicti reges facere potuerunt ut de dominicis boscis pratis molendinis, preter hoc quod non talliat homines predicti manerii nisi quando dominus rex talliet maneria et dominica sua; et homines de Bramptun' pro falso clamio in misericordia. Et quia convictum est per predictam inquisicionem quod predicti homines de Bramptun fugaverunt ballivos vicecomitis domini regis ibi missos cum ballivis predicti Henrici ad distringendum eos quod permitterent se talliari per preceptum domini regis et quod violenter averia ea occa-

---

[35] *pars* interlined.

[36] *et* interlined.

sione capta a ballivis predicti vicecomitis abstulerunt, ideo in misericordia pro transgressione. Et Johannes Kechel Johannes le Sire Elyas Nolly et Hugo de Mynill', quatuor ex illis transgressoribus qui venerunt, committuntur gayole pro predicta transgressione.

This case—apart from the interesting, if violent, reaction of the men of Brampton to the collection of a tallage—is important for the light it throws upon the privileges of the tenants of the royal demesne. The essential principle is that a royal manor in another's hand should be held "in the same state in which the lord king held it." During the thirteenth century, and later, tenants of recently alienated royal manors frequently complained that their new lords had changed their status by substituting "villein customs" for the rent they had formerly been paying. This case shows that such a change was not necessarily subversive of the tenants' rights. If the king had possessed the right, when the manor was in his hands, of exacting rent or services at will, the same right would pass to the new lord of the manor. (Compare no. 8, above.) The view is sometimes expressed, in modern works, that the royal courts tended to favor the lord as against the "tenants of ancient demesne" in this kind of dispute, because the courts often decided in favor of the lord who had changed from rent to services after receiving the grant of his royal manor. If all these cases were as fully reported as the present one, the charge of favoritism might be very difficult to sustain.

24. Ass. Roll No. 175, m.3d. Pleas and Assizes at Exeter, 28 Henry III (1244).

Assisa venit recognitura si Joel de Westchingl' avunculus Joelis filii Sywardi fuit seisitus in dominico suo ut de feodo de quarta parte dimidie virgate terre cum pertinenciis in Blaketorinton' die quo etc. et si etc.; quam terram Joel' filius Jordani tenet. Qui venit et dicit quod non debet ei ad hoc breve respondere quia predicta terra est de dominico domini regis in Blaketorinton' ubi tale breve non currit; et dicit similiter quod predictus Joel' de Westchingl' non obiit seisitus de predicta terra ut [37] de feodo. Et Joel' filius Sywardi dicit quod obiit ut de feodo et cartam inde habuit, et de hoc ponit se super juratam.

Juratores dicunt quod predictus Joel' de Westchingl' avunculus predicti Joelis obiit seisitus de predicta terra ut de feodo et post terminum, et quod predictus Joel' est propinquior heres ejus. Et ideo consideratum [est] quod predictus Joel' filius Siwardi recuperavit seisinam suam versus eum; et predictus Joel' filius Jordani in misericordia per plegium

[37] *ut* repeated in original.

Willelmi de Wamford et Rogeri Pigge. (*In margin,* misericordia, *struck through.*)

Compare no. 26, below.

25. Ass. Roll No. 175, m.20d. Pleas and Assizes at Exeter, 28 Henry III (1244).

Thomas de Luschote petit versus Robertum de Blakeford' et Aviciam uxorem ejus dimidium ferlingum terre cum pertinenciis in Branton' ut jus suum etc. per breve secundum consuetudinem manerii; [38] et unde quidam Theobaldus pater ipsius Thome fuit seisitus ut de feodo et jure tempore regis Johannis patris domini regis capiendo inde espleta ad valenciam etc.; et de ipso Theobaldo descendit jus predicte terre isti Thome ut filio et heredi; et quod tale sit jus suum offert etc.

Et Robertus pro se et Avicia cuius loco etc. venit et deffendit jus suum quando etc. Et quia non potest constare justiciariis de consuetudine predicti manerii, ideo dictum est vicecomiti quod ipse audiat loquelam et faciat inde justiciam.

Compare no. 15, above. In the earlier case between these two parties, the itinerant justices delivered judgment.

26. Ass. Roll No. 175, m.23d. Pleas and Assizes at Exeter, 28 Henry III (1244).

Assisa venit recognitura si Margeria la Zusche Alanus la Zusche Robertus de Cadeleg' et Robertus le Blund injuste etc. disseisiverunt Jollanum filium Jordani de libero tenemento suo in Blakethorinton' post primam etc.; et unde queritur quod disseisiverunt eum de quadam montana que continet circiter decem acras.

Et Alanus et alii veniunt et dicunt quod non debent ei ad hoc breve respondere quia manerium de Blakethorinton' fuit antiquum dominicum domini regis ubi tale breve non currit. Et preterea idem Jollanus nichil ostendit de feoffamento de predicta terra. Et ideo consideratum est quod Alanus et alii inde sine die; et Jollanus in misericordia. Custodiatur. Et perquirat sibi per parvum breve secundum consuetudinem regni [39] si voluerit. Plegii Johannis [40] de misericordia sua Willelmus de Wammeford' et Radulfus de Apse. (*In margin,* misericordia.)

Compare no. 24, above.

27. Ass. Roll No. 56, m.15d. Pleas and Assizes at Wycombe, 32 Henry III (1247).

Assisa venit recognitura si Willelmus Gernun frater Agnetis uxoris

[38] *per breve secundum consuetudinem manerii* interlined.

[39] This word is abbreviated as *r'* in original; recte, *manerii.*

[40] Recte, *Jollani.*

Willelmi le Brade fuit seisitus in dominico suo etc. de uno mesuagio cum pertinenciis in Buk' die quo etc. et si etc.; quod mesuagium Rogerus Uggesoule et Letoria uxor ejus tenent. Qui veniunt et vocant inde ad warantum Rogerum de Wymbervill' qui presens est et eis warantizat. Et dicit quod assisa non debet inde fieri quia dicit quod burgus de Bukingham fuit antiqum dominicum domini regis ubi tale breve non currit. Et Willelmus le Brade et Agnes non possunt hoc dedicere. Et ideo consideratum est quod predictus Rogerus inde sine die; et ipsi Willelmus et Agnes in misericordia per plegium Willelmi le Grey. (*In margin,* misericordia.)

Compare nos. 4 and 17, above.

28. Ancient Correspondence, vol. XI, no. 7. A letter from the bailiffs of Brill to the king's council concerning a dispute settled in the lord king's court of Brill, 1245–1246.[41]

Viris providis [et] discretis et dominis reverendissimis domini regis consiliariis ballivi domini regis de Brehull' salutem et tam debitam quam devotam reverenciam. [Vestre do]minacioni duximus intimandum nos die Lune proxima ante festum beati Thome ul[timo pret]eritum preceptum domini regis in hec verba susscepisse: Henricus dei gracia r[ex A]nglie etc. ballivis suis de Brehull' salutem. Gravem nuper a Ricardo d[e . . . .]l[42] accepimus querelam quod vos eum pro vestre volunt[atis l]ibito dissaisivistis,[43] unde plurimum admiramur. Et ideo vobis mandamus quod nobis per litteras vestras per eundem Ricardum sine dilacione distincte et aperte scire faciatis qua racione vel occasione ipsum de terra sua, si ita est, dissaisiveritis. Teste me ipso apud Clarendun xiij.[44] die Decembris [anno regni] regis xxxj.

Nos vero inquantum possimus volentes mandatis domini regis obedire taliter resspondemus quod quidam Radulfus filius Willelmi de Brehull' preceptum domini regis nobis detulit in hec verba: Henricus dei gracia rex Anglie etc. ballivis suis de Brehull' salutem. Precipimus vobis quod sine dilacione et secundum consuetudinem manerii nostri de Brehull' plenum rectum teneatis Radulfo filio Willelmi de quatuordecim acris terre cum pertinenciis in Brehull', unde Johannes de la Huse novem acras Agatha que fuit uxor Walteri de Myldunhal' quatuor acras Ricardus le Turnur dimidiam acram et Petrus filius Simonis

[41] This document is illegible in a few places owing to the presence of holes in the manuscript. The letter has been divided into paragraphs which do not appear in the original.

[42] This is *Ricardus filius Walteri de Myldunhal',* as will appear.

[43] *dissaivistis* in original.

[44] This number might be read as *xxij.*

dimidiam acram terre ei deforciant, ne amplius inde clamorem audiamus pro defectu recti. Teste me ipso apud Wyngchecumb' xx. die Julii anno regni regis xxix.

Istis vero in predicto brevi nominatis ad curiam domini regis de Brehull' vocatis, et habitis dilacionibus secundum consuetudinem manerii de Brehull' et tandem habitis omnibus dilacionibus que sibi competebant, vocarunt dicti defor[c]iatores in warantum quamdam Isabellam filiam Walteri de Myldunhal' que quidem [45] Isabella intravit in plenum warantum dicte terre. Tandem debitis et consuetis dilacionibus eidem Isabelle secundum consuetudinem manerii de Brehull' concessis, vocavit eadem Isabella in warantum Ricardum fratrem suum qui quidem intravit in warantum prout fuit vocatus. Tandem debitis et consuetis dilacionibus eidem Ricardo et secundum consuetudinem manerii concessis, vocavit idem Ricardus in warantum quamdam Ascelinam; unde datus fuit dies dicto Ricardo ad warantum suum habendum, scilicet ad proximam curiam. Qui quidem Ricardus nec venit nec ressponsalem misit ad illam curiam.[46] Curia vero consulta super hoc posuit loquelam in resspectu usque ad proximam curiam ad quam necdum venit predictus Ricardus nec ressponsalem misit, et sic fecit unicam defaltam, unde predicta terra judicio tocius curie capta fuit in manum domini regis.

Predicto vero Radulfo ad eandem curiam preceptum domini regis d[efe]rente in hec verba: Henricus dei gracia rex Anglie etc. ballivis suis de Brehull' salutem. Precipimus vobis quod juste et sine dilacione faciatis habere Radulfo filio Willelmi recordum et racionabile judicium suum de loquela que est coram vobis in curia nostra [47] de Brehull' per breve nostrum inter ipsum Radulfum petentem et Ricardum filium Walteri et Isabellam filiam Walteri tenentes de tresdecim acris terre et dimidia cum pertinenciis in Brehull' sicut loquela illa racionabiliter deducta est in eadem curia, ne amplius inde clamorem audiamus pro defectu justicie. Teste me ipso apud Rading' primo die Octobris anno regni regis xxxj.[48] Ad proximam aliam sequentem curiam [49] necdum venit predictus Ricardus nec ressponsalem misit, et sic aliam fecit defaltam.[50]

Nos vero predicto Ricardo parcentes misimus ad eum tres viros fide-

[45] *quidam* in original.

[46] *ad illam curiam* interlined.

[47] This word is abbreviated in a form which could be read and extended as either *nostra* or *vestra*. The usage of the scribe would warrant either reading.

[48] Recte, *xxx*?

[49] *curiam* interlined.

[50] The sense requires the entire paragraph to be read as if it were one sentence.

dingnos curie nostre ut requirerent ab eo utrum vellet replegiare feodum suum vel non vellet, qui quidem Ricardus resspondebat quod replegiare noluit. Curia vero super hoc consulta propter iteratam defaltam adjudicavit predicto Ricardo perdere [51] saysinam et predicto Radulfo saysinam recuperare. Taliter autem d[ed]ucta est predicta loquela in predicta [curia]. In cuius rei testimonium [*hoc prese*]ns scriptum clausum singnatum singnis quorumdam sociorum nostrorum vestre [dom]inacioni duximus transmittendum.

This letter illustrates the judicial supervision and redress exercised by the council which Henry III accused the baronial council, in 1261, of failing to provide for the tenants of the royal demesne. The case was initiated by the little writ of right close according to the custom of the manor (whose full text is given), and judgment was made by the *curia domini regis de Brehull'*. The last writ quoted by the bailiffs gives the text of the writ *de habendo recordum et racionabile judicium* which the printed Register of Writs associates with the ancient demesne. This letter is one of the earliest descriptions, in any detail, of the legal procedure in a manorial court of the royal demesne. It should be noted that the tenement in dispute is termed *feodum suum;* and yet the plea rolls usually refer to land in the royal manor of Brill as socage. Compare no. 2, above.

---

[51] *perdedere* in original.

CHAPTER VII

Conclusion

In concluding this review of the royal demesne of the medieval English monarchy from the Conquest to the death of Henry III, we shall first summarize the conclusions of the foregoing discussion and estimate the constitutional significance of the royal demesne in the period and, finally, touch upon problems outside the chronological limits or the immediate scope of the present work.

The nature of the royal demesne of the Norman settlement is of crucial importance both for an understanding of the Anglo-Norman monarchy and for a proper assessment of the role of the royal demesne in English medieval history as a whole. The *Terra Regis* of Domesday Book, like the royal demesne throughout the Middle Ages, has not hitherto been made the subject of special study, although nearly all historians of the period have touched on it in connection with broader problems in which they were interested. A review of the evidence has led us to the conclusion that the royal demesne was not, in 1086, set apart from the rest of the realm, as it came to be at a later period. The royal demesne was not an immunity as a whole, although many royal manors, just like many private manors, were exempt from geld or otherwise specially privileged. So also, there was no fundamental distinction between one and another kind of royal demesne. There was no "ancient demesne" consisting of "the manors of St. Edward" which in any significant way were set apart or treated differently from the rest of the *Terra Regis*.

Among the older royal manors, particularly those which had from the beginning been held by the kings of Wessex and had descended to Edward the Confessor and William the Conqueror, special privilege might flourish better than among royal manors of recent acquisition. But the same may be said of large and ancient ecclesiastical manors. Immunity was both royal and private, and it was a matter of degree. The normal condition of the royal demesne was the same as that of the demesne manors of the barons and prelates. The degree to which a manor—whether royal or private—was exempt from geld or separate from the regular administration of shire and hundred, was dependent upon the will of the king and not upon anything inherently "royal" in the *Terra Regis*. It is a mistake to read back into the eleventh-century political ideas and distinctions of which that age was ignorant. Neither with regard to the administration, taxation, nor economic exploitation of the royal demesne can the king as greatest landlord be distinguished from the king as suzerain ruler, in any fundamental way. The "public" authority and "private" rights of the feudal monarchy were fused in the person of the *dominus rex*.

The great extent and value of the Conqueror's royal demesne, approaching one-fourth of the total value of the landed wealth of England, and providing the monarchy with a direct seignorial interest in many shires where Edward had held few manors or none at all, are fundamental to the political power of the Anglo-Norman monarchy. Beyond this basic importance of the royal demesne, its economic exploitation raises a special problem. The seignorial policy of the monarchy, the attitude of the Anglo-Norman kings toward the peasantry of their demesne manors, must be determined in order to account properly for later developments which have been alleged to result from preferential treatment of royal peasants by the king who was "the best of landlords." We have found, on the contrary, that the royal peasantry were subject to a thoroughgoing exploitation at the hands of royal officials and farmers which argues strongly against special favor or preferential treatment. The attitude of the king in this respect, as elsewhere, was the same as that of any other lord. On the other hand, the early development, in England, of a mature financial system owes much to the freedom with which new financial and administrative methods could be developed in connection with the exploitation of the widespread royal demesne and then extended to the general administration of the whole realm.

The huge landed endowment of the Anglo-Norman monarchy was, in the first half of the twelfth century, dissipated rapidly. This undoubted fact seems inexplicable only if later ideas are read back into the period. Alienation of the royal demesne did not amount to loss of the wealth represented by alienated manors. The seignorial rights and wealth of the king as landlord were transformed into the rights and revenues of the king as feudal lord of his vassals. The exploitation of royal manors by royal officials—an exploitation which involved the danger of enhancing shrieval power and the inevitable loss of a "middle man's" profits under the medieval system of farming—was replaced by the exploitation of the rights of lordship, the profits of justice, and of the incidents of feudal tenure.

The administrative and legal reforms of the reign of Henry II are, from the beginning, closely associated with the administration and exploitation of the royal demesne, where the monarchy was relatively unrestricted by the limitations of custom or the contractual element in feudalism. While these reforms applied equally to the royal demesne and to the rest of the realm, they nevertheless resulted in the growth of a royal demesne which was both distinct from the rest of the realm and also beginning to be treated as one whole, an entity from which the monarchy drew strength clearly separate from the power it possessed by virtue of the feudal rights of the king as overlord. There were two reasons for this development. First, the administration and exploitation of the demesne was centralized under the Exchequer; second, the monarchy developed upon the demesne a new "nonfeudal" tax which increased its demesne revenues at the same time that it served to mark off more clearly the boundary between the royal demesne and the rest of the realm.

The judicial and administrative reforms of Henry II underlay the growth of the idea of the inalienability of the royal demesne, which first appears in the administrative practice of the reigns of Richard I, John, and Henry III. By the middle of the thirteenth century, the concept of "the ancient demesne of the crown"—the endowment of the monarchy, set apart from the rest of the realm, thought of as especially pertaining to the office rather than the person of the king—is fully developed. The privileges of the tenants of the ancient demesne were the result of royal policy and not a survival of pre-Conquest conditions upon the manors held by Edward the Confessor or William the Conqueror. Legal protection of tenure and services of the peasantry on royal manors, and also upon manors once royal but later alienated, represents a successful effort of the monarchy to extend its demesne rights and increase its judicial profits.

The extension of royal justice to the unfree peasants of alienated manors was a radical break with feudal ideas, although it was done in the name of custom and justified by appeals to the past. The custom of the king's demesnes governed the tenure and services of the tenants of the ancient demesne, whether in the king's or others' hands. But appeals to custom or to the past must not obscure the central fact that this protection, this supremacy of the custom of the manor over the will of the lord, was effected by the monarchy and existed only by virtue of the peasants' access to royal justice. The constitutional significance of the privileges of the ancient demesne lies in the fact that they are the by-product of an effort of the monarchy to increase its revenues and extend its authority down past the line of freedom (below which the common law did not penetrate). The ultmiate end of such a process would be to transform an essentially feudal society into one in which the relationship between the ruler and his subjects was essentially that of the modern state—relatively unrestricted by the intervening rights of feudal lords. Such a revolution could not be accomplished by one act, in one reign, or in one century; nor could its scope include the whole of the realm. The process was piecemeal and slow, and the important point to emphasize is that the royal demesne provided the starting point, the area in which such a transformation of the realm could begin. Both the slowness of the process and the rationalizations of royal policy provided by Bracton and his followers have led historians to view the privileges of the ancient demesne as essentially a survival and as evidence of the force of custom and the static nature of medieval society. It has been our thesis, and is now submitted as our conclusion, that the very reverse was true. The real nature of the royal demesne in English constitutional history was dynamic and not static in that it provided the monarchy its best opportunity for shaping and creating medieval society to serve its own interests. Thus, the royal demesne is intimately connected with the growth of the distinction between crown and king, which is basic to the evolution of the monarchy from one which is more feudal than national to one that is more national than feudal. In a real sense the royal demesne is the heart of the realm—a realm which the monarchy was consistently trying to consolidate and bring wholly under its full authority, subject only to the limitations imposed by the legal rights of its subjects.

The constitutional significance of the royal demesne, then, is to be found in the light it can throw upon the nature and policy of the medieval monarchy.

Much work remains to be done on a variety of problems connected with the history of the royal demesne as it affects the medieval English monarchy. The Anglo-Saxon crown lands and the royal demesne after 1272 remain to be studied in detail. There is need for a thorough investigation of the social and economic conditions within the manors of the Domesday *Terra Regis*—an investigation which will take full account of the regional differences in the general social structure of eleventh century England. Royal tallage has not received the treatment it deserves. Its relationship both with other twelfth century "prerogative" taxes and with the later parliamentary taxation should be worked out. An intensive study of the administrative history of the royal demesne in the twelfth and thirteenth centuries would throw new light on the evolution of governmental institutions by describing the functions and duties of sheriffs, bailiffs, keepers, and escheators with respect to the royal demesne. This administrative history would have to deal with the practice of farming and subfarming estates to the tenants of royal manors. And this subject would provide a new approach to the problem of the immunity of the ancient demesne in the thirteenth century. Exemption from common amercements of shire and hundred, from suit to the public courts, from parliamentary taxation, and from the authority of the sheriff and his officials, was not a simple heritage of "Anglo-Saxon freedom." Nor was it absolute. The ancient demesne may have been exempt from parliamentary taxation in the days of Fitzherbert and Coke, but the important point is that in the beginning it was not. The royal demesne, urban and rural, together with the nonroyal boroughs represented in parliament, for a time made up a parliamentary "estate" of the realm, the creation of royal policy. All of these subjects lie outside the scope or chronological limits of the present work, and they all provide a neglected approach both to the medieval English monarchy and to the growth of the realm. The history of the royal demesne is found at the center of both.

APPENDIX F

A List of Abbreviations of Works Frequently Cited

I. SOURCES

A. Documents and Official Records

Ass. Roll	Public Record Office, Assize Roll.
Book of Fees	*Liber Feodorum: The Book of Fees Commonly Called Testa de Nevill,* 3 vols. (Public Record Office), London, 1920–1931.
Cl.R.	*Close Rolls of the Reign of Henry III, 1227–1272,* in 14 vols. (Public Record Office), London, 1902–1938.
C.R.R.	Public Record Office, Curia Regis Roll.
C.R.R.	*Curia Regis Rolls of the Reigns of Richard I and John,* edited by C. T. Flower, 8 vols. (Public Record Office), London, 1922–1938.
D.B.	*Domesday Book: Seu Liber Censualis Willelmi Primi Regis Angliae.* Text, vols. I and II, edited by Abraham Farley, n.p., 1783; Indices and Introduction, vol. III, and *Additamenta,* vol. IV, edited by Sir Henry Ellis (Record Commission), n.p., 1816.
Mem. Roll 1 John	*The Memoranda Roll for the Michaelmas Term of the First Year of the Reign of King John (1199–1200),* edited by H. G. Richardson (Pipe Roll Society, New Series, vol. XXI), London, 1943.
P.R.	*Magnum Rotulum Scaccarii, vel Magnum Rotulum Pipae, de Anno Tricesimo-Primo Regni*

	Henrici Primi, edited by Joseph Hunter (Record Commission); *The Pipe Roll of 31 Henry I* (reproduced in facsimile from the edition of 1833), London, 1929.
	The Great Rolls of the Pipe for the Second, Third, and Fourth Years of the Reign of King Henry the Second, edited by Joseph Hunter (Record Commission); *The Pipe Rolls of 2–3–4 Henry II* (reproduced in facsimile from the edition of 1844), London, 1930.
	Pipe Rolls of the reign of Henry II (Publications of the Pipe Roll Society, vols. I, II, IV–IX, XI–XIII, XV, XVI, XVIII, XIX, XXI, XXII, XXV–XXXIV, and XXXVI–XXXVIII), London, 1884–1925.
	Pipe Rolls of the reigns of Richard I and John (Pipe Roll Society, New Series, vols. I–III, V–X, XII, XIV–XVI, XVIII–XX, XXII, and XXIII), London, 1925—(continuing).
	The Great Roll of the Pipe for the Twenty-Sixth Year of the Reign of King Henry the Third, edited by H. L. Cannon (Yale Historical Publications, vol. V), New Haven, 1918.
Plac. Abbrev.	*Placitorum in domo capitulari Westmonasteriensi asservatorum Abbreviatio,* abstracted *t. Eliz.* by Arthur Agarde (Record Commission), n.p., 1811.
Red Book Exch.	*The Red Book of the Exchequer,* edited by Hubert Hall, 3 vols. (Rolls Series), London, 1896.
Richardson and Sayles, *Proc. without Writ*	Richardson, H. G., and Sayles, George, editors, *Select Cases of Procedure without Writ under Henry III* (Selden Society, vol. LX), London, 1941.
Rot. Cur. Reg.	*Rotuli Curiae Regis,* edited by Sir Francis Palgrave, 2 vols. (Record Commission), n.p., 1835.
Rot. de Dom.	*Rotuli de Dominabus et Pueris et Puellis de XII Comitatibus,* with introduction and notes by J. H. Round (Pipe Roll Society, vol. XXXV), London, 1913.

Rot. Hund.	*Rotuli Hundredorum temp. Hen. III & Edw. I,* edited by W. Illingworth, 2 vols. (Record Commission), n.p., 1812–1818.
Rot. Litt. Claus.	*Rotuli Litterarum Clausarum,* edited by T. D. Hardy, 2 vols. (Record Commission), n.p., 1833–1844.
Rot. de Obl. et Fin.	*Rotuli de Oblatis et Finibus in Turri Londinensi asservati, Tempore Regis Johannis,* edited by T. D. Hardy (Record Commission), n.p., 1835.
Rot. Orig.	*Rotulorum Originalium in Curia Scaccarii Abbreviatio,* 2 vols. (Record Commission), n.p., 1805–1810.
Lincolnshire and Worcestershire Eyre	Stenton, D. M., editor, *Rolls of the Justices in Eyre . . . for Lincolnshire 1218–9 and Worcestershire 1221* (Selden Society, vol. LIII), London, 1934.
Gloucestershire, Warwickshire, and Staffordshire Eyre	Stenton, D. M., editor, *Rolls of the Justices in Eyre . . . for Gloucestershire, Warwickshire and Staffordshire, 1221, 1222* (Selden Society, vol. LIX), London, 1940.

B. Treatises, Collections, Literary Works, Etc.

Bigelow, *Plac. Ang.-Norm.*	Bigelow, M. M., editor, *Placita Anglo-Normannica,* Boston, 1879.
Bracton, *De Leg. et Cons.*	Bracton, *De Legibus et Consuetudinibus Angliae,* edited by G. E. Woodbine, 4 vols., New Haven, 1915–1942.
Bracton's Note Book	*Bracton's Note Book,* edited by F. W. Maitland, 3 vols., London, 1887.
Glanvill, *De Legibus*	Glanvill, *De Legibus et Consuetudinibus Regni Angliae,* edited by G. E. Woodbine (Yale Historical Publications, Manuscripts and Edited Texts, vol. XIII), New Haven, 1932.
Liebermann, *Gesetze*	Liebermann, F., editor, *Die Gesetze der Angelsachsen,* Erster Band: Text und Ubersetzung, Halle, 1898–1903.
Robertson, *Anglo-Saxon Charters*	Robertson, A. J., editor, *Anglo-Saxon Charters* (Cambridge Studies in English Legal History, edited by H. D. Hazeltine), Cambridge, 1939.

Scac. Dial. — *De Necessariis Observantiis Scaccarii Dialogus,* edited by Arthur Hughes, C. G. Crump, and Charles Johnson, Oxford, 1902.

Select Charters — Stubbs, William, editor, *Select Charters and Other Illustrations of English Constitutional History* (9th edition, revised, edited by H. W. C. Davis), Oxford, 1929.

II. SECONDARY WORKS

A. Books

Baigent and Millard, *Basingstoke* — Baigent, F. J., and Millard, J. E., *A History of the Ancient Town and Manor of Basingstoke,* Basingstoke, 1889.

Cam, *Liberties & Communities* — Cam, H. M., *Liberties & Communities in Medieval England,* Cambridge, 1944.

Eyton, *Dorset Survey* — Eyton, R. W., *A Key to Domesday . . . Analysis and Digest of the Dorset Survey,* Dorchester, 1878.

Jacob, *Studies* — Jacob, E. F., *Studies in the Period of Baronial Reform and Rebellion, 1258–1267* (Oxford Studies in Social and Legal History, vol. VIII, edited by Paul Vinogradoff), Oxford, 1925.

Jolliffe, *Const. Hist.* — Jolliffe, J. E. A., *The Constitutional History of Medieval England,* New York, 1937.

Madox, *Firma Burgi* — Madox, Thomas, *Firma Burgi or an Historical Essay concerning the Cities Towns and Boroughs of England,* London, 1726.

Maitland, *D.B. and Bey.* — Maitland, F. W., *Domesday Book and Beyond,* Cambridge, 1897.

McKechnie, *Magna Carta* — McKechnie, W. S., *Magna Carta a Commentary on the Great Charter of King John* (2d edition, revised), Glasgow, 1914.

Mitchell, *Taxation* — Mitchell, S. K., *Studies in Taxation under John and Henry III* (Yale Historical Publications, Studies, vol. II), New Haven, 1914.

Pollock and Maitland, *Hist. Eng. Law* — Pollock, Sir Frederick, and F. W. Maitland, *The History of English Law before the Time of Edward I,* 2 vols. (2d edition), Cambridge, 1898.

Poole, *Obligations*	Poole, A. L., *Obligations of Society in the XII and XIII Centuries,* Oxford, 1946.
Powicke, *Henry III*	Powicke, F. M., *King Henry III and the Lord Edward,* 2 vols., Oxford, 1947.
Round, *Feud. Eng.*	Round, J. H., *Feudal England,* London, 1895.
Round, *Commune of London*	Round, J. H., *The Commune of London and Other Studies,* Westminster, 1899.
Stenton, *Anglo-Saxon England*	Stenton, F. M., *Anglo-Saxon England* (2d edition; Oxford History of England, vol. II), Oxford, 1947.
Stephenson, *Bor. and Town*	Stephenson, Carl, *Borough and Town* (Mediaeval Academy of America), Cambridge, 1933.
Stubbs, *Const. Hist.*	Stubbs, William, *The Constitutional History of England,* 3 vols. (vol. I, 5th edition; vol. II, 3d edition; vol. III, 4th edition), Oxford, 1887–1891.
Tait, *Med. Eng. Bor.*	Tait, James, *The Medieval English Borough* (Publications of the University of Manchester, Historical series, No. LXX), Manchester, 1936.
Vinogradoff, *Villainage*	Vinogradoff, Paul, *Villainage in England,* Oxford, 1892.
Vinogradoff, *Eng. Soc.*	Vinogradoff, Paul, *English Society in the Eleventh Century,* Oxford, 1908.

B. Articles and contributions to composite works

Cam, *"Manerium cum Hundredo"*	Cam, H. M., *"Manerium cum Hundredo:* the Hundred and the Hundredal Manor," *English Historical Review,* XLVII (1932), 353–376, reprinted in *Liberties & Communities,* pp. 64–90.
Jacob, "Complaints"	Jacob, E. F., "The Complaints of Henry III against the Baronial Council in 1261," *English Historical Review,* XLI (1926), 559–571.
Mills, "Exchequer Procedure"	Mills, M. H., "Experiments in Exchequer Procedure," *Transactions of the Royal Historical Society,* 4th Series, VIII (1925), 151–170.
Postan, "Labour Services"	Postan, M., "The Chronology of Labour Services," *Transactions of the Royal Historical Society,* 4th Series, XX (1937), 169–193.
Round, *Domesday Studies*	Round, J. H., "Danegeld and the Finance of Domesday," *Domesday Studies* (edited by P. E. Dove, 2 vols.; London, 1888–1891), I, 77–142.

Stephenson, "Taxation and Representation"	Stephenson, Carl, "Taxation and Representation in the Middle Ages," *Anniversary Essays in Mediaeval History by Students of Charles Homer Haskins* (edited by C. H. Taylor; Boston, 1929), pp. 291–312.
Turner, "Sheriff's Farm"	Turner, G. J., "The Sheriff's Farm," *Transactions of the Royal Historical Society,* New Series, XII (1898), 117–149.
V.C.H.	*The Victoria History of the Counties of England,* edited by William Page et al., Westminster and London, 1900—(continuing).

Index